Scaling and Sustaining Pre-K–12 Stem Education Innovations

Systemic Challenges, Systemic Responses

Christine M. Massey and Amy Stephens, *Editors*

Committee on Pre-K–12 STEM Education Innovations

Board on Science Education

Division of Behavioral and Social Sciences and Education

Consensus Study Report

NATIONAL ACADEMIES PRESS 500 Fifth Street, NW Washington, DC 20001

This activity was supported by a contract between the National Academy of Sciences and the National Science Foundation (49100423C0013). Any opinions, findings, conclusions, or recommendations expressed in this publication do not necessarily reflect the views of any organization or agency that provided support for the project.

International Standard Book Number-13: 978-0-309-72602-3
International Standard Book Number-10: 0-309-72602-6
Digital Object Identifier: https://doi.org/10.17226/27950
Library of Congress Control Number: 2025932293

This publication is available from the National Academies Press, 500 Fifth Street, NW, Keck 360, Washington, DC 20001; (800) 624-6242; http://www.nap.edu.

Copyright 2025 by the National Academy of Sciences. National Academies of Sciences, Engineering, and Medicine and National Academies Press and the graphical logos for each are all trademarks of the National Academy of Sciences. All rights reserved.

Printed in the United States of America.

Suggested citation: National Academies of Sciences, Engineering, and Medicine. 2025. *Scaling and Sustaining Pre-K–12 STEM Education Innovations: Systemic Challenges, Systemic Responses*. Washington, DC: National Academies Press. https://doi.org/10.17226/27950.

The **National Academy of Sciences** was established in 1863 by an Act of Congress, signed by President Lincoln, as a private, nongovernmental institution to advise the nation on issues related to science and technology. Members are elected by their peers for outstanding contributions to research. Dr. Marcia McNutt is president.

The **National Academy of Engineering** was established in 1964 under the charter of the National Academy of Sciences to bring the practices of engineering to advising the nation. Members are elected by their peers for extraordinary contributions to engineering. Dr. John L. Anderson is president.

The **National Academy of Medicine** (formerly the Institute of Medicine) was established in 1970 under the charter of the National Academy of Sciences to advise the nation on medical and health issues. Members are elected by their peers for distinguished contributions to medicine and health. Dr. Victor J. Dzau is president.

The three Academies work together as the **National Academies of Sciences, Engineering, and Medicine** to provide independent, objective analysis and advice to the nation and conduct other activities to solve complex problems and inform public policy decisions. The National Academies also encourage education and research, recognize outstanding contributions to knowledge, and increase public understanding in matters of science, engineering, and medicine.

Learn more about the National Academies of Sciences, Engineering, and Medicine at **www.nationalacademies.org**.

Consensus Study Reports published by the National Academies of Sciences, Engineering, and Medicine document the evidence-based consensus on the study's statement of task by an authoring committee of experts. Reports typically include findings, conclusions, and recommendations based on information gathered by the committee and the committee's deliberations. Each report has been subjected to a rigorous and independent peer-review process and it represents the position of the National Academies on the statement of task.

Proceedings published by the National Academies of Sciences, Engineering, and Medicine chronicle the presentations and discussions at a workshop, symposium, or other event convened by the National Academies. The statements and opinions contained in proceedings are those of the participants and are not endorsed by other participants, the planning committee, or the National Academies.

Rapid Expert Consultations published by the National Academies of Sciences, Engineering, and Medicine are authored by subject-matter experts on narrowly focused topics that can be supported by a body of evidence. The discussions contained in rapid expert consultations are considered those of the authors and do not contain policy recommendations. Rapid expert consultations are reviewed by the institution before release.

For information about other products and activities of the National Academies, please visit www.nationalacademies.org/about/whatwedo.

COMMITTEE ON PRE-K–12 STEM EDUCATION INNOVATIONS

CHRISTINE M. MASSEY (*Chair*), Senior Researcher, University of California, Los Angeles
HYMAN BASS,[1] Samuel Eilenberg Distinguished University Professor of Mathematics and Mathematics Education, University of Michigan
JASON T. BLACK, Associate Professor in Business Information Systems, Florida A&M University
TINA CHEUK, Assistant Professor of Elementary Science Education, California Polytechnic State University, San Luis Obispo
CHRISTINE M. CUNNINGHAM, Senior Vice President of STEM Learning, Museum of Science in Boston
XIMENA DOMINGUEZ, Executive Director of Learning Sciences and Early Learning Research, Digital Promise
KARA JACKSON, Professor of Mathematics Education, University of Washington, Seattle
AMERY D. MARTINEZ, CTE Curriculum Specialist, Denver Public Schools, Colorado
KRISTEN D. McKINNEY, Innovation Coach, Sedalia 200 School District, Missouri
MEIXI, Assistant Professor in Comparative Education and International Development, University of Minnesota – Twin Cities
THOMAS T. PETERS, Executive Director, South Carolina's Coalition for Mathematics & Science, Clemson University
ANTHONY J. PETROSINO, JR., Associate Dean for Research and Outreach, Professor of Learning Sciences, Southern Methodist University
ROBERT J. SEMPER, Chief Learning Officer, Exploratorium
MIRAY TEKKUMRU-KISA, Senior Policy Researcher, RAND
MARCELO AARON BONILLA WORSLEY, Associate Professor of Computer Science and Learning Sciences, Northwestern University

Study Staff

AMY STEPHENS, Study Director, Associate Board Director
AUDREY WEBB, Program Officer
SAMUEL CRAWFORD, Research Associate (*as of December 18, 2023*)
BRITTANI SHORTER, Senior Program Assistant
HEIDI SCHWEINGRUBER, Board Director

---

[1] Member of the National Academy of Sciences

BOARD ON SCIENCE EDUCATION

SUSAN R. SINGER (*Chair*), President, St. Olaf College
SUE ALLEN, Deputy Director, Clean Conferencing Institute
MEGAN BANG, Professor of Learning Sciences and Psychology, Northwestern University
VICKI L. CHANDLER, Provost, Minerva Schools at Keck Graduate Institute
KIRSTEN ELLENBOGEN, President and CEO, Great Lakes Science Center
MAYA M. GARCIA, Chief Program Officer, Beyond100K
DAVID GOLDSTON, Director, MIT Washington Office
G. PETER LEPAGE, Andrew H. and James S. Tisch Distinguished University Professor of Physics, Emeritus, Cornell University
WILLIAM PENUEL, Professor of Learning Sciences and Human Development, University of Colorado Boulder
STEPHEN L. PRUITT, President, Southern Regional Education Board
K. RENAE PULLEN, K–6 Science Curriculum Instructional Specialist, Caddo Parish Schools, Louisiana
K. ANN RENNINGER, Dorwin P. Cartwright Professor of Social Theory and Social Action, Swarthmore College
FRANCISCO RODRIGUEZ, Chancellor, Los Angeles Community College District
MARCY H. TOWNS, Bodner-Honig Professor of Chemistry, Purdue University
DARRYL N. WILLIAMS, Senior Vice President, Science and Education, The Franklin Institute

Study Staff

HEIDI SCHWEINGRUBER, Senior Board Director
AMY STEPHENS, Associate Board Director
MARGARET KELLY, Senior Program Coordinator

Reviewers

This Consensus Study Report was reviewed in draft form by individuals chosen for their diverse perspectives and technical expertise. The purpose of this independent review is to provide candid and critical comments that will assist the National Academies of Sciences, Engineering, and Medicine in making each published report as sound as possible and to ensure that it meets the institutional standards for quality, objectivity, evidence, and responsiveness to the study charge. The review comments and draft manuscript remain confidential to protect the integrity of the deliberative process.

We thank the following individuals for their review of this report:

LAURA M. AKESSON, Department of Physics and Astronomy, George Mason University
ANGELICQUE TUCKER BLACKMON, Research and Evaluation Division, Innovative Learning Center
SHAFIQ CHAUDHARY, Math and Science Bureau, New Mexico Public Education Department
JOSHUA CHILDS, College of Education, University of Texas at Austin
CYNTHIA E. COBURN, School of Education and Social Policy, Northwestern University
PHILLIP HERMAN, Regional Educational Laboratory Central, Mathematica
NANCY HOPKINS-EVANS, Program Impact, BSCS Science Learning
CAROL O'DONNELL, Smithsonian Science Education Center, Smithsonian Institution

WILLIAM R. PENUEL, School of Education, University of Colorado Boulder
DARRYLL J. PINES, Office of the President, University of Maryland, College Park
CHRISTIAN D. SCHUNN, Psychology, Learning Sciences, and Intelligent Systems, University of Pittsburgh
JOSEPH TAYLOR, Department of Leadership, Research, and Foundations, University of Colorado, Colorado Springs.
JENNIFER TYRELL, STEM Workforce Development, Oak Ridge Institute for Science as Education

Although the reviewers listed above provided many constructive comments and suggestions, they were not asked to endorse the conclusions or recommendations of this report nor did they see the final draft before its release. The review of this report was overseen by **SUZANNE M. WILSON,** University of Connecticut, and **ENRIQUETA C. BOND,** Burroughs Wellcome Fund. They were responsible for making certain that an independent examination of this report was carried out in accordance with the standards of the National Academies and that all review comments were carefully considered. Responsibility for the final content rests entirely with the authoring committee and the National Academies.

Acknowledgments

The Committee on Pre-K–12 STEM Education Innovations faced a monumental charge mandated by Section 10311 of the CHIPS and Science Act of 2022 to study the interrelated factors that foster or hinder the widespread implementation of promising science, technology, engineering, and mathematics (STEM) education practices, programs, models, and technologies. Through a contract with the National Science Foundation (NSF), the committee embarked on the project with the goal of making recommendations to various federal, state, and local educational agencies, programs, and other relevant stakeholders to address pervasive systematic barriers. Considering the breadth of the task, this report represents the work of thousands of people in numerous roles and contexts within and adjacent to STEM education.

This congressionally mandated study would not have been possible without sponsorship from NSF, and we would like to thank both our technical point of contract, Margret Hjalmarson, and our contracting officer's representative, Sarah-Kathryn McDonald, for working so diligently to ensure that this project ran smoothly. And a special thanks to Margret for her participation during many of our open sessions and providing any necessary insights along the way.

We also would like to extend thanks to the congressional staffers from both the Democratic and Republican House Science Space and Technology Committee who recognized the importance of equitable access to high-quality STEM education and included this study within the scope of the CHIPS and Science Act of 2022.

The committee benefited from the expertise of dozens of individuals, most of whom have made STEM education their lives' work, who presented at one of three information gathering meetings.

- The goal of the first committee meeting in September 2023 was to clarify the statement of task as well as the kinds of recommendations that would be most useful to the entities specifically called out in the charge. We thank the following individuals for their participation: Patti Curtis (U.S. Department of Education), Margret Hjalmarson (NSF), Cate Jonson (House Science, Space and Technology Committee, Research and Technology Subcommittee, Republican), Victoria Rubin (House Science, Space and Technology Committee, Republican), and Dahlia Sokolov (House Science, Space and Technology Committee, Democratic).
- The goal of the second committee meeting in December 2023 was to consider impact, opportunities, and barriers to implementation across contexts. The committee extends thanks to: Jeremy Babendure (SciTech), Pam Buffington (Regional Educational Laboratory Northeast and Islands), Alice Klein (WestEd), Calvin Mackie (STEM NOLA), Lee Meadows (Alabama STEM Advisory Council), Kathy Perkins (PhET Simulations), Katie Rich (Regional Educational Laboratory Midwest), Julie Riordan (Regional Educational Laboratory Northeast and Islands), Prentice Starkey (WestEd), Michael Vargas (Arizona STEM Acceleration Project), and Jeff Weld (Iowa STEM Advisory Council).
- The goal of the entirely virtual third committee meeting in February 2024 was to highlight the needs of both in-service and preservice STEM teachers, as well as those of certain student populations, that need to be considered when designing and implementing innovations for STEM education. The committee wishes to thank: Jody Bintz (BSCS Science Learning), Laura Booker (Tennessee Education Research Alliance), Kathy DeerInWater (American Indian Science and Engineering Society), Megan Franke (University of California Los Angeles), Richard Ingersoll (University of Pennsylvania), Michael Marder (University of Texas at Austin), Gina Svarovsky (Notre Dame University), Jonte Taylor (Pennsylvania State University), Karen Thompson (Oregon State University), and Chris Wilson (BSCS Science Learning).

The Education Development Center (EDC) was tasked with identifying and reviewing promising, evidence-based Pre-K–12 STEM education programs that have scaled and demonstrated evidence of impact. The committee is immensely grateful for the work that they were able to accomplish in such a brief period of time. We would like to thank Andres Henriquez for his enthusiasm to engage with us about this project from the beginning and Rebecca Lewis for her management of the project at EDC. A special thank you goes out to her team, which included Jennifer Jocz, Madelyn Johnson, and Erin Stafford. Thank you for your time, patience, promptness in responding to committee (and staff) queries, and hard work.

The committee also sends endless gratitude to the authors of several commissioned papers that form part of the body of this work: Sarah L. Woulfin, Daniel Dawer, Lauren McKenzie, and Michaela Pernetti from the University of Texas at Austin; Lori Connors-Tadros and GG Weisenfeld from the National Institute for Early Education Research; and Sadhana Puntambekar from the University of Wisconsin–Madison.

Lastly, special thanks are due to the staff of this project who worked together to support the committee in coming to consensus and ushered the report through all its iterations into its current form. Amy Stephens, associate board director for the Board on Science Education (BOSE), directed the study and played a key role throughout the entire study process. Audrey Webb, program officer for BOSE, and Samuel (Niko) Crawford, research associate with BOSE, provided critical assistance through the project. Brittani Shorter, senior program assistant with BOSE, managed the study's logistical and administrative needs. Heidi Schweingruber, director of BOSE, provided thoughtful advice and many helpful suggestions throughout the entire study.

Staff of the Division of Behavioral and Social Sciences and Education also provided help: Laura Yoder substantially improved the readability of the report; Kirsten Sampson Snyder expertly guided the report through the report review process; and Bea Porter masterfully guided the report through production. The committee also wishes to express its sincere appreciation to Anne Marie Houppert in the National Academies Research Center for assistance with conducting literature searches.

Contents

Preface		xix
Summary		1
1	Introduction	13
	CHARGE TO THE COMMITTEE, 16	
	STUDY APPROACH, 17	
	MAJOR FEATURES OF THE CURRENT CONTEXT, 29	
	REPORT ORGANIZATION, 31	
	REFERENCES, 32	
2	Landscape of STEM Education Learning Opportunities: Federal, State, Local, and Regional Roles	35
	MAPPING THE STRUCTURE OF U.S. EDUCATION SYSTEM, 36	
	FEDERAL AGENCIES AND CURRENT STEM EDUCATION IMPROVEMENT INITIATIVES, 38	
	ROLE OF STATES IN PRE-K–12 STEM EDUCATION, 49	
	LOCAL-LEVEL ACTORS, 57	
	REGIONAL ACTORS, 64	
	SUMMARY, 68	
	REFERENCES, 69	
	ANNEX 2-1: TRACKED COSTEM FEDERAL PRE-K–12 STEM EDUCATION PROGRAMS AND INVESTMENTS, 75	

3   History of Federal and National STEM Education
    Improvement Efforts   87
    LAUNCH OF SPUTNIK TO *A NATION AT RISK*
        (1958–1983), 88
    FROM *A NATION AT RISK* TO NO CHILD LEFT BEHIND
        (1983–2001), 93
    NO CHILD LEFT BEHIND TO THE EVERY STUDENT
        SUCCEEDS ACT (2001–2015), 101
    FROM EVERY STUDENT SUCCEEDS ACT TO NOW:
        THE CURRENT STATE OF STEM EDUCATION
        (2015–PRESENT), 107
    SUMMARY, 108
    REFERENCES, 109

4   Approaches to Scaling and Sustaining Innovations   113
    CONCEPTUALIZING SCALE AS MULTIDIMENSIONAL, 114
    SCALING INNOVATIONS, 122
    SUMMARY, 138
    REFERENCES, 140

5   Navigating the Landscape of STEM Innovation and
    Implementation   145
    THE INNOVATION DEVELOPMENT LANDSCAPE, 146
    THE INNOVATION IMPLEMENTATION LANDSCAPE, 157
    NEGOTIATING THE TERRAIN BETWEEN THE LANDSCAPES
        OF INNOVATION DEVELOPMENT AND
        IMPLEMENTATION, 158
    SUMMARY, 173
    REFERENCES, 174

6   Technology in STEM Education and the Emerging Frontier   177
    TECHNOLOGIES DESIGNED TO SUPPORT STEM
        LEARNING AND TEACHING, 178
    EMERGING FRONTIERS: ARTIFICIAL INTELLIGENCE
        IN EDUCATION, 184
    CLOSING DIGITAL DIVIDES AND CREATING EQUITABLE
        STEM LEARNING OPPORTUNITIES
        FOR ALL STUDENTS, 186
    MANAGING THE RAPID PACE OF EMERGING
        TECHNOLOGIES IN EDUCATION, 189
    SUMMARY, 193
    REFERENCES, 193

| 7 | Promising Pre-K–12 STEM Education Innovations | 199 |

IDENTIFYING PROMISING PRE-K–12 STEM INNOVATIONS, 200
INNOVATION-LEVEL FACTORS THAT SUPPORT SCALING, 205
CHALLENGES TO SCALING PROMISING INNOVATIONS, 217
SUMMARY, 218
REFERENCES, 219

| 8 | Enabling and Constraining Factors and the Need for System Change | 221 |

ENABLING AND CONSTRAINING FACTORS, 222
AFFORDANCES OF RESILIENT SYSTEMS, 230
NEED FOR SYSTEM CHANGE, 233
SUMMARY, 234
REFERENCES, 235

| 9 | Conclusions, Recommendations, and Research Agenda | 239 |

CONCLUSIONS, 240
RECOMMENDATIONS, 248
RESEARCH AGENDA, 253
FINAL REFLECTION, 256
REFERENCE, 257

Appendix A	Biosketches	259
Appendix B	Development of the Compendium (online only)	269
Appendix C	Compendium (online only)	285

Boxes, Figures, and Tables

BOXES

1-1   Statement of Work, 16

2-1   Office of Elementary and Secondary Education (OESE), 39
2-2   ESSA Funds: Categories, Calculations, and Flow-Through, 40
2-3   Institute of Education Sciences Authorizing Legislation, Role and Responsibilities, 43
2-4   REL Regions, 44
2-5   National Science Foundation (NSF), 48
2-6   Teaching Institute for Exemplary STEM (TIES), 66
2-7   State STEM Ecosystem Functions, 67

3-1   History of Goals for the Regional Educational Laboratory (REL) Program, 91
3-2   Race to the Top (RTTT) Program, 102

4-1   Pre-K Mathematics, 126
4-2   Tennessee Math Coaching Project, 129
4-3   Inquiry Hub Partnership, 134
4-4   Ambitious Science Teaching Networked Improvement Community (AST NIC), 136

5-1   The Role of the Private Sector, 156

xvii

6-1 Recommendations on AI and the Future of Teaching and Learning, 192

7-1 Strategic CSforALL Resource & Implementation Planning Tool (SCRIPT), 208
7-2 IRCEDE STEM for Our Youngest Learners, 209
7-3 Beauty and Joy of Computing (BJC), 210
7-4 Science Teachers Learning from Lesson Analysis (STeLLA), 212
7-5 Making Sense of SCIENCE (MSS), 213
7-6 NURTURES, 214
7-7 AlgebraByExample, 215
7-8 Exploratorium California K–12 Science Leader Network, 217

FIGURES

1-1 STEM learning ecology, 27

2-1 The nested ecology of STEM policy actors, 37

3-1 Statewide Systems Initiatives (SSI) activities, 97
3-2 Leadership and Assistance for Science Education Reform (LASER) model, 99
3-3 MSP model, 106

8-1 Aligning factors across the system to enable scaling and sustaining innovations, 231

TABLES

2-2-1 Competitive Assessment Grants, 41
2A-1 CoSTEM Federal STEM Education Programs and Investments Directly or Indirectly Impacting Pre-K–12, 75

5-1 STEM Investments across Federal Agencies, 148

6-1 Technologies to Support Learning and Teaching, 179

7-1 Nominated Innovations by Domain and Grade Band, 205
7-2 Nominated Innovations by Audience, 206

8-1 Considerations Related to Scaling and Sustaining Innovations, 232

B-1 Individual Programs Invited to Self-Nominate, 272
B-2 Organizations Contacted, 277
B-3 List of Nominations Received, 279
B-4 Rubric, 282

Preface

For many decades, the United States has been a deep wellspring for creative design, insightful research, practical wisdom, and persistent ingenuity aimed at innovations to improve learning and teaching in science, technology, education, and mathematics (STEM)-related fields. At the same time, only a limited number of students routinely experience the benefits of many of these efforts. What do we need to understand and what actions should we undertake in order to activate the best of what has been discovered and created to improve STEM education for all students in the United States? This is at the heart of the charge that was given to our consensus committee under a congressional mandate within the CHIPS and Science Act of 2022. Our committee was charged with assembling a compendium of successful evidence-based education practices, models, programs, and technologies, and identifying the state of evidence on the interconnected factors that foster and hinder their capacity for widespread and sustained implementation. In doing this work, we were to consider the full range of STEM-related disciplines across all grade bands from preschool through the end of high school and at all levels of the educational system, from local classrooms through national policies.

Given the scale and complexity of public education in the United States, this was a daunting undertaking, but we consistently found inspiration in reminders of what is at stake. The shining promise of public education in the United States is that every child will have the opportunity to learn about the world around them and to participate in the remarkable human enterprise of invention and discovery, to cultivate their own interests and talents, and to prepare for a productive future as a community member and citizen.

This promise is intended for all children, whether they are naturally drawn to STEM fields or need some encouragement to approach them, whether their ambitions are customary or uncommon in their setting, and whether their families and communities are prosperous or struggling. Thus, first and foremost, our inspiration was serving children and youth, from early childhood through the threshold of adulthood.

We also drew inspiration from the many enthusiastic, creative, and dedicated innovators and designers who have made a deep study of STEM teaching and learning and have pioneered new approaches and resources. In addition to reviewing their published work and publicly accessible resources, we also communicated directly with researchers and developers through correspondence, interviews, and in-person presentations at our committee's open sessions. We gained insights from their reflections on how they have sustained their efforts, often in the face of unexpected obstacles, and forged new pathways to develop and expand their projects and to adapt them to new settings and participants. For many, these efforts have been their life's work, and it was our privilege to learn from the full arc of their experience.

We were equally inspired by hardworking, resourceful educational leaders and teachers who are deeply committed to enhancing their professional practice and bringing new and better learning opportunities to all of the students under their care. No one knows more than teachers and educational leaders about the myriad challenges posed by the hard work of providing high-quality STEM education to all students. And yet many of them remain eager to explore new STEM education innovations, put them into practice, and figure out how to make them even better.

They are also joined in this work by people who stand outside the formal education system but who share a compelling vision for advancing opportunities for young people to become engaged in programs and activities related to STEM and to deepen and broaden the kinds of learning experiences available to them. Champions from local communities and businesses, museums and science centers, and foundations have seen the need for fresh opportunities in their communities and have launched into action to activate new resources and forge broader networks of support for STEM education, both in schools and in out-of-school programs.

The work of a consensus committee is demanding and painstaking. Answering our particular charge required a willingness to tackle a series of difficult, high-stakes questions in all of their complexity. The committee had to seek out and process a wide range of evidence and use it to probe and frame our assumptions and conclusions. We also needed to engage in extended discussions to compare and connect our varied knowledge and perspectives, with the goal of achieving a deeper understanding of the broad, complicated landscape of Pre-K–12 STEM education than any one of us was able to command on our own. We had to figure out collectively how to organize and sequence our analysis of a nonlinear and somewhat chaotically interconnected set of systems and processes.

Fortunately, the members of our committee brought a wealth of knowledge and experience to our work. In contrast to the more typically "siloed" nature of many people's careers, individual committee members' careers have been characterized by an unusual and impressive breadth and variety of work across different roles, initiatives, and organizations over the course of their professional lives. The committee included scientists and mathematicians who have become deeply involved in Pre-K–12 education; school-based educators who have been active in overseeing or advising on curriculum, instruction, and assessment at classroom, district, and state levels; people who have served as classroom teachers or program directors as well as academic researchers and university faculty; and researchers and teachers with extensive experience with the needs of particular students and cultural communities. For nearly all of the issues or questions that emerged, we had one or more committee members who were able to speak to them in depth as scholars and also from first-hand experience. This range of expertise allowed us, both individually and collectively, to illuminate potential relationships, connections, interactions, and contexts that are not always obvious from more limited perspectives.

Our committee strove to create a report that is educative, insightful, and responsive to the available evidence. We hope that our report gives voice to the knowledge and experiences of people who do the work of creating, implementing, and supporting new resources and ways of doing things in STEM education. We also hope that this report will build on the solid foundations that they have provided to activate and mobilize new and improved STEM learning opportunities throughout the STEM education landscape. Many varied and creative approaches to questions of teaching and learning have been developed and investigated, and, as a nation, we have also made progress in promoting evidence-based improvements. But the United States has consistently under-invested in the kinds of research methodologies and organizational structures that would allow us to better understand and address the contexts and variables that facilitate or hinder widespread distribution and effective adaptation to new contexts in actual practice. While the committee examined many individual innovations and initiatives in particular contexts, our conclusions and recommendations are aimed at a systemic perspective, since that is where the committee saw the most persistent obstacles and the most promising models for large-scale change.

I am deeply grateful for the exceptional generosity shown by each of the committee members in sharing their time, talents, knowledge, and wisdom as we prepared this report. Despite the many other demands on them, they somehow found time and brought their best efforts to developing a shared understanding that expanded and deepened as we all learned from each other. They also showed remarkable good humor, diligence, and persistence as we worked through draft after draft of the report's components. They joined Zoom meetings from across the globe, responded to emails in the wee hours of the night, and were generally undeterred as they simultaneously dealt with extreme weather, rampant viruses, family needs, and more.

Finally, I think I speak for the whole committee in thanking the extraordinary National Academies of Sciences, Engineering, and Medicine staff members who supported our team. Dr. Amy Stephens, our fearless and unflappable study director, provided expert guidance and astounding hard work that kept us motivated and on track every step of the way. Dr. Heidi Schweingruber, director of the Board on Science Education (BOSE), regularly provided deep insights into the broader contexts surrounding this report and helped us understand and use the National Academies' processes, standards, and resources to the fullest. Samuel (Niko) Crawford, Brittani Shorter, and Audrey Webb accompanied us on this journey with inspiring energy and superb organization and support. It has been a pleasure and a privilege to work with each of you, and we thank you for your contributions to this report and to the larger mission of BOSE.

Christine M. Massey, *Chair*
Committee on Pre-K–12 STEM Education Innovation

Summary[1]

In the history of the United States, science, technology, engineering and mathematics—the disciplines that are linked together in the acronym STEM—have been uniquely powerful engines of growth and development. Harnessing the power of these disciplines and shaping and deploying them in ways that promote the wellbeing of all citizens and long-term stewardship of the natural world requires a well-informed population of critical thinkers that understands the STEM disciplines. To ensure that the United States continues to be a global leader in STEM literacy, innovation, and employment, it is essential that all Americans have lifelong access to high-quality STEM education.

Over several decades, the federal government has allocated resources to the improvement of STEM education. This has led to the development of a rich variety of educational innovations (i.e., programs, practices, models, and technologies), all in the service of supporting teaching and learning within the STEM disciplines. Although a number of these innovations have had the potential to impact learners on a broad scale, that potential often remains unrealized, and there are still ongoing questions of how to address the expansive goals of Pre-K–12 STEM education across the different grade bands, inclusive of all learners.

The Board on Science Education of the National Academies of Sciences, Engineering, and Medicine in response to a mandate within the CHIPS and Science Act of 2022 with support from the National Science Foundation

---

[1] This summary does not include references. Citations for the information presented herein are provided in the main text.

convened an expert committee to examine the interconnected factors at local, regional, and national levels that foster or hinder the widespread implementation of promising, evidence-based, Pre-K–12 STEM education innovations, identify gaps in the research, and provide guidance on how to address barriers to implementation.[2] The 15-member expert committee had extensive expertise across the STEM disciplines (science, engineering, mathematics, computer science, and data science) in various settings (rural and urban) and with different roles and spheres of influence (local, regional, and national).

The committee explored the available evidence on what it takes to successfully develop, implement, scale, and sustain Pre-K–12 STEM education innovations. In particular, the committee focused on the barriers to widespread implementation and looked for examples of innovations that found solutions to implementation challenges. Significantly, the committee examined the education system at various levels to better understand how the structure of the system itself can facilitate or hinder the scalability of promising, evidence-based, Pre-K–12 STEM education innovations.

Overall, the committee found that investments in innovations in STEM education have resulted in numerous promising programs. However, these programs vary in their success in reaching large numbers of students across different educational contexts. Perhaps more importantly, it is not clear that assembling an array of discrete innovative programs will result in the kind of robust, coherent, large-scale, systemic change that is likely needed to create the kinds of major improvements in student outcomes that many policy leaders seek.

PRE-K–12 STEM EDUCATION LANDSCAPE AND POLICY CONTEXT

Understanding how innovations in STEM education can take hold and result in improved outcomes for large numbers of learners requires an understanding of the larger educational landscape in the United States. The formal K–12 education system in the United States is organized across federal, state, and local levels. The federal government and states influence education through regulations and through financial support for education programs that often comes with particular guidance or restrictions for receipt and use of the funding. States are constitutionally responsible for public elementary and secondary education, and, as a result, most policy-making and governance of schools happen at this level. School districts, in turn, implement policy set by both the federal government and the state,

---

[2]The full statement of task appears in Box 1-1 in Chapter 1.

and also make numerous decisions about policy and practice that impact what happens in schools and classrooms.

Often policy and decision makers at the various levels of the system (including teachers) may not share the same priorities and goals with the result that there is misalignment in policies and priorities across federal, state, district, and school levels. These misalignments create obstacles to implementing coherent educational programs and are especially challenging when it comes to integrating innovative programs into existing structures and local contexts. In particular, the decentralized system means that it is difficult to propagate large-scale improvement across the country, and it presents a challenge for how the federal government can incentivize large-scale, sustained, and well-resourced improvement efforts.

Influence of Accountability

Currently, K–12 education is shaped by the past 25 years of accountability-based improvement efforts that began at the federal level with the passage of the No Child Left Behind (NCLB) Act in 2001. This legislation marked a number of critical changes in the federal education policy landscape and significantly increased the role of states in holding schools responsible for the academic progress of all students. State accountability systems serve to provide transparent data for instructional improvement, make visible learning gaps across equity groups, and encourage innovations in assessment practices. However, the high-stakes assessments have often narrowed the curriculum with an intense focus on English Language Arts and mathematics and emphasis on teaching approaches that result in high performance on standardized tests. This narrow focus can create barriers to implementation of some innovations in STEM education.

Preschool and Out-of-School Time

The challenges of disconnection across levels of the formal education system are compounded for preschool and for learning in out-of-school programs. Both of these sectors function almost independently from K–12 formal education. Each state designs its own preschool system through authorizing legislation and funding, and determines eligibility, quality standards, and monitoring. Because of this, the governance is highly variable and fragmented. Young children are served through a variety of programs (e.g., federal programs like Head Start, state-funded preschool, and various community agencies), which vary in their alignment to K–12 standards and curriculum.

Out-of-school time learning spaces comprise a vast range of environments and situations, including youth development programs, museums, libraries, zoos, botanical gardens, science centers, and community centers.

Out-of-school spaces not only provide opportunities for learners to engage in Pre-K–12 STEM education innovations but also are important spaces for innovation development. These settings can support experimentation as well as the development of resources (e.g., professional development, curriculum) that can translate into formal Pre-K–12 educational settings. Yet, these settings are often entirely disconnected from the formal education system.

SCALING AND SUSTAINING PROMISING PRE-K–12 STEM EDUCATION INNOVATIONS

Within this complex, disconnected system, the challenge becomes how an innovation that is successful in a single location or for a particulate group of students can be expanded to reach more students in more places. This is often thought of as a question of "scale."

What Is "Scale"?

Many discussions of scale focus solely on increasing numbers of participants (spread), and common measures of scale often focus on number of beneficiaries, presence of materials, and time spent using the materials. However, scale can also mean depth of implementation (i.e., extent to which the innovation is intended to create or entails substantial shifts in the core of educational practice), sustainability (i.e., innovation endures over time in the original and new contexts when the initial circumstances run their course), and ownership (i.e., extent to which knowledge of and authority over the innovation is deepened and expanded over time). These additional ways of understanding scale are important because spread alone does not support educators or researchers in knowing whether an innovation is resulting in the desired improvement and for whom, whether the innovation is sustained as enactors change, and why or why not.

In fact, Pre-K–12 STEM education innovations can be designed for different purposes. They can be designed to have deep impact with a more local focus, designed explicitly for large-scale impact with less attention to depth, or designed to be some combination of both. Targeted innovations can be just as impactful as those designed for broad reach.

The more ambitious an innovation is—that is, the more it requires a substantial change to "business as usual" in order to be implemented—the more difficult it may be to sustain or to scale. If an innovation requires only superficial or minor changes to current practice, its adoption and assimilation by practitioners might be more easily achieved. However, the changes may not result in meaningful and long-lasting improvements. In fact, there is a tension between adoption of innovations that spread easily but may have limited impact and those that are harder to implement yet show robust evidence of impact in the settings where they have been developed.

Features of Innovations That Facilitate Scaling

There are some key characteristics of innovations that appear to facilitate scaling. First, innovations with a strong core program (that is clearly stated) with room for adaptation to different contexts and learners are more likely to scale. Second, an innovation is more likely to scale when the goals and practices of the program align with the goals, priorities, and existing practices of the adopting organization or individual (e.g., district, school, educator, or out-of-school setting). Third, professional learning[3] or other activities that build the capacities of individuals or organizations to implement the innovation are key. Finally, partnerships can be valuable for scaling in a variety of ways. If an innovation is developed by an entity outside of the K–12 system, such as a university or a nonprofit, partnering with districts, schools, and teachers as the innovation is designed and enacted can provide developers with in-depth insights into how contextual factors influence implementation and outcomes. These insights can guide subsequent improvements. In moving forward with implementation, external partners such as philanthropy or local business and industry can be valuable sources of resources, funding, and support.

ENABLING AND CONSTRAINING FACTORS

Many promising and innovative projects are not sustained in a significant way beyond their original instantiation. This is true for innovations that originate as research studies and those that emerge as educators on the ground work to expand and improve their practice. In some cases, the promising innovation does not gain traction beyond where it is developed because there is no strategy for sharing the innovation more widely. However, some innovations may also be developed in ways that do not take

---

[3] As noted below, the committee recognizes that, as evidence-based practices have evolved with regard to the most effective ways to enable teachers to expand their knowledge and refine their practice in support of students' learning, there has been a shift away from short-term professional development workshops or passive lectures and toward sustained, interactive learning experiences that include opportunities for educators to practice, customize, and reflect on how they can apply new learning in their schools and classrooms. The term "professional learning" is increasingly being used to refer to the latter approach. This report generally uses the term professional learning in line with current best practices, except when describing the work of others, in which case their own terms and descriptors are retained. Because various local, state, and national education agencies; funders; and other organizations may use one or the other, the committee's recommendations include both terms.

into consideration variation across educational contexts—essentially there is a disconnect between the context where the innovation is developed and the contexts where it will need to be implemented. Collaboration across multiple sites and iterative cycles of design across time can be a model for addressing this kind of disconnect. In fact, innovations that have shown promise for scaling and sustaining are often developed with input from practitioners about the needs of educators and students and with explicit attention to the varying contexts in which the innovation could be implemented.

Research Incentives and Constraints

The incentives and constraints faced by researchers in obtaining funding and establishing the efficacy and effectiveness of new innovations can pose obstacles to developing flexible innovations that are more easily scalable. Research designs and methodologies that clearly show impact may push against designing flexible innovations. In addition, some researchers may lack the expertise to flesh out the kinds of supports that are needed in the initial design and/or evaluation to support more widespread implementation and allow adaptation to a broad set of contexts and student populations.

Once a program has scaled broadly, it is challenging to monitor and evaluate. When a program is being implemented and adapted in many different contexts, it is difficult to draw conclusions across sites and learners. Additionally, the cost of evaluating something at this scale in a deep way can be prohibitive.

The Realities of Educational Contexts

The complexity of educational environments creates additional challenges that can negatively affect successful scaling and sustainability efforts. If a program is designed to align with specific policies or to meet specific goals in a particular context, there can be a large threat to scaling if these goals vary across contexts. There is also a threat to sustainability when policies or priorities change and are not in line with the direction of the program.

Also, scaling and sustainability are aided by the buy-in and capacity building of individuals and organizations. If individuals championing the program at an organization or those trained to implement it leave, it can hinder continuity and efforts to scale the program. For programs that are sustained over time, it can be a challenge to keep materials up to date with advances in STEM fields or to update delivery technologies, as these would require additional development and testing.

Capacity of Educators and Education Leaders

The preparation and development of preservice and in-service STEM educators and education leaders does not routinely include opportunities to learn how to identify, evaluate, and implement innovations and adapt them for the needs of different students. This makes high-quality professional learning supports for those charged with enacting innovations essential. However, professional learning for the initial cohort of implementers is not sufficient for supporting sustainable implementation, and the sustainability of an innovation is easily threatened by turnover in the enactors. Thus, whether the innovation entails a minor or substantial change to "business as usual," it is critical to build in structured opportunities to "onboard" new enactors.

Alignment with Existing STEM Initiatives and Priorities

The alignment of a particular STEM innovation with existing educational improvement efforts in a state, district, or school can shape whether and how an innovation is implemented. If an innovation aligns well with existing priorities, it may be easier to implement. If it contradicts existing priorities, it may meet resistance and fail. By aligning with—or building upon—other improvement strategies and reducing the perceived burden of educational reform, education leaders and decision makers can better leverage innovative STEM programs to advance educational improvement. In fact, one of the major challenges to improving STEM education through individual innovations is how to ensure that different programs are coherent and are leading to lasting change to the system.

THE FEDERAL ROLE IN SUPPORTING AND ADVANCING INNOVATIONS IN STEM EDUCATION

Although the federal role in STEM education is limited, some previous federal initiatives did make significant progress. For example, the systemic initiatives funded by National Science Foundation in the 1990s built significant capacity in states and districts for supporting high-quality STEM education. Many of these efforts, particularly those with robust (and co-ordinated) plans, showed promise leading to improvement; however, they were often not sustained when federal funding was eliminated.

Currently, federal funding agencies that support development of innovations in STEM education prioritize sequential studies of scaling innovations (i.e., pilot studies, efficacy studies, effectiveness studies, scale-up studies), whereby the innovation is implemented in tightly prescribed ways, in increasingly heterogeneous sites and/or populations, and in service of specified outcomes. However, federal funding is not widely available to investigate the sustainability of innovations.

RECOMMENDATIONS

Based on the findings and conclusions summarized above, the committee developed a set of recommendations for federal, state, and local actors. These recommendations focus on building the capacity of educators and the education system for implementing innovations, enhancing the research infrastructure for developing innovations that are scalable and sustainable, developing methods to support systemic and continuous improvement, and understanding how to monitor progress.

Building Capacity and Monitoring Progress

The first four recommendations point to roles that federal agencies can play in building capacity within states to support implementation efforts. To build capacity, there needs to be significant investment in the professional development of the various enactors who are the main implementors of STEM education innovations (e.g., teachers, administrators) and designers (including researchers) as well as significant investment in building partnerships within the system to support organizational capacity. Building connected systems of teachers and administrators, curriculum specialists and developers, technology specialists, community learners and partners, and researchers, and creating new roles and spaces for them to work and learn together, is foundational for supporting organizational capacity. Moreover, previous systemic efforts showed greater promise when given the opportunity to build strong plans that enable systems-level change that can be sustained, many of which require time to take shape and then be implemented.

> Recommendation 1: The U.S. Department of Education should allocate funding for teacher professional learning and development in all STEM disciplines, to include science, technology, engineering, mathematics, computer science, and other emerging STEM-focused subjects (e.g., data science). As part of the funding allocation, states will need to provide a plan for the use of funding for professional learning and development that is based on established best practice (e.g., curriculum-embedded, sustained over time), metrics to achieve the goals (e.g., measures of quality teacher professional learning and development), and data that show evidence for achieving those goals. The funding should be renewable up to ten years, and if states have not shown improvement by year four, they must revise their plan.

Recommendation 2: The National Science Foundation should develop a new generation of Pre-K–12 STEM education systemic initiatives with the goal of building infrastructure, capacity, and expertise to harvest promising evidence-based innovations, prepare them for wider implementation in new settings, and fund backbone organizations to organize the resources and support systems needed to carry out the implementations in schools. Funding should have a long enough time horizon (e.g., renewable up to ten years) for new structures and relationships to be iteratively refined and to take root in ways that could be sustained.

Recommendation 3: In alignment with the authorizing language of the CHIPS and Science Act of 2022 (P.L. 117–167, Sec. 10395), the National Science Foundation's Directorate for Technology, Innovation, and Partnerships should partner with the Directorate for STEM Education (EDU) to fully leverage the expertise of the EDU Federal Advisory committee and ensure the inclusion of program officers with expertise in Pre-K–12 STEM education in the evaluation of proposals related to supporting multidisciplinary research centers for scaling promising Pre-K–12 STEM education innovations.

Recommendation 4: In an effort to facilitate coordination across federal agencies that implement, scale, and sustain Pre-K–12 STEM education innovations, the National Science and Technology Council's Committee on STEM Education (CoSTEM) should identify key metrics for scaling and sustaining innovations and identify an appropriate schedule for reporting them to the public, exploring where the data should be reported (e.g., science.gov, National Center for Education Statistics, National Center for Science and Engineering Statistics) to keep the data evergreen. CoSTEM should use these data to inform future iterations of the strategic plan and coordinate consistent investments across the federal agencies.

Building a Research Infrastructure for Scalable and Sustainable Innovations

The committee also points to the need for additional research for better understanding the interrelated factors associated with sustaining Pre-K–12 STEM education innovations. The next three recommendations point to how federal actors can further develop the research infrastructure, helping researchers to fill the gaps in the current research base.

Recommendation 5: The U.S. Department of Education and the National Science Foundation should create a new funding category that allows for the study of sustainability of STEM education innovations, which could allow for a deeper understanding of the dimensions of scaling. This should include developing system-level measures of STEM education innovations that attend to the interrelated actors, structures, and interactions that shape how innovations take hold in multiple, diverse contexts for different learners with an eye toward equity.

Recommendation 6: The U.S. Department of Education and the National Science Foundation should encourage practice-initiated partnerships and planning grants that will connect teams of researchers, designers, and practitioners with expertise and experience in different aspects of innovation development and implementation, either within a project or across successive related projects. These projects should include considerations of implementation and adaptation for different learners across multiple, diverse contexts early in the development process.

Recommendation 7: The U.S. Department of Education and the National Science Foundation should continue to encourage research and development in early STEM education: specifically, efforts that tackle integrating professional learning and development opportunities with curricula that address the many domains of learning that educators are expected to promote in early childhood, planning grants to support practice-initiated partnerships, and focus on coherence and alignment across preschool and elementary grades.

State and Local Actors: Systemic Change and Continuous Improvement

The next five recommendations are directed toward state and local actors in the Pre-K–12 education system. The recommendations focus on including strategies for making processes for continuous improvement the norm and creating partnerships to connect and align all the relevant roles and forms of expertise.

Recommendation 8: School and district leaders should adopt and/or evaluate a networked continuous improvement framework, emphasizing iterative assessment and refinement of strategies to meet the evolving educational landscape. This involves a cycle of planning, implementing, evaluating, and adjusting, with engagement of pertinent individuals to ensure ongoing relevancy. Data-driven analysis and feedback mechanisms should allow for real-time monitoring and responsive adaptation. Embracing this approach fosters a culture of innovation, learning, dexterity, responsiveness, and resilience within the schools and across the district.

Recommendation 9: To understand the implementation and scaling of Pre-K–12 STEM education innovations, state and district partners should develop data systems that capture information about opportunities to learn, including time for instruction, allocation of resources and funding, access to and enrollment in Pre-K–12 STEM education innovations, and qualifications of teachers and characteristics of teachers. These data should be disaggregated to examine trends by subgroups of students and by school characteristics.

Recommendation 10: To ensure continuous improvement in Pre-K–12 STEM education innovations, school and district leaders should engage with professional learning and development providers to offer curriculum-embedded, ongoing opportunities within and across years that includes specific emphasis on new teachers to ensure that their learning is commensurate with those who participated in opportunities in years prior.

Recommendation 11: Local school and district leaders should initiate and sustain partnership agreements across all levels of the STEM education learning ecosystem (e.g., teachers, teacher educators, education researchers, designers of Pre-K–12 STEM education innovations, families, etc.) in order to combine STEM education expertise and local knowledge to attend to specific problems of practice and advance sustained development and implementation of promising, evidence-based, Pre-K–12 STEM education innovations.

Regional Actors and Impact

The final set of recommendations acknowledge some of the broader range of actors that can have regional impact as they support the implementation, scaling, and sustaining of Pre-K–12 STEM education innovations.

Recommendation 12: Leaders of local and regional Pre-K–12 systems should work to strengthen learning opportunities in STEM education among key actors in the STEM education learning ecosystem (e.g., teachers, school/district leaders, school board leaders, teacher educators, professional development providers, universities and colleges, museums, nonprofits, families, etc.) with an emphasis on building relational connections among communities and sharing knowledge.

Recommendation 13: In their support of Pre-K–12 STEM education innovations, the federal government, philanthropic organizations, and business and industry should provide support to projects that include designers of curricula partnering with education leaders, teachers, families/communities, and researchers to co-design resources that are evidence-based, meaningful, accessible, and able to be feasibly implemented to support STEM teaching and learning. Attention should be given to features that can lead to meaningful STEM learning, while also considering components needed to ensure resources can be sustained and adapted for use by others.

1

Introduction

The world is rapidly changing. Harnessing advances in science and technology to navigate pressing local and global challenges in an increasingly technological society requires a population that understands science, technology, engineering, and mathematics (STEM) disciplines. This holds particular significance amid present-day challenges and impacts of technologies related to artificial intelligence (see U.S. Department of Education Office of Educational Technology's policy report, *Artificial Intelligence and the Future of Teaching and Learning: Insights and Recommendations*, 2023). As technology continues to shape our information landscape, the focus on developing a well-informed, engaged populace of critical and ethical thinkers is essential.

In response to these challenges, various governmental and nongovernmental agencies have put forth visionary and expansive goals for the U.S. STEM education system. A 2011 report from the National Academies of Sciences, Engineering, and Medicine, *Successful K–12 STEM Education: Identifying Effective Approaches in Science, Technology, Engineering, and Mathematics*, argued that the goals for U.S. STEM education include:

- Expand the number of students who ultimately pursue advanced degrees and careers in STEM fields and broaden the participation of women and minorities in those fields.
- Expand the STEM-capable workforce and broaden the participation of women and minorities in that workforce.
- Increase STEM literacy for all students, including those who do not pursue STEM-related careers or additional study in the STEM disciplines.

In these goals, the 2011 report mirrors the priorities put forth by the Office of Science and Technology Policy (OSTP) during the Obama Administration, which aims to "advance a wide range of initiatives, programs, projects, and activities that unleash the power of science, technology, and innovation for the benefit of Americans and people around the world."[1] This was amplified in the 2018 National Science & Technology Council Committee on STEM Education strategic plan *Charting a Course for Success: America's Strategy for STEM Education,* which specified "a vision for a future where all Americans will have lifelong access to high-quality STEM education and the United States will be the global leader in STEM literacy, innovation, and employment" (p. 4).

As highlighted above, the purposes of STEM and advancing formal STEM education have been tied to political and economic goals with an emphasis on a workforce wellversed in basic STEM content. This workforce was needed to exercise various, seemingly repeatable, processes across an array of contexts. In some respects, STEM workers were valued based on their knowledge and their ability to complete pre-defined tasks. In more recent years, however, a shift has been observed where STEM workers are being valued for their ideas and ways of thinking. Instead of solely focusing on the capacity of STEM workers to retain certain forms of knowledge, there has been a growing interest in fostering learning experiences that expansively contribute to creativity in thought and in practice, that expand the purposes and goals of STEM education, and that understand STEM learning as part of larger goals of human development toward more socially and ecologically just and healthy societies (National Academies of Sciences, Engineering, and Medicine [NASEM], 2024). Part of this shift is based on the recognition that many of the challenges that our society faces will require untold amounts of creativity and innovation.

More recently, in 2022, the U.S. Department of Education launched *Raise the Bar: STEM Excellence for All Students initiative*[2] designed to strengthen STEM education nationwide by prioritizing three goals for STEM education:

- Ensure all students from Pre-K to higher education excel in rigorous, relevant, and joyful STEM learning.
- Develop and support our STEM educators to join, grow, and stay in the STEM field.

---

[1] See https://obamawhitehouse.archives.gov/administration/eop/ostp/initiatives#:~:text=OSTP%20works%20to%20advance%20a,%2C%20and%20Mathematics%20(STEM)%20Education

[2] See https://www.ed.gov/news/press-releases/us-department-education-launches-new-initiative-enhance-stem-education-all-students

- Invest in STEM education strategically and sufficiently using American Rescue Plan and other federal, state, and local funds.

These goals are inherently aspirational, but their fulfillment has often been compromised by privileged access of some groups and marginalization of others, notably people of color (see NASEM, 2023, 2024) and students with disabilities (see National Center for Science and Engineering Statistics [NCSES], 2023). For example, although the U.S. STEM workforce gradually became more diverse between 2011 and 2021, including Black, Latino/a, and American Indian/Alaska Native populations, these populations still accounted for a smaller percentage of the total STEM workforce: 9 percent Black, 15 percent Latinx, and less than 1 percent American Indican/Alaska Native (NCSES, 2023). And whereas the number of women earning a STEM degree has grown, gender parity does not exist for some disciplines such as engineering, computer science, and mathematics and statistics (National Science Board, 2019).

How these goals can be addressed in different grade bands, inclusive of all learners, requires thoughtful design and implementation of practices and structures with a clear and intentional focus on equity while, at minimum, broadening participation for those who have been historically excluded from formal institutionalized STEM learning. This necessitates examining these disparities from a systemic lens, acknowledging the multiple barriers (e.g., structural inequities and cultural exclusion/narrow views of STEM) inherent in the system that can be observed at various levels (i.e., region, state, district, school, and classroom). That is, disparities in teacher expectations and other school- and classroom-level factors—such as access to adequate laboratory facilities, resources, and supplies—contribute to gaps in STEM achievement for underrepresented groups (National Research Council [NRC], 2011), as do the norms and practices of the discipline, and stereotypes and implicit biases (NASEM, 2021a, 2024). The culture of the school or district environment also plays an important role, with research showing that when school and district administrators are supportive of STEM education innovations, they can help to provide the necessary resources for activities and support to empower educators to enable high-quality STEM learning (NASEM, 2021b, 2022).

Despite all these STEM initiatives and the creation of various STEM programs, implementation depends on the availability of resources, time, knowledgeable educators, policies, practices, and buy-in from participants and decision makers throughout the education system. As a result, there is a need to understand better how these factors impact the scaling and sustainability of STEM education innovations across Pre-K through 12th grade, with attention to examples that have successfully addressed the potential barriers.

CHARGE TO THE COMMITTEE

Sponsored by the National Science Foundation (NSF) in response to a mandate within the CHIPS and Science Act of 2022, the Board on Science Education (BOSE) of the National Academies convened an expert committee to examine the interconnected factors that foster or hinder the scalability of promising, evidence-based STEM education innovations and identify barriers and gaps in research (see Box 1-1). The 15-member Committee on Pre-K–12 STEM Education Innovations has extensive knowledge across STEM disciplines (science, engineering, mathematics, computer science, and data sciences) in various settings (rural and urban) with different spheres of influence (local, regional, and national). A subset of members works within out-of-school-time institutions that provide resources and services for formal Pre-K–12 settings, such as developing curriculum and providing professional development. Moreover, many committee members are trained scientists and mathematicians in addition to their work in education.

Many of the committee members deeply understand the broader policy landscape and have also been practitioners or worked closely with them. Committee members also bring a wealth of experience in developing programs designed to broaden participation in STEM, including designing systems, curricula, or policies that support the participation of traditionally marginalized and/or underresourced communities and students with disabilities. Their expertise covers the full spectrum of Pre-K–12 from early

---

BOX 1-1
Statement of Work

An ad hoc committee of the National Academies of Sciences, Engineering, and Medicine will conduct a consensus study to:

1. Review the research literature and identify research gaps regarding the interconnected factors that foster and hinder successful implementation of promising, evidence-based PreK-12 STEM education innovations at the local, regional, and national level;
2. Present a compendium of promising, evidence-based PreK-12 STEM education practices, models, programs, and technologies;
3. Identify barriers to widespread and sustained implementation of such innovations; and
4. Make recommendations to the National Science Foundation, the Department of Education, the National Science and Technology Council's Committee on Science, Technology, Engineering, and Mathematics Education, state and local educational agencies, and other relevant stakeholders on measures to address such barriers.

STEM education to secondary school, with differing orientations to the STEM disciplines and the integration of STEM content.

STUDY APPROACH

The committee met five times over 11 months in 2023 and 2024 to gather information on the interrelated factors at local, regional, and national levels that can foster or hinder the scaling of promising, evidence-based innovations. During this time, the committee reviewed the published literature on its charge and had opportunities to engage with many experts. Additionally, the committee commissioned three papers and a larger landscape paper during the information-gathering phase; the latter served as the basis for the compendium.

Study Process

The committee deliberated and came to consensus on the best ways to respond to its charge. Evidence was gathered from presentations and a review of the existing literature. The committee requested a literature search by the National Academies research center for information on Pre-K–12 STEM education innovations since 2000 with particular attention to barriers and challenges with implementation. In this search, STEM was defined as the individual disciplines (science, mathematics, engineering), including computer science and data science, as well as interdisciplinary and integrated approaches (see deeper discussion of this issue in the subsequent section Defining STEM) and covered the spectrum from preschool/prekindergarten through 12th grade.

Over the course of this study, committee members benefited from discussions and presentations by the many individuals who participated in the three fact-finding meetings. At the first meeting, the committee had the opportunity to engage with the sponsoring agency, NSF, speak with congressional staffers involved in the genesis of the legislation for this consensus study, and hear from the U.S. Department of Education. These conversations allowed the committee to gain clarity on the statement of work and the issues that are of most interest to the sponsoring agency, to understand the motivations leading to the development of this congressionally mandated consensus study, and to hear about ongoing national-level STEM education innovation initiatives already underway. Through this discussion with the congressional staffers, it was made clear that Congress's intention was for the report's emphasis to be placed on the scaling and sustainability of promising, evidence-based innovations; this intention was coupled with a desire to understand why innovations are not scaling and what supports are needed for innovations that have the potential to scale to achieve that goal. Subsequent meetings took up the theme of how to establish standards of evidence for what counts as a promising innovation as well as evidence that an innovation has scaled and has been sustained.

During the second meeting, the presentations centered on the broader system. The first panel began with taking an expansive view of the system, focusing first on STEM Ecosystems as an approach to leverage relationships across various stakeholders to solve a community-based problem and then on how states within a particular region can learn and share information about the implementation of high-impact practices (i.e., examining the work of the U.S. Department of Education's Regional Educational Labs [RELs][3]). The second panel examined state-led STEM initiatives from two angles: similar initiatives across different state contexts as well as two different initiatives deployed within the same state. This allowed the committee to consider how innovations can be activated throughout a system and the relationships that are leveraged, with attention to the local, more nuanced variability that exists. The final panel further honed in on a particular facet within the educational system—the development of STEM education innovations. In particular, the committee heard from researchers involved in developing specific STEM education innovations (Pre-K Mathematics and PhET Simulations) to interrogate how the developers sought to scale and sustain their evidence-based innovations, including the challenges faced and successes achieved.

The third and final fact-finding meeting, which was entirely virtual, examined teacher professional learning and what it means to center the needs of all students. On the first day, the panel focused on centering the needs of all students, elevating research on multilingual learners, students with disabilities, and engaging learners from Indigenous communities and tribal nations. On the second day, a set of panels presented evidence on professional learning. The first panel delved into innovations within pre-service teacher preparation programs and the need for induction supports. The second panel examined in-service teacher professional learning innovations, focusing on programs and models that have shown widespread impact.

During the fourth and fifth meetings, discussions about the evidence engaged the full committee, and members shared their expertise in designing and implementing Pre-K–12 STEM education innovations. Throughout the committee's deliberations, there was a constant tension between the large body of positive descriptive evidence, the lack of extensive causal evidence (particularly with respect to scaling and sustaining innovations), the impassioned calls for the expansion of Pre-K–12 STEM education innovations, and the numerous approaches for the implementation of innovations that

---

[3]For more information on RELs, see www.ies.ed/gov/ncee/rel/about

have already been established. The committee worked to reconcile the perspectives to provide guidance to the field. This report synthesizes the committee's findings based on the evidence reviewed and the expertise of its members.

The committee commissioned three papers to provide a more in-depth analysis of key issues. Sarah Woulfin (The University of Texas at Austin) and colleagues authored a paper analyzing the locus of control in U.S. educational policy. The paper examined the different actors within the K–12 state educational system with a particular focus on how these actors impact STEM teaching and learning (i.e., foster or serve as a potential barrier). Lori Connors-Tadros (National Institute for Early Education Research [NIEER]) and GG Weisenfeld (NIEER) provided a comprehensive overview of the U.S. Pre-K STEM educational policy landscape. The paper began with a discussion of how Pre-K is situated within the early childhood system and the implications for policy, governance and funding, and opportunities for STEM support in Pre-K programs. The final paper, by Sadhana Puntambekar (University of Wisconsin–Madison), focused on the historical context implementing promising tools and technologies within K–12 education and the implications for STEM learning.

Developing the Compendium

In addition to articulating the evidence on the interrelated factors that support promising, evidence-based innovations to scale, the committee was charged with developing a compendium of promising, evidence-based Pre-K–12 STEM education practices, models, programs, and technologies. The committee recognized that this was a major undertaking and commissioned the Education Development Center (EDC) to conduct a study to review the Pre-K–12 STEM education research literature and current landscape to identify innovative projects and projects with the potential for impact and scale.

The committee met several times with EDC to ensure that the development of the compendium would provide the committee with the insights that were needed to understand how the innovations approached scale and were able to sustain implementation successfully. As EDC conducted the work, they recognized that there would need to be a consistent set of standards and descriptors and that the innovations had to be consistent with the charge and have connections to formal public education settings. The development of the compendium also needed to be completed on a relatively short timeline. EDC developed a process whereby innovation developers or leaders were required to actively submit current program information via an online form to be considered for inclusion in the compendium. Although EDC did considerable outreach to lead people and organizations related to potential innovations, not all responded while the submission process was open. As a result, the compendium is not a comprehensive catalog. Appendix B describes the methodology EDC employed to carry out this work, and Appendix C presents the compendium.

Because this process was limited by both time and available funds, the effort is not exhaustive nor was it guided by the more nuanced definition of scale articulated by the committee. Moreover, it is a snapshot that will undoubtedly change as new innovations are developed and others mature and gather more evidence. The process was designed with the idea that it could be the seed for an ongoing effort to collect and update notable resources—this is beyond the auspices of the National Academies or this committee. In its fact-finding and deliberations, the committee also considered prominent programs and resources for which information was available through other sources (e.g., published literature and the What Works Clearinghouse), in addition to those that were evaluated for the compendium.

Defining Key Terms

There were several terms that the committee had to grapple with in understanding and interpreting the charge; below is a deeper discussion of some of these terms.

Defining STEM

The committee spent substantial time thinking through STEM and the various ways in which the term has been used and its connotations. The acronym STEM refers broadly to the whole scientific enterprise—basic research, applications, workforce, education—by naming its major constituent fields together.

Science is a vast enterprise dedicated to the fundamental empirical study of the natural and experiential worlds, and the discovery and explanation of patterns and regularities. It comprises numerous subdisciplines, broadly divided into physical and biological sciences, with many different methodologies for systematically gathering and evaluating evidence. Becoming a scientist generally requires many years of theoretical study and empirical practice focused on some subdomain of science.

Technology has many forms and functions. Throughout the history of science, new technologies have drawn on scientific knowledge to produce increasingly powerful tools for observation and analysis that have vastly expanded the capacity of human senses. In this respect, technology, like engineering, is an applied science. More recently, the knowledge-building discipline corresponding roughly to computer science has emerged, devoted to the study of algorithms, coding them, and digitizing information. Technologies based in these developments have expanded not just the physical capabilities of humans but also cognitive capacities. These can free human agents to rise to higher levels of performance. New developments in artificial intelligence (AI) have shown promise that it can not only provide technical support but also, sometimes, become a full partner in the discovery of new scientific knowledge. Because of technology's many pathways and roles, it has no uniformly developed model for professional preparation.

Engineering is an applied science in that it uses scientific knowledge to design and build tools intended to serve social needs and desires, tools that, like technology, enlarge human capability. Engineering is the act of creating artifacts, processes, or systems that advance technology and address human needs using principles of the sciences, mathematics, computing, and operations. It involves the knowledge of the mathematical and natural sciences (biological and physical) gained by study, experience, and practice that are applied with judgment and creativity to develop ways to utilize the materials and forces of nature for the benefit of mankind. It requires a systematic and often iterative approach to designing objects, processes, and systems. While science education provides the knowledge and curiosity-driven practices to understand the world, collegiate engineering education is more like professional preparation, analogous to medicine or law.

Mathematics is a conceptual rather than an empirical field that also serves as an enabling discipline for all of science, engineering, and technology in that it provides concise and precise analytic language and models with which to quantitatively express scientific discoveries about the natural and built worlds. Moreover, purely deductive reasoning on these models can sometimes expand scientific knowledge beyond what is easily perceptible. Mathematics research, like scientific research, is basic and curiosity-driven. The fundamental distinction between mathematics and science is their contrasting models of reasoning: deductive versus inductive. Mathematics research is mostly done either in academic environments, where it is combined with teaching, or in mission-oriented contexts, using applications of mathematics to other fields, like computer science, biology, medicine, cryptography, image processing, etc.

STEM. In the 1990s, the linguistic assemblage of STEM was found to be a useful term in discussions of federal policy concerning education and the workforce, and it continues to be so used.[4] It was originally SMET, reflecting the perceived order of importance of the fields; the change in 2001 to STEM has been attributed to Judith Ramaley, Assistant Director

---

[4]It should be noted that the earliest uses of the phrase can be linked to a "STEM Institute" developed by Charles Vela in the 1990s (Raupp, 2019).

for Education and Human Resources at the NSF, who made the change "on aesthetic grounds and conceptual grounds" (Lyons, 2020, p. 226).

As Lyons (2020) described, using the acronym provided momentum in three ways. First, it provided the impression of a consolidation of resources, increasing the capacity for lobbying, media attention, and curriculum leverage. Second, it promoted engineering into curriculum conversations. Third, there is the power associated with the inclusion or exclusion of other disciplines (inclusion of Medicine [STEMM] or inclusion of Arts [STEAM]); however, this has been carried out piecemeal rather than considering how closely aligned conceptually the disciplines are. (See Chapter 3 for a more detailed discussion of how accountability has shaped STEM education and the prioritization of content areas within STEM.)

Visibly, these four fields are quite different in form, function, and practice. Yet they are substantially related and are deeply synergistic. Indeed, there are compelling arguments that many of the significant challenges we face in the 21st century may be most powerfully approached by integrated teams of professionals with deep expertise in various STEM disciplines. However, it does not automatically follow that Pre-K–12 curriculum and pedagogy also pursue full integration of all aspects of STEM. The common use of language like "STEM workforce" and "STEM education" tempts people to think that STEM is a singular entity, rather than an assemblage of related and interdependent components. In particular, some discussions of "integrated STEM education" seem to suggest (mistakenly) that STEM is itself a scientific subject. With respect to STEM education, there is a need to carefully consider and orchestrate the relationships among learning opportunities within the core individual disciplines and opportunities that integrate them in purposeful ways.

In practice, the integration of concepts, methods, and tools from different STEM disciplines has often been connected with particular pedagogies, such as problem-based learning and modeling (e.g., Hmelo-Silver, 2004; Lehrer & Schauble, 2012). While there may be some natural affinity, it is important to point out that the research on learning and teaching that supports these pedagogical practices is separate from the notion of integrating STEM disciplines, and does not require or depend on a commitment to combine content or tools from one or more STEM fields. Moreover, the core organizing concepts, bodies of interconnected knowledge, epistemologies, discourse, and practices within individual disciplines have distinctive characteristics and follow unique learning trajectories (NASEM, 2018). Research indicates that it is essential that students have sufficient opportunities to build these knowledge bases and competencies in systematic ways over multiple years (Clements & Sarama, 2021; Rich et al., 2020). This stands in contrast to a checklist mentality sometimes observed when teachers feel pressured by school administrators or curriculum pacing guides to fit a lot of diverse content into the school day, and are encouraged to add different bits to an activity to "cover" math, science, technology, and language arts in a single class period. For example, the fact that students might use a tool to measure something while doing a science investigation and then write a paragraph describing their procedure and findings does not mean that they were engaged in systematically advancing their understanding and proficiency with important grade-band appropriate concepts and skills in each of these disciplines.

Taken together, the committee recognizes the variability in integration and also realizes that the evidence on the effectiveness of these integrated approaches is still emerging (English, 2016; National Academy of Engineering [NAE] & NRC, 2014). Thus, the committee does not subscribe to a single integrated approach. Instead, the group examined the evidence on STEM education innovations, including those located in individual domains and those that were designed to be integrated in some fashion.

Innovations

It was important for the committee to come to a clear understanding of what might be meant by "innovations" as it appears in the statement of work. One possible interpretation is the notion of novelty, something that is new. But as the committee reflected on the use of this word in the context of the charge—coupled with the language of promising, evidence-based practices, programs, models, and technologies—and following the conversation with congressional staffers, it was clear that a different frame would better serve the purposes of the present work. The committee came to use this word not just to connote the act of invention or a general change, but also as a capacious term to indicate the varied novel approaches, curricula, programs, methods of analysis, etc. that serve as the specific objects of analysis focused on in this report. The committee also connected innovation with progress and improvement, noting that even if an innovation might not be deemed wholly "new," it *might* be new to some individuals, or the instantiation of an innovation might be new. As such, the committee defines **an innovation** as an idea or potential solution intended to positively alter one or more intended learning outcomes. This framing is consistent with the U.S. Department of Education's Office of Innovation and Improvement, which recognizes the inherent contradiction between developments that are innovations (new and untested) versus ones that are solidly evidence-based.[5] The committee determined that for an innovation to be considered as promising, there needed to be some evidence

---

[5] See https://www2.ed.gov/about/offices/list/oii/about/definition.html

of its potential to scale and some evidence of beneficial impacts on student learning or teacher practice.

This led the committee to think not just about the individuals involved in the design or development of an innovation but also those who are involved in the implementation of the innovation. The committee identified four groups: *beneficiaries* (the recipients of the innovation), *designers* (those who design the innovation), *enactors* (those who directly enact the innovation), and *enablers* (those who support the enactors). This characterization allows one to recognize the ways in which an individual may wear multiple hats or have various roles in the innovation and that there can also be a shifting or handing off of roles over time (see Chapter 4 for a more nuanced discussion).

Scale and Implementation

The committee also discussed issues of scale and implementation. The statement of task asks the committee to consider barriers to widespread and sustained implementation of innovations and through the conversation with congressional staffers, as suggested above, emphasis on issues of scale was clarified as a driving motivation. The committee defined *scale* as the degree to which an innovation is enacted or implemented. The committee explored the ideas of implementation and scale through a framework offered by Coburn (2003) and discusses the conceptualization of scale and what it means for scaling innovation in Chapter 4. In particular, the committee defined scale as multidimensional. Although many discussions of scale focus solely on increasing number of participants (spread), the committee also considered dimensions such as depth of implementation (i.e., the extent to which the innovation is intended to create or entails substantial shifts in the core of educational practice), sustainability (i.e., innovation endures over time in the original and new contexts when the initial circumstances run their course), and ownership (i.e., extent to which knowledge of and authority over the innovation is deepened and expanded over time).

The committee defined *implementation* as the process by which actors enact a designed innovation in a particular context, in service of the intended learning outcomes, and can be understood in relation to the four dimensions of scale. In considering *widespread implementation*, the committee recognized that this could be accomplished by supporting the learning of a broader population in a specific setting than was initially engaged (e.g., "spreading" from one school in a district to a set of schools; from one set of students in an afterschool setting to a broader set of students) or supporting learning in additional settings from where the innovation was initially implemented (e.g., "spreading" to a different district, state). *Sustained implementation* meant that the implementation took hold over time, even in the face of changes. These innovations could also include those developed for a particular population or to address a specific problem of practice that was not designed to spread beyond the intended context.

Attending to Equity

A critical issue in considering how innovations spread and are sustained in new settings and with new participants is understanding who gains access to new opportunities, how they are supported, and the degree to which new implementations continue to demonstrate effectiveness in serving the needs of different communities and groups of learners. If dimensions of equity and inclusiveness are not attended to, it is likely that patterns in the uptake of innovations in STEM education will replicate or even increase existing disparities.

Along with a variety of other resources, the committee drew on overlapping equity frameworks developed in two recent National Academies consensus study reports to focus and frame considerations of equity in relation to the scaling and sustainability of STEM education innovations. *Science and Engineering in Preschool through Elementary Grades: The Brilliance of Children and the Strengths of Educator*s (NASEM, 2022) outlined four approaches to equity: (1) increasing opportunity and access to high-quality science and engineering learning and instruction; (2) emphasizing increased achievement, representation, and identification with science and engineering; (3) expanding what constitutes science and engineering; and (4) seeing science and engineering as part of justice movements. *Equity in K–12 STEM Education* (NASEM, 2024) described five equity frames that can serve as decision-making guides: (1) reducing gaps between groups, (2) expanding opportunity and access, (3) embracing heterogeneity in STEM classrooms, (4) learning and using STEM to promote justice, and (5) envisioning sustainable futures through STEM.

In reviewing the scaling of innovations in STEM education, our committee encountered a variety of approaches exemplified in individual innovations, many of which expressed explicit goals with respect to equity. The large majority of innovations—particularly those with a long enough track record to have achieved some success in scaling and sustaining their innovations and in producing evidence to document their processes and outcomes—focused on expanding access and opportunity, including availability of social and material resources; and increasing achievement, representation, and self-identification as someone who can learn and participate in STEM. Some projects, especially those that have focused on particular sociocultural contexts or the needs of particular groups of learners, such as multilingual students or neurodivergent students, have explored ways of making STEM learning experiences more accessible to all students (e.g., with emerging technologies) and have promoted a wider variety of ways in which children and youth can make sense of and find meaning in STEM concepts and practices. Projects focused on promoting justice and cultivating sustainable futures through STEM are generally more recent, and the committee found few examples that had specific evidence that could illuminate whether and in what ways issues of scalability or sustainability are different for these approaches.

Considering the Full Landscape of Learning Opportunities in STEM

In its work, the committee needed to describe implementation of innovations and the interrelated factors at local, regional, and national levels. Part of beginning that work was consideration of the variety of spaces in which an innovation can be designed and implemented, recognizing that this is different across the Pre-K–12 continuum. Although the committee prioritized STEM outcomes in formal education spaces, it was important to consider the variety of participants and actors engaged throughout the process including families, communities, business and industry, higher education, and out-of-school time organizations (i.e., STEM learning ecology). The committee began from a sociocultural lens to consider the dynamic forces at play that shape how individuals and collectives learn (see Figure 1-1). A sociocultural lens examines multiple levels of influence from the immediate surroundings to broader-culture, placed-based, and historical contexts (Bronfenbrenner, 1994; Nasir et al., 2020, 2021; Rogoff, 2003).

It is important to note that Figure 1-1 does not capture every kind of institution and the complex inter-institutional relations, but it provides a starting point to visualize the landscape in which learners move and participate. The layers within the system include:

- *Place (light yellow)*: Place refers to the histories, futures, ideologies, values, and cultural practices of that place and in the context in which learning happens. Rather than a backdrop, place is the foundational base context of learning (NASEM, 2022), mediating everyday interactions in teaching and learning, community spaces, and various institutional norms at multiple levels.
- *Learners within Classrooms and Homes (light yellow)*: Learners sit at the center. Children in Pre-K–12 education systems are the primary learners under this label; they are often the target end-beneficiaries of many STEM innovations and the focus of a program or model. Here, we use "learners" in the plural for two reasons. First, "learners" recognizes that humans learn in systems of dynamic sociocultural interactions that include other key social others such as teachers, peers, and families (Lee, Shin, & Bong, 2020). Learning is always relational, mutually constituted, social, cultural, and situated

INTRODUCTION 27

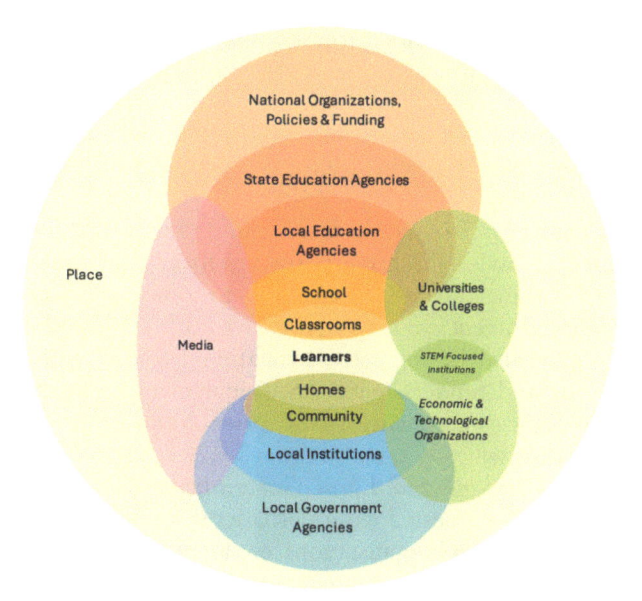

FIGURE 1-1 STEM learning ecology.
SOURCE: Committee generated.

in place (NASEM, 2022). Learning conceptualized as a collective endeavor helps us to see the ways children learn across classrooms and homes (Gutiérrez & Rogoff, 2003), in ways that individual views of learning and accomplishment often fail to account for. Second, the committee sees teachers as other key learners within STEM Pre-K–12 innovations, with teacher learning and leadership as important actors and levers in educational theories of change.

"Learners" and "place" are both colored light yellow to highlight ways the specificity of place within learning and interaction continually mediates children's and teachers' sensemaking and participation. STEM learning is always influenced by the situated histories, futures, natural, social, and built environments, cultural practices, ideologies, ethics, and politics of a particular place and time (NASEM, 2018, 2022, 2024).

- *Schools and Communities (yellow)*: One layer out from the dynamic learning interactions in homes and classrooms are school and communities. School-level actors include educational leadership (e.g., instructional leaders, department heads, teacher groups, principals) whereas community actors include afterschool programs, clubs, parent groups, community centers, and faith-based groups in which families participate.

Together, these yellow circles learners within homes, classrooms, schools, and communities make up various parts of the microsystem of STEM learning.

Moving out in proximity to the learner are the more distal systems. These are sometimes referred to as the exosystem, which are interacting factors that more indirectly influence the development of learners.

- *Local, State, and Federal Educational Agencies and Organizations (orange)*: Individual schools in the Pre-K–12 education systems are nested within, and are accountable to, school districts and state educational agencies, as governed by both state and federal law. They may also be impacted by national STEM education organizations and funders (e.g., U.S. Department of Education, Institute of Education Sciences, NSF, private and other philanthropic organizations).
- *Local Institutions and Local Governments (blue)*: Children and their families are nested within broader systems of local institutions (e.g., neighborhood organizations, community centers, playgrounds), STEM-rich learning spaces (e.g., museums, libraries, other community groups), and county and city governments. Leaders, cultural brokers, and organizers play important roles in the adoption and dissemination of STEM education innovations both vertically within and horizontally across organizations (Akkerman & Bruining, 2016; Ishimaru et al., 2016).
- *STEM Focused Institutions including Universities and Colleges and Economic and Technological Organizations (green)*: Two other key bodies of actors include (a) postsecondary institutions such as universities and colleges that support STEM learning and training of teachers as well as partnerships across the system, including professional societies, and (b) workforce development agencies, businesses, corporations/not for profits, philanthropies, and other economic and technological supports/tools for STEM learning within and beyond the classroom.
- *Media (pink)*: Various media outlets play an important role in knowledge dissemination for Pre-K–12 STEM innovations. For innovations to scale, knowledge dissemination is a key factor that supports public engagement with STEM learning opportunities, documentation of impact, and spread within and across levels of the system.

Although these layers are described separately, this approach underscores the dynamic nature of development and how each layer is co-constituted and interconnected. That is, while federal and school district policies and priorities (exosystem) influence school practices in classrooms (microsystem), what happens in classrooms at the microsystems level can also shape the local- or federal-level policies and discourses about what STEM is and related learning outcomes (Spillane, Reiser, & Reimer, 2002).

The committee also considered the landscape when the unit of analysis is an innovation itself, rather than learners. From a lens of scale and sustainability, landscape here refers to the relationships among various Pre-K–12 actors, designers, and enablers within and across levels of the system, the ways various actors interact, and their spheres of influence. Given that the U.S. education system has a local locus of control (i.e., states, districts, and schools have the power to make decisions), the federal government plays an indirect role in education. And although schools are most directly responsible for educating students, what goes on in classrooms is influenced and affected by a variety of factors within and beyond a single school, district, and state, as decisions are made that influence how innovations can scale and sustain, the impact the innovations can have, and the tensions/misalignments that can arise within the system. In probing this tension, the committee examined how partnerships within the educational system can be a mechanism through which innovations can scale and be sustained, and considered the necessary supports needed for the various local contexts (e.g., building the necessary organizational and relational infrastructure) and the conditions that support or hinder its development, implementation, scale, spread, depth, and sustainability.

MAJOR FEATURES OF THE CURRENT CONTEXT

In addition to grappling with many of the complexities of the statement of work, the committee also recognized the need to acknowledge particular features of the current context that serve to shape the scale and sustainability of innovations: the changing student demographics and increasing demands on the teacher workforce and the rapidly evolving technological landscape. These factors are important to consider as opportunities to learn in Pre-K–12 STEM education are unevenly distributed and the experiences individuals have vary based on a myriad of factors (NASEM, 2024). What follows is a discussion of these features and their impacts on Pre-K–12 STEM education.

Changing Student Demographics and Increasing Demands on Teacher Workforce[6]

Over the past two decades, there have been a number of shifts that have impacted the expectations for Pre-K–12 teachers: policy shifts, an

---

[6]This section draws heavily from the National Academies report on *Changing Expectations for the K–12 Teacher Workforce: Policies, Preservice Education, Professional Development, and the Workplace* (2020).

increasingly diverse student body, and the composition of the workforce itself. There have been marked changes with respect to the expectations for teachers in the classroom: they are required to attend to new curricular standards and participate in the selection and adaption of instructional materials, all while being held accountable for student performance (NASEM, 2020). There has also been an increasing emphasis on technology, both in terms of how teachers use technology as a vehicle for learning as well as for communication with families and as a medium for sharing ideas for educators (NASEM, 2020).

These increasing demands are happening while the diversity of the student population has rapidly shifted. The majority of students in U.S. K–12 schools identify as members of minoritized communities. As a result, teachers need to evaluate their teaching practices to ensure that they are creating environments that are supportive for all learners and foster trusting and caring relationships among students and with teachers (NASEM, 2020). This demand to create a learning environment that responds to the experiences of all students in combination with these compounded expectations for learning (given the policy shifts) call for innovative approaches to instruction that may differ substantially from their own experiences as students or their preservice education (NASEM, 2020).

Lastly, all of this is happening within the content of a hyper-localized teacher labor market that is seeing substantial staffing challenges and teacher turnover. Although teachers develop a number of valuable skills during their preparation, there still remains a mismatch in terms of the preparation teacher candidates seek out and the job opportunities available. A common finding across states is that staffing challenges are generally far greater for schools serving students living in poverty, students who are low-achieving, students of color, rural schools, those geographically far from teacher education programs, and in high-needs subjects, such as science, technology, engineering, mathematics, and special education (NASEM, 2020).

These longstanding issues can present challenges for the implementation of Pre-K–12 STEM education innovations. Although the subsequent chapters do not take these issues up in substantial detail, they connect to an important undercurrent that can have far-reaching impact, particularly the preparation of teachers and their perception as professionals in education.

Acknowledging the Rapidly Evolving Technological Landscape

The promise of technology is that, when used and implemented well, it could be a game-changer in K–12 classrooms: there would be equitable access for all learners to develop the skills needed to succeed, and teachers and schools would have the data available to make decisions about students' learning, informing both individualized instruction and policies (see Chapter 6). It is important to remember that the use of technology in schools and districts does not guarantee learning, but rather, is a tool that mediates it. Critical use of technologies in the service of *learning* requires continuous updates, integration with existing systems, and regular troubleshooting—all of which require ongoing professional development to build and expand professional capacity among teachers.

The COVID-19 pandemic provided an opportunity to work toward this goal through the Elementary and Secondary School Emergency Relief (ESSER) funding program, which many districts used to invest in educational software and systems (see Chapter 2). However, with ESSER funding having ended in September 2024, schools now have to make decisions about the best use(s) of the technology given the prospect of diminishing resources. This means districts, schools, and teachers are facing increased pressure to utilize the most up-to-date technology while many struggle with implementation, or are unable to quickly adapt. The growing inequities for school districts that have been historically underfunded will become more pronounced as the chasm around technology access and usage continues to widen, further disadvantaging students who already face significant educational barriers. Additionally, the pace of research cannot keep up with the changing technology, which leaves districts, schools, and teachers implementing technology without fully understanding the intended use or the potential impacts on learning as they do not have the necessary evidence to make evidence-informed decisions. The rapid evolution and increase of technology use in the classroom means that teachers must frequently adapt through professional development, mentorships, and time spent with colleagues to keep pace with the continuous growth, continually considering which technologies for what purposes.

REPORT ORGANIZATION

This report is intended to describe what is known about promising, evidence-based Pre-K–12 STEM education innovations and how those can be taken to scale and sustained. To understand the interconnected factors that foster and hinder successful innovations at local, regional, and national levels, the committee needed to first set the stage.

Chapter 2 characterizes the landscape of the public Pre-K–12 education system[7] including the various actors at different levels of the system (federal, state, and local levels, including district and regional), including their roles and responsibilities.[8] Building from an understanding of the system overall, the committee then describes the history of federal and national

---

[7]Note that the scope of the committee's statement of work is centered on formal education spaces. This resulted in a limited focus on informal learning.

[8]Note that there is limited research on higher levels of the system. The committee draws on websites as appropriate.

STEM education improvements in Chapter 3, recognizing that many of the reforms were born out of a need to address concerns with the state of K–12 education and the implications for the competitiveness of the STEM workforce. In Chapter 4, the committee provides a framework for understanding what it means to scale and sustain a STEM education innovation. The chapter begins with articulating a multidimensional framework for conceptualizing scale and then goes on to discuss various approaches to scaling innovations.

Chapter 5 extends the discussion of scaling innovations by describing the inherent tensions that can exist between the landscapes of innovation and implementation. Central to understanding this landscape is recognizing that there is an important distinction to be made between the configurations of actors, decision makers, and financial resources that are typically involved in the development of evidence-based innovations as compared to the configurations that come into play as innovations are implemented, sustained, and spread across settings and populations. Together, these chapters provide an understanding of the current state of Pre-K–12 STEM education and the various actors at different levels of the system and what it takes to scale and sustain innovations—addressing bullet one of the committee's charge.

To address bullet two, Chapter 6 highlights the evolving technological landscape, providing a discussion of how technology has had a profound impact on education, whereas Chapter 7 presents the findings from the compendium, emphasizing the factors that fostered and hindered successful implementation of the identified promising, evidence-based, Pre-K–12 STEM education innovations.

The report culminates in Chapter 8, which pulls together the various enabling and constraining factors highlighted throughout, discussing the affordances of durable systems that can allow for innovations to scale and sustain and the need for system change—addressing bullet three of the committee's charge.

Building from the evidence covered throughout the report, Chapter 9 presents the committee's consensus conclusions and recommendations, and identifies key areas for future research.

REFERENCES

Akkerman, S., & Bruining, T. (2016). Multilevel boundary crossing in a professional development school partnership. *Journal of the Learning Sciences*, 25(2), 240–284.

Bronfenbrenner, U. (1994). Ecological models of human development. *International Encyclopedia of Education*, 3(2), 37–43.

Clements, D. H., & Sarama, J. (2021). STEM or STEAM or STREAM? Integrated or interdisciplinary? In C. Cohrssen & S. Garvis (Eds.), *Embedding STEAM in early childhood education and care*. Palgrave Macmillan.

Coburn, C. E. (2003). Rethinking scale: Moving beyond numbers to deep and lasting change. *Educational Researcher, 32*(6), 3–12.

English, L. D. (2016). STEM education K–12: Perspectives on integration. *International Journal of STEM Education, 3*(1), 3.

Gutiérrez, K. D., & Rogoff, B. (2003). Cultural ways of learning: Individual traits or repertoires of practice. *Educational Researcher, 32*(5), 19–25.

Hmelo-Silver, C. E. (2004). Problem-based learning: What and how do students learn? *Educational Psychology Review, 16*(3), 235–266.

Ishimaru, A. M., Torres, K. E., Salvador, J. E., Lott, J., Williams, D. M. C., & Tran, C. (2016). Reinforcing deficit, journeying toward equity: Cultural brokering in family engagement initiatives. *American Educational Research Journal, 53*(4), 850–882.

Lee, H. J., Shin, D. D., & Bong, M. (2020). *Considering sociocultural influences. Promoting motivation and learning in contexts: Sociocultural perspectives on educational interventions.* Information Age Publishing.

Lehrer, R., & Schauble, L. (2012). Seeding evolutionary thinking by engaging children in modeling its foundations. *Science Education, 96*(4), 701–724.

Lyons, T. (2020). Seeing through the acronym to the nature of STEM. *Curriculum Perspectives, 40*, 225–231.

Nasir, N. S., Lee, C. D., Pea, R., & McKinney de Royston, M. (2021). Rethinking learning: What the interdisciplinary science tells us. *Educational Researcher, 50*(8), 557–565. https://doi.org/10.3102/0013189X211047251

Nasir, N. S., McKinney de Royston, M., Barron, B. J. S., Bell, P., Pea, R., Stevens, R., & Goldman, S. (2020). Learning pathways: How learning is culturally organized. In N. S. Nasir, C. D. Lee, R. Pea, & M. McKinney de Royston (Eds.), *Handbook of the cultural foundations of learning* (pp. 195–211). Routledge.

National Academies of Sciences, Engineering, and Medicine (NASEM). (2018). *How people learn II: Learners, contexts, and cultures.* The National Academies Press. https://doi.org/10.17226/24783

___. (2020). *Changing expectations for the K-12 teacher workforce: Policies, preservice education, professional development, and the workplace.* The National Academies Press.

___. (2021a). *Call to action for science education: Building opportunity for the future.* The National Academies Press. https://doi.org/10.17226/26152

___. (2021b). *Cultivating interest and competencies in computing: Authentic experiences and design factors.* The National Academies Press. https://doi.org/10.17226/25912

___. (2022). *Science and engineering in preschool through elementary grades: The brilliance of children and the strengths of educators.* The National Academies Press. https://doi.org/10.17226/26215

___. (2023). *Closing the opportunity gap for young children.* The National Academies Press.

___. (2024). *Equity in K-12 STEM education: Framing decisions for the future.* The National Academies Press.

National Academy of Engineering, & National Research Council. (2014). *STEM integration in K–12 education: Status, prospects, and an agenda for research.* The National Academies Press. https://doi.org/10.17226/18612

National Center for Science and Engineering Statistics. (2023). *Diversity and STEM: Women, minorities, and persons with disabilities 2023* (Special report No. NSF 23-315). National Science Foundation. Available: https://ncses.nsf.gov/wmpd

National Research Council. (2011). *Successful K–12 STEM education: Identifying effective approaches in science, technology, engineering, and mathematics.* The National Academies Press. https://doi.org/10.17226/13158

National Science Board. (2019). *Higher education in science and engineering. Science and engineering indicators 2020* (Report No. NSB-2019-7). https://ncses.nsf.gov/pubs/nsb20197/

National Science and Technology Council, Committee on STEM Education, National Science & Technology Council, the White House. (2018). *Charting a course for success: America's strategy for STEM education.* A Report by the Committee on STEM Education of the National Science & Technology Council. https://files.eric.ed.gov/fulltext/ED590474.pdf

Raupp, A. B. (2019, August 4). STEM education's lost decade and tenor: Contemporary insights into a popular, global movement. *Medium.* https://medium.com/datadriveninvestor/stem-educations-lost-decade-and-tenor-3f741bd728e6

Rich, K. M., Spaepen, E., Strickland, C., & Moran, C. (2020). Synergies and differences in mathematical and computational thinking: Implications for integrated instruction. *Interactive Learning Environments, 28*(3), 272–283.

Rogoff, B. (2003). *The cultural nature of human development.* Oxford University Press.

Spillane, J. P., Reiser, B. J., & Reimer, T. (2002). Policy implementation and cognition: Reframing and refocusing implementation research. *Review of Educational Research, 72*(3), 387–431.

U.S. Department of Education. (2022). *Raise the bar: STEM excellence for all students.* https://www2.ed.gov/about/inits/ed/raise-the-bar/stem-excellence.pdf

U.S. Department of Education, Office of Educational Technology. (2023). *Artificial intelligence and the future of teaching and learning: Insights and recommendations.* https://www2.ed.gov/documents/ai-report/ai-report.pdf

2

Landscape of STEM Education Learning Opportunities: Federal, State, Local, and Regional Roles

Numerous educational reform[1] efforts at the federal and state levels have attempted to change the nature of science, technology, engineering, and mathematics (STEM) instruction and disrupt persistent patterns regarding students' short-and long-term STEM outcomes. Yet structural features of the U.S. education system present barriers as well as opportunities for STEM education innovations to take root and scale. For instance, district and school leaders have limited time to create new systems and routines that boost educators' capacity to teach STEM in ambitious ways. And teachers may lack opportunities to learn how to shift STEM pedagogical practices, or innovate, to serve all students in engaging, equitable ways. At the same time, individuals find ways to make positive change. Various actors, positioned across multiple levels of the education system and facing different institutional and organizational conditions, deploy their agency while enacting STEM innovations. These actors not only engage in different responsibilities but hold different levels of power and authority for motivating the implementation of various innovations.

---

[1] The development and implementation of innovations in Pre-K–12 STEM education sometimes intersects with larger reform efforts in U.S. education. Advancing significant reform initiatives, such as changing STEM teaching and learning as called for in the Framework for Next Generation Science Standards, typically depends on introducing and aligning a variety of specific innovations at different levels of the education system, such as new models of assessment, new curricula, and new professional learning programs for educators. As a result, some but not all innovations are also aligned with educational reforms, and the report may use the term reform in relation to such cases. The report does not refer to large-scale reform initiatives writ large as innovations in and of themselves.

This chapter begins with mapping the landscape of the public education system actors and the role of each one in STEM learning. For each level—federal, state, local, school, and regional—the chapter goes on to explain which actors engage in which types of activities related to STEM innovations and discusses how that shapes implementation. Throughout, the chapter explains the spheres of influence of various actors who affect the direction and depth of efforts to improve STEM teaching and learning.

MAPPING THE STRUCTURE OF U.S. EDUCATION SYSTEM

The structure of the U.S. public education system affects the implementation of STEM innovations. As represented in Figure 2-1, the education policy system includes organizations and actors situated at federal, state, district, and school levels. Outside of the formal system, there are also numerous organizations and actors interfacing with the education system at every level. As these policy actors design, authorize, monitor, and implement STEM reforms and innovations, their specific locations within this nested structure shape their agency, constraints, access to resources, and capacity to effect change. Policy actors frequently interface with one another, both through interactions that descend across levels such as setting mandates, offering incentives, or monitoring progress, and interactions that ascend across levels, such as reporting data or interpreting and framing policy directives from above. Additionally, the roles of regional actors in the STEM policy process are highlighted as they are linked to actors at various system levels through policy networks (Hodge, Salloum, & Benko, 2020). In some instances, regional actors engage system actors directly to shape policy agendas, advocate for specific policies, or support policy implementation; in other cases, they serve as bridges between implementing actors by facilitating the flow of information, resources, and expertise.

Examining the STEM learning ecology presented in Chapter 1, Figure 2-1 is focused on STEM policy actors. Each of the multiple, nested levels of the education system contains regulations, ideas, and resources related to STEM education innovations. However, different innovations are coupled to the policy system in diverse ways. Crucially, institutional and organizational elements permeate across levels of the system, shaping the nature of implementation. For instance, ideas and resources from the state level related to STEM innovations often move to the district and then school levels, shaping systems, practices, and outcomes. For example, federal accountability policies issue mandates regarding collecting and analyzing data on students' mathematics proficiency. Individual states, however, make specific decisions and develop plans regarding which mathematics assessments and cut scores to use (Pelsue, 2017). Next, districts within a state make concrete decisions on preparing students for these mathematics

Regional actors

Textbook publishers, curriculum companies
· Create STEM instructional materials and assessments

STEM education organizations
· Disseminate learning standards
· Lead teacher professional development

Community and industry partners
· Expand extracurricular opportunities
· Offer student internships
· Cultural institutions

Private foundations and business community
· Invest in STEM programs

Federal

U.S. Department of Education
· Monitor and support states and districts
· Distribute Title I and other federal funds

State

State Legislatures

Education Commissioner
· Messaging on STEM

State Board of Education
· Set state education regulations
· Write and approve curriculum standards
· Adopt instructional materials

State Education Agency
· Create initiatives
· Select frameworks and curricula
· Manage assessment systems

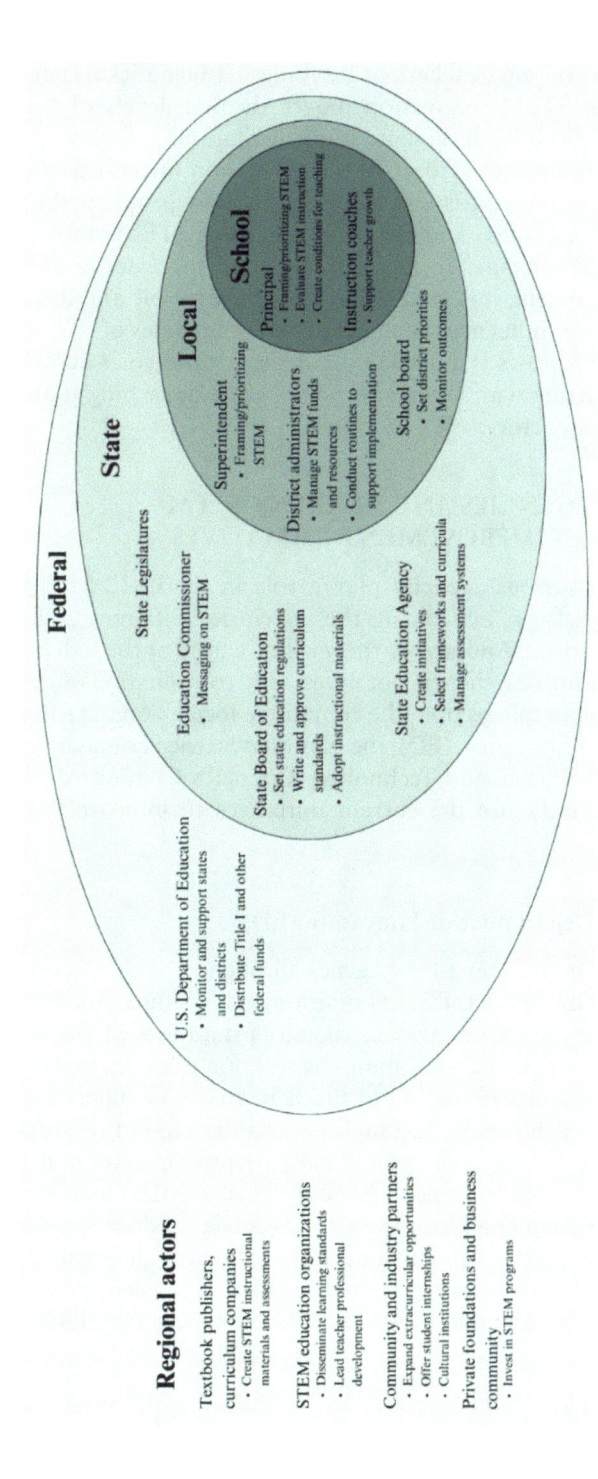

Local

Superintendent
· Framing/prioritizing STEM

District administrators
· Manage STEM funds and resources
· Conduct routines to support implementation

School board
· Set district priorities
· Monitor outcomes

School

Principal
· Framing/prioritizing STEM
· Evaluate STEM instruction
· Create conditions for teaching

Instruction coaches
· Support teacher growth

FIGURE 2-1 The nested ecology of STEM policy actors.
NOTE: In some states, the state education agency mirrors the actions of the state board of education. Additionally, although regional actors are positioned outside of the circles, they have influence throughout the nested system and should be conceptualized as woven throughout.
SOURCE: Adapted from Woulfin et al., 2024.

assessments and how to support teachers in teaching mathematics in particular ways. As a given STEM innovation moves through levels of the system, it may mutate in both its design and implementation.

Throughout this chapter with respect to the discussion of the various roles of the different actors, emphasis will be placed on how people within each level advance (or block) ideas and resources regarding STEM innovations to foster (or impede) change. To better understand successes in and barriers to STEM improvement, it is vital to consider how people and their ground-level, daily practices influence the dynamics and outcomes of STEM innovation efforts. What follows is a discussion of the various roles across the education system, starting with federal agencies before describing state, district, local, and regional actors.

FEDERAL AGENCIES AND CURRENT STEM EDUCATION IMPROVEMENT INITIATIVES

At the federal level, various agencies play a role in Pre-K–12 STEM education improvement efforts, influencing the system for different audiences tied to specific priorities. And across the various actors at the federal level, even with similar priorities, there is not necessarily coordination of the programs across agencies. In this section, the committee focuses on the roles of the U.S. Department of Education (ED), the National Science Foundation (NSF), and the National Science and Technology Council's Committee on STEM Education (CoSTEM) and the current initiatives to improve Pre-K–12 STEM education.[2]

U.S. Department of Education (ED)[3]

Established in 1979 as a Cabinet-level agency through the U.S. Department of Education Organization Act, ED sets priorities and disburses funding to state education agencies (SEAs) as well as monitors state uses of federal funds. It also has taken up rigorous education research for practices to support high-quality teaching and learning. All of this is in service of supporting access to opportunity for each person, accomplished via the support of SEAs and initiatives to improve local school quality. ED currently operates under the governance of the Every Student Succeeds Act (ESSA), a 2015 bipartisan reauthorization of the longstanding Elementary and Secondary Education Act (ESEA; see Chapter 3 for a deeper discussion). Although many different offices make up ED, particular attention is given to the Office of Elementary and Secondary Education (OESE) and the Institute of Education Sciences (IES).

---

[2]These actors were specifically called out in the committee's statement of work.
[3]This section was developed from www.ed.gov

Office of Elementary and Secondary Education (OESE)

OESE, comprising ten offices, serves as the primary federal policy interface with state departments of education in efforts to support and improve local K–12 education agencies. Box 2-1 outlines the roles and responsibilities of OESE paraphrased from the authorizing legislation.

A large part of federal support for state and local education agencies (LEAs) comes through funding through the Office of Formula Grants. To receive formula funds from ED, called Title or covered funds, states must submit plans. All 50 states, the District of Columbia, and Puerto Rico have successfully submitted consolidated plans for funding, meaning that each of these agencies has adopted state-level math and science standards and aligned assessments, and provide targeted interventions to schools that underperform on state math assessments, among other non-STEM related indicators. Outside of basic formula funding, when annual congressional appropriations exceed the trigger amounts noted in each Title category under ESSA, the Office of Discretionary Grants and Supports Services develops and

---

BOX 2-1
Office of Elementary and Secondary Education (OESE)

Authorizing Legislation
U.S. Department of Education Organization Act (1979)

Role
The mission of OESE is to empower states, districts, and other organizations to meet the diverse needs of every student by providing leadership, technical assistance, and financial support.

Responsibilities
OESE is responsible for directing, coordinating, and recommending policy for programs designed to:

- Help state and LEAs improve the achievement of preschool, elementary, and secondary school students;
- Support equal access to services to help every child achieve with particular attention to children who are from low-income families, have disabilities or developmental delays, are educationally disadvantaged, or are English Learners, Native American, migrant, homeless, or in foster care;
- Advance educational improvement at the state and local levels; and
- Provide financial assistance to LEAs whose local revenues are affected by federal activities.

SOURCE: Based on www.ed.gov

administers competitive funding programs. Box 2-2 shows the kinds of funding available through ESSA as well as how funds are calculated and flow.

Separate from ESSA funding but still under the governance of OESE, Congress appropriated three rounds of funding for the Elementary and Secondary School Emergency Relief Fund (ESSER): Coronavirus Aide, Relief, and Economic Security (CARES) Act of 2020, Coronavirus Response and Relief Supplemental Appropriations (CRRSA) Act of 2021, and the American Rescue Plan (ARP) Act of 2021. Each round flowed to SEAs in the same proportion as Title I-A funds; however, these funds were not constrained to ESSA guidelines. The first two rounds of funding were intended to support state and LEAs as they responded to challenges to teaching and learning amid COVID-19. ARP and ESSER focused primarily on

---

BOX 2-2
ESSA Funds: Categories, Calculations, and Flow-Through

State Formula-Funded, or Covered, Grant Programs (FY 2023)

- Title I-A: Improving Basic Programs Operated by Local Educational Agencies (18.4B)
- Title I-B: State Assessment Grants (390M)
- Title I-C: Education of Migratory Children (375.6M)
- Title I-D: Prevention and Intervention Programs for Children and Youth Who are Neglected, Delinquent, or at Risk (49.2M)
- Title II-A: Supporting Effective Instruction (2.2B)
- Title III-A: English Language Acquisition, Enhancement, and Academic Achievement (890M)
- Title IV-A: Student Support and Academic Enrichment Grants (1.4B)
- Title IV-B: 21st Century Community Learning Centers (1.3B)
- Title V-B Rural Education (215M)

For each Covered Program, any appropriation at or below the trigger level gets funneled to formula funding to support SEAs in meeting basic ESSA requirements.

Discretionary Funding Description

Any appropriation above the trigger amount turns into pre-established discretionary funds ED can use as competitive grants programs to encourage evidence-based innovation beyond basic ESSA stipulations. Across programs, only a few have a history of receiving appropriations over the threshold. Below is a list of the funded competitive grant programs relevant to STEM education and their most recent allocations.

reopening and recovering from the impact. ESSER funding officially expired in September 2024.

In addition to the various funding mechanisms described, OESE also provides technical assistance through the Comprehensive Center Network (CCNetwork) and supports the sharing and scaling of effective practices across regions. The CCNetwork is made up of the National Comprehensive Center as well as 19 Regional Comprehensive Centers (RCC). Together, this network provides technical assistance to state, regional, local, and tribal education agencies (SEAs, REAs, LEAs, and TEAs) to build capacity in educational systems. The RCCs work closely with the states in their region to identify educational system needs before developing, implementing, and evaluating evidence-based solutions.

- Teacher and School Leader Incentive Grants (Title II, Part B, Subpart 1)
- Supporting Effective Educator Development (Title II, Part B, Subpart 4)
- School Leader Recruitment and Support (Title II, Part B, Subpart 4)
- STEM Master Teacher Corps (Title II, Part B, Subpart 4)
- Education Innovation and Research (Title IV, Part Subpart 1)
- Preschool Development Grants (Title IX, Part B)

Competitive Assessment Grants

The most well-funded competitive grant program relevant to STEM education is the Competitive Assessment Grants (CAG) program in Title 1-A to promote the redesign of state assessment systems to more closely align with instruction to promote useful and usable data. The table below (Table 2-2-1) represents the nine CAGs awarded to states related to science or math. The remaining 34M in competitive assessment grants were used for English Language Arts-related assessment systems.

Table 2-2-1 Competitive Assessment Grants

2019–2022 Total	58M	19 grants
Math Total	2.5M	1 grant
Math w/ELA Total	9.5M	4 grants
Science Total	12M	4 grants

SOURCE: Based on https://www.nea.org/sites/default/files/2023-01/final-fy23-appropriations-for-education-related-discretionary-programs-with-state-tables.pdf (2023 Appropriations) and https://oese.ed.gov/offices/office-of-discretionary-grants-support-services/

Institute of Education Sciences (IES)[4]

In 2002, the Education Sciences Reform Act of 2002 expanded the research capability of ED through the establishment of IES. Currently operating directly under the supervision of the Secretary of Education, IES is organized into four centers: (a) National Center for Education Evaluation and Regional Assistance (NCEE), (b) National Center for Education Research (NCER), (c) National Center for Education Statistics (NCES), and (d) National Center for Special Education Research (NCSER; the most recent center as of 2004). IES aims to connect research, policy, and practice in education through the production of sustained, usable, and rigorous scientific evidence. Box 2-3 outlines the role and responsibility of IES; note that the authorizing legislation specifically calls out responsibilities related to mathematics and science teaching and learning. Congress appropriated $734 million to IES initiatives in 2023.

National Center for Education Evaluation and Regional Assistance (NCEE)

NCEE is made up of two divisions: The Evaluation Division, responsible for evaluating any ED programs, and the Knowledge Use Division, responsible for dissemination and technical assistance. The Knowledge Use Division operates within two teams: The Regional Educational Laboratories (RELs) and the Knowledge Synthesis Team, which operates the What Works Clearinghouse, the National Library of Education, and the Education Resources Information Center.

The RELs collaborate with school districts, state departments of education, and other education stakeholders through research-practice partnerships to help generate and apply evidence, with the goal of improving learner outcomes. There are currently ten REL regions (see Box 2-4). The RELs engage partners in the design, execution, and evaluation of REL activities. The partnership activities are intensive, narrowly focused on a high-leverage topic within a specific state, and characterized by effective communication, cooperation, and mutual understanding of the context, content, and intended outcomes of the work. The work of the RELs is to produce clear, objective, and peer-reviewed research products designed to be actionable for partners and national audiences, including the development of toolkits that support the scaling up of best practices. RELs provide training, coaching, and technical support for use of research as well as work to disseminate research and evidence in a timely, accessible, and actionable manner. See Chapter 5 for additional discussion.

National Center for Education Research (NCER)

NCER, in pursuit of rigorous evidence about what works in education, employs several mechanisms to achieve its goals. Across initiatives,

---

[4]This section summarized from https://ies.ed.gov/

BOX 2-3
Institute of Education Sciences Authorizing Legislation, Role and Responsibilities

Authorizing Legislation
   Education Sciences Reform Act (2002)
   Educational Technical Assistant Act (2002)
   National Assessment of Educational Progress Authorization Act (2002)

Role
   The role of the Institute of Education Sciences within ED is to support the synthesis and, as appropriate, the integration of education research to promote quality and integrity using accepted practices of scientific inquiry; to obtain knowledge and understanding of the validity of education theories, practices, or conditions; and to promote scientifically valid research findings that can provide the basis for improving academic instruction and lifelong learning

Responsibilities
   IES can carry out the following responsibilities itself, through grants, or cooperative agreements:

- Maintain published peer-review standards and standards for the conduct and evaluation of all research and development
- Promote the use of scientifically valid research within the federal government, including active participation in interagency research projects
- Ensure that research conducted under the direction of the Research Center is relevant to education practice and policy
- Synthesize and disseminate the findings and results of education research conducted or supported by the Research Center
- Carry out research on successful state and local education reform activities, including those that result in increased academic achievement and in closing the achievement gap
- Conduct research on technology in education, including research into how technology affects student achievement, how teachers use technology, which technologies are most effective and cost-efficient under what conditions, and long-term research into cognition and learning issues as they relate to the uses of technology
- Conduct research on methods of mathematics and science teaching that are most effective, cost efficient, and able to be applied, duplicated, and scaled up for use in elementary and secondary classrooms, including in low-performing schools, to improve the teaching of, and student achievement in, mathematics and science

SOURCE: Based on https://ies.ed.gov/

BOX 2-4
REL Regions

The RELs operate within ten different regions of the United States and its territories. What follows is a list of the regions with states and territories served in each.

Appalachia: Kentucky, Tennessee, Virginia, and West Virginia

Central: Colorado, Kansas, Missouri, Nebraska, North Dakota, South Dakota, Standing Rock Reservation, and Wyoming

Mid-Atlantic: Delaware, District of Columbia, Maryland, New Jersey, and Pennsylvania

Midwest: Illinois, Indiana, Iowa, Michigan, Minnesota, Ohio, and Wisconsin

Northeast & Islands: Connecticut, Maine, Massachusetts, New Hampshire, New York, Puerto Rico, Rhode Island, Vermont, and Virgin Islands

Northwest: Alaska, Idaho, Montana, Oregon, and Washington

Pacific: American Samoa, Commonwealth of the Northern Mariana Islands, Federated States of Micronesia, Guam, Hawaii, the Republic of Palau, and the Republic of the Marshall Islands

Southeast: Alabama, Florida, Georgia, Mississippi, North Carolina, and South Carolina

Southwest: Arkansas, Louisiana, New Mexico, Oklahoma, and Texas

West: Arizona, California, Nevada, and Utah

SOURCE: Taken from https://ies.ed.gov/ncee/rel/About

NCER identifies, develops, and evaluates promising education innovations to support scale-up of the most effective practices, programs, or policies. Additionally, NCER promotes high-quality research through training in educational research. To stimulate research and development in context nationwide, NCER funds the creation of National Education Research and Development Centers (R&D Centers)—temporary R&D initiatives comprised of interdisciplinary teams housed at various universities and research engines nationwide. R&D Centers typically run for five years.

Although none of the 13 active R&D Centers pursues work related to STEM education or scaling effective practices, several of the 21 completed R&D Centers have produced research relevant to the committee. However, of the 34 funded R&D Centers since 2002, only a small percentage have been specific to STEM Education.[5]

National Center for Education Statistics (NCES)

NCES is one of 13 federal statistical agencies, and, like the Census Bureau, it collects and analyzes national longitudinal data for public use. This organization sets psychometric, statistical, and data confidentiality standards, collects statistical information through surveys, such as the National Teacher and Principal Survey, and provides technical assistance related to measurement and data systems, among other goals. Additionally, NCES is responsible for the biennial administration of the National Assessment of Education Progress (NAEP)—which measures student achievement in math and reading (as well as science in grades 4, 8, and 12)—with guidance from the National Assessment Governing Board and the cooperation of states.

As part of the technical assistance offered by NCES, the Statewide Longitudinal Data Systems Grant Program (SLDS) provides funding to states and territories to develop the interconnected data systems needed to gather information about teaching and learning broadly. Established under the Educational Technical Assistant Act of 2002, the intent is to promote more functional local and SEAs that can better respond to student performance and educator needs measured more reliably over time, filling in gaps to provide more resources toward disadvantaged students. Although SLDS grants are given to only a few states, any state can receive technical assistance from check-in calls to site visits from the SLDS State Support Team to help build robust data systems.

National Center for Special Education Research (NCSER)

Authorized by the Individuals with Disabilities Education Act (IDEA) in 2004, NCSER is the newest division (with grant awards starting in 2006) within IES charged with researching the needs of and best practices to support students with disabilities, infants, and toddlers to improve services

---

[5]The National Center on Cognition and Science Instruction operated from 2008 to 2013, prior to the formation and adoption of state-level science standards based on the 2012 *Framework for K–12 Science Education* (National Research Council [NRC], 2012), to modify FOSS and Holt through iterative cycles of adaptation and then test them in two parallel large-scale randomized controlled trials (RCT). Likewise, the National Research and Development Center on Cognition and Mathematics Instruction housed at WestEd from 2010 to 2015 also modified middle grade math curricular materials and conducted large-scale RCTs. During the same timeframe, Vanderbilt University ran the National Research and Development center on Scaling Up Effective Schools to identify innovations that effectively enabled large urban schools to provide quality education for historically low-performing groups.

at scale. Like NCER, NCSER carries out its work through research grant programs, special education research and development centers, partnerships, research training programs, and research networks. A few notable projects have come out of NCSER, including several longitudinal studies (see Wagner et al., 2006 for an overview of the National Longitudinal Transition Study-2 and Carlson et al., 2009 for an overview of the Pre-Elementary Education Longitudinal Study).

Department of Health and Human Services (HHS)[6]

Within HHS, the Administration for Children and Families runs the Office of Early Childhood Development (ECD). This office supports (a) holistic efforts to meet the diverse needs of families across the country as they raise children from birth to school age and (b) recruits, prepares, and retains a strong workforce ready to meet the demands of the wide range of available programs.

Pertinent to the committee are the Preschool Development Birth through Five grants, funded by HHS but co-administered by ECD and the Office of Early Learning within ED, to promote strategic planning and coordination efforts across existing state programs. These grants are intended to support the transition from early childhood education to kindergarten across state systems by creating partnerships between systems to increase collaboration between Pre-K and elementary educators, align curricular strategies, and support family navigation between systems. Although not particular to content in its current iteration, there is room for discipline-specific support in future grant cycles.

Head Start uses a federal to local funding model to promote locally responsive early education programs for low-income families. Again, although this federal program does not support STEM specific outcomes, students enrolled in Head Start tend to have better high school graduation and college enrollment rates. More short term, Head Start shows content-specific benefits for enrolled students that, while statistically significant for students at the end of their programs, generally fade throughout early grades in elementary. In developing the workforce of early childhood educators across states, HHS has proposed an increase in Head Start worker salaries that could improve wages by up to $10,000 a year.

National Science Foundation (NSF)[7]

NSF is a federal grant-making agency that funds research related to teaching and learning in STEM. In particular, it supports both basic and

---

[6]This section summarized from https://www.acf.hhs.gov/ecd
[7]This section summarized from https://new.nsf.gov/funding/find-by-directorate

applied research to progress science and engineering, promote societal well-being, and provide national defense. NSF is organized into Divisions within Directorates, with the Directorate for STEM Education and the Directorate for Technology, Innovation, and Partnerships (TIP) being the most pertinent to Pre-K–12 STEM education (see Box 2-5). In addition to the funding opportunities provided through the Directorates described next, NSF and the White House Office of Science and Technology Policy support the Presidential Awards for Excellence in Mathematics and Science Teaching (PAEMST) and Presidential Awards for Excellence in Science, Mathematics, and Engineering Mentoring (PAESMEM) programs.[8] These programs can play a critical role in highlighting individuals in LEAs and teachers who support innovative STEM programming to make change for students.

Directorate for STEM Education (EDU)

Although there are a number of different divisions within EDU, the Division on Equity for Excellence in STEM and the Division on Research on Learning in Formal and Informal Settings (DRL) lead the work most pertinent to this report.[9] DRL "invests in improving STEM Education for people of all ages by promoting innovative research, development, and evaluation of learning and teaching across all STEM disciplines in formal and informal learning settings."[10] Within this Division, the Discovery Research Pre-K–12 (DRK12) and the EDU Core Research programs supports research and development to enhance STEM learning and teaching for Pre-K–12 students. The programs aim to award on average $50 million annually to roughly 50–60 exploratory, design and development, impact, implementation, measurement and assessment, or synthesis projects, in either teaching or learning strands.

Technology, Innovation, and Partnerships Directorate (TIP)

In the CHIPS and Science Act of 2022, the same legislation that mandated the work of the committee, authorized the TIP Directorate. TIP has three broad focus areas: (a) fostering innovation and technology ecosystems, (b) accelerating research to impact, and (c) partnering to engage the nation's diverse talent. Given the recent development of TIP, none of the activities to date has foregrounded public K–12 STEM education as an avenue to develop the STEM workforce.

---

[8] See https://paemst.nsf.gov/ and https://paesmem.nsf.gov/

[9] It is important to note that EDU/DRL also includes the Advanced Informal STEM Learning (AISL) program, which also funds programs that could be of interest to this study. However, because the funding more indirectly flows into formal Pre-K–12 education settings, it is not discussed in detail.

[10] See https://www.nsf.gov/edu/drl/about.jsp

> **BOX 2-5**
> **National Science Foundation (NSF)**
>
> **Authorizing Legislation**
> National Science Foundation Act of 1950
>
> **Role**
> The role of NSF is to promote the progress of science; to advance national health, prosperity, and welfare; to secure the national defense; to strengthen basic research and education in the sciences, including independent research by individuals; and to avoid undue concentration of such research and education
>
> **Responsibilities**
>
> - Develop and encourage the pursuit of a national policy for the promotion of basic research and education in the sciences
> - Initiate and support basic scientific research in the mathematical, physical, medical, biological, engineering, and other sciences
> - Appraise the impact of research upon industrial development and upon the general welfare
> - Initiate and support specific scientific research activities in connection with matters relating to the national defense
> - Award scholarships and graduate fellowships in the mathematical, physical, medical, biological, engineering, and other sciences
> - Foster the interchange of scientific information among scientists in the United States and foreign countries
> - Evaluate scientific research programs undertaken by agencies of the federal government
> - Maintain a register of scientific and technical personnel and in other ways provide a central clearinghouse for information covering all scientific and technical personnel in the United States
>
> SOURCE: Based on https://new.nsf.gov/funding/find-by-directorate

National Science and Technology Council's Committee on STEM Education (CoSTEM)

Within the Executive Office of the President, the Office of Science and Technology Policy (OSTP) exists to both advise the president on and coordinate among nearly 200 programs across roughly 20 federal agencies regarding science and technology–related affairs. OSTP supports the National Science and Technology Council, a cabinet-level advisory group liaising between Congress, federal programs, and the White House to both elevate current science and technology in policy decisions and to support consistency in vision and policy across the federal government. The council works in six committees, with CoSTEM primarily responsible for coordinating STEM education efforts across federal programs.

CoSTEM was established in 2011 through the America COMPETES Reauthorization Act and is responsible for coordinating STEM education efforts across federal programs. This is accomplished through setting the vision through the federal five-year strategic plan. The most recent plan, which was established in 2018 and active through 2023, pursued three goals: (a) Foundational STEM Literacy, (b) Broadening Participation in STEM, and (c) STEM workforce preparation through four pathways: (a) strategic partnerships, (b) interdisciplinary STEM,[11] (c) computational literacy, and (d) operational transparency and accountability.

Across federal agencies that are coordinated through CoSTEM, there are nearly 200 programs that focus on STEM education and workforce development.[12] In 2022–2024, an estimated $14.5 billion flowed from federal programs to support STEM education and transition to the STEM workforce. Of those investments, $4.75 billion impacted Pre-K–12 education either directly or indirectly and $1.7 billion supported efforts primarily for Pre-K–12 STEM education (see Annex Table 2A-1).[13] Of those efforts, NSF ($814.4 million) made the largest investment, outpacing ED ($731.6 million) by $82.8 million. The next largest investment came from HHS under the National Institute of Health in the form of the Science Education Partnership Awards ($98.1 million), a competitive grant program that supports resources and authentic learning experiences aligned to state standards for STEM subjects.

ROLE OF STATES IN PRE-K–12 STEM EDUCATION

Although federal agencies do have some influence on state educational priorities and activities, each state has the power to direct its own education system with oversight from a variety of actors at each state level. State educational agencies (SEA) play crucial roles in education policy as they direct funding, respond to mandates from the federal government and their own state legislatures, and oversee compliance. SEA officials function as system actors who make decisions related to STEM innovations, including creating grant programs to prepare and develop STEM educators and vetting lists

---

[11] For more information, see the CoSTEM report *Convergence education: A guide to transdisciplinary stem learning and teaching* available at https://www.whitehouse.gov/wp-content/uploads/2022/11/Convergence_Public-Report_Final.pdf

[12] These programs support a variety of different STEM education initiatives either within schools or in out-of-school time settings, aimed at Pre-K–12, undergraduate, graduate, or transitioning students and/or educators.

[13] Just over 40 of the 244 CoSTEM tracked investments went to formal Pre-K–12 institutions.

of approved mathematics and science instructional materials.[14] Traditionally, within the Pre-K–12 space, those individuals who are responsible for decision making for Pre-K are separate from those responsible for decision making about what is happening within K–12. What follows is a discussion of the key state-level actors within the formalized Pre-K system followed by the K–12 state-level actors.

The Formalized Pre-K System[15]

Young learners are served through a diverse range of early childhood programs before they enter Kindergarten; these include private or religiously affiliated preschools, federally funded preschool programs such as Head Start, state-funded prekindergarten programs, childcare settings, and home daycares. Across the different preschool programs, access to and the quality of STEM learning experiences varies greatly, with children in public preschool programs serving lower income communities often having less access to high-quality STEM learning experiences and/or resources (e.g., Morgan et al., 2023; NASEM, 2024a; Piasta, Pelatti, & Miller, 2014).

Before delving into specific roles and responsibilities of states in supporting Pre-K education, there are a few contextual considerations. First, it is important to note that the wholistic approach to early childhood education has strengths and includes features that could in fact help address some of the challenges seen within K–12 (Larimore, 2020); for instance, preschool teachers often form home-school collaborations, draw from families' insights and experiences, and create caring and collaborative classroom cultures, which have been found to be necessary and conducive for deeper STEM learning (NASEM, 2023, 2024a). At the same time, however, STEM has not been a focus of accountability initiatives in preschool, which often drive the attention given to curriculum and professional learning[16] experiences provided to teachers. Similar to early elementary educators, preschool

---

[14]State roles vary from state to state. Many do not have the ability to create their own grant programs. Further, only about half of the states have lists of approved instructional materials, whereas others leave these decisions entirely up to local districts.

[15]Portions of this text were drawn from the commissioned paper by Connors-Tadros and Weisenfeld (2024).

[16]The committee recognizes that, as evidence-based practices have evolved with regard to the most effective ways to enable teachers to expand their knowledge and refine their practice in support of students' learning, there has been a shift away from short-term professional development workshops or passive lectures toward sustained, interactive learning experiences that include opportunities for educators to practice, customize, and reflect on how they can apply new learning in their schools and classrooms. The term "professional learning" is increasingly being used to refer to the latter approach. This report generally uses the term professional learning, in line with current best practices, except when describing the work of others, in which case their own terms and descriptors are retained.

teachers are rarely provided with high-quality professional learning opportunities to facilitate children's STEM engagement and learning specifically and the support to integrate STEM learning into an increasingly crowded preschool curriculum as well as training on culturally responsive teaching practices (NASEM, 2024a).

Role of States

In the United States, state-level agencies manage a variety of early care and education (ECE) programs serving children from birth through age five (Franchino & Loewenberg, 2019), including publicly funded preschool programs (Friedman-Krauss et al., 2020). These agencies administer almost $40 billion in federal funding and more than $8 billion in state funding, plus other state investments for young children (before school entry), including preschool children (Connors-Tadros et al., 2021).

The state's role in the education of young children before kindergarten is growing with the expansion of state-funded Pre-K increasing from 700,000 four-year-olds served in state-funded preschool programs in 2001 to its current peak of 1.63 million children in 2022–2023 (Friedman-Krauss & Barnett, 2024). The formal Pre-K early education system is unique, and distinct from childcare, in that its primary focus is on education grounded in child development and developmentally appropriate practice, focusing on the whole child and all domains of development and learning. Pre-K is authorized and funded separately from the K–12 system. Each state designs its Pre-K system through authorizing legislation, and funding, and determines eligibility, quality standards, and monitoring.

The governance of programs serving preschool children at the state level is highly variable and can be fragmented, partly due to the differing federal, state, and local funding sources and associated regulations (Friedman-Krauss et al., 2024). For example, in Alabama, three state agencies oversee five different programs serving preschool-aged children, and in Washington state, one state agency oversees five programs serving preschool-aged children (Education Commission of the States, 2020). An increasing number of states are moving to consolidate programs serving young children, before school entry, to increase access to programs and the efficiency of administering and funding programs, many of which have different federal, state, or local funding sources and regulations (Walsh, Smith, & Mercado, 2023).

Authority and Oversight of State Pre-K

The authority and oversight of state-funded Pre-K can be housed in different state agencies, such as the SEA, the state human services agency, a separate child-serving agency, and in a few cases, a public-private partnership entity. For the 44 states and Washington, D.C. that operate state-funded Pre-K, the programs are administratively housed in the SEA in the majority of states. Though it varies greatly, authority for Pre-K within the SEA could allow for greater coordination and alignment of Pre-K with K–12 policy, including STEM-related standards or initiatives (policy alignment with STEM is discussed in more detail below.) For example, in Kansas, the state-funded preschool program is housed in the Early Childhood Unit, in the state Department of Education, Division of Learning, Special Education and Title Services.[17] A unique example of coordinated decision making across state agencies is the West Virginia Universal Pre-K program,[18] administratively housed in the SEA, but required by legislation to have shared leadership across the Departments of Health and Human Services (HHS) and the SEA.

Pre-K is administered by a separate state agency for young children in some states.[19] These state agencies' major purpose is to provide oversight to the state-funded Pre-K program and depending on the specific state legislation, coordinate with other programs for young children. A separate state agency elevates early childhood to a cabinet-level position, with similar authority to the state's Secretary of Education. For example, the Alabama Department of Early Childhood Education[20] implements state-funded Pre-K and Head Start and other programs serving children from birth through age eight.

Less common is when state-funded Pre-K is housed in the health and human services department, currently in just three states (North Carolina, North Dakota, and Washington[21] state); or oversight is located or co-located across several entities, as in South Carolina where authority for state-funded Pre-K is split between the SEA and First Steps[22] which is both

---

[17] See https://www.ksde.org/Agency/Division-of-Learning-Services/Special-Education-and-Title-Services/Early-Childhood

[18] See https://wvde.us/early-and-elementary-learning/wv-universal-pre-k/

[19] Alabama, Colorado, Connecticut, Georgia, Massachusetts, Michigan, Hawaii, New Mexico, and Oregon are examples of states that have set up a separate state agency to oversee Pre-K. In addition, Arizona's First Things First program is overseen by the Early Childhood Development and Health Board; the Louisiana Board of Elementary and Secondary Education oversees the Louisiana, 8(g) program; the Head Start Collaboration Office has authority over Minnesota Head Start; and the Utah State Board of Education, Department of Workforce Services, Office of Child Care oversees its state Pre-K program. For more information, see Friedman-Krauss et al. (2024).

[20] See https://children.alabama.gov/

[21] One of the Pre-K programs, the Early Childhood Education and Assistance Program operates under the authority of the Department of Children, Youth and Families, but the SEA has administrative authority over the other Pre-K program, Transition to Kindergarten.

[22] See https://www.scfirststeps.org/

a state agency and nonprofit entity. The SEA oversees the public-school Pre-K programs, and First Steps oversees the community-based preschools.

Funding Sources and Funding Mechanisms of State-funded Pre-K

Funding for Pre-K programs is a combination of federal, state, and local dollars (Parker, Diffy, & Atchison, 2018). In 2022–2023, states spent on average, $7,277 per child (Friedman-Krauss et al., 2024). When adding other reported spending (not all states could report all funds), the state average per-child expenditures increased to $8,294 (Friedman-Krauss et al., 2024). This is much lower than the comprehensive Head Start program ($13,840 per child) and substantially lower compared to the average per-child K–12 spending of $18,426 (2022–2023) (Friedman-Krauss et al., 2024).

State dollars are typically general fund appropriations. Some states and cities use "sin taxes" such as lottery (Georgia), soda tax (Philadelphia), and tobacco/nicotine tax (California and Colorado) to fund Pre-K programs or quality services to support them. About a quarter of the state Pre-K programs use the school funding formula (SFF),[23] at least in part, to fund programs (Friedman-Krauss et al., 2024). To distribute funds, some programs use the same mechanism as the SFF, distributing state dollars to school districts who then subcontract with nonpublic schools to operate in mixed-delivery settings. Other states use grants to distribute contracts through a competitive bidding process, and others award contracts to any eligible provider.

Federal dollars come from several different U.S. departments, including ED for Title I and IDEA Part C and Part B and HHS for Head Start, Child Care Development Fund, and Temporary Assistance for Needy Families (NASEM, 2018). Each funding source has rules defining who is eligible to receive the funds, how the dollars can be used, and who is the direct recipient is. For example:

- Head Start funds flow directly to programs or agencies, not the state.
- Title I is controlled by public school districts that decide if it is used for Pre-K.[24]

---

[23] For more information about school funding formulas and Pre-K, see Barnett, W. S., & Kasmin, R. (2018). Fully funding Pre-K through K–12 funding formulas. *State Education Standard, 18*(1), 22–28.

[24] For more information, see U.S. Department of Education. (2024). *Serving children through Title I, Part A of the Elementary and Secondary Education Act of 1965, as amended: Non regulatory guidance.* https://oese.ed.gov/files/2024/02/Title-I-Preschool-Early-Learning-Guidance-Revised-2023-FINAL.pdf

- IDEA funding is targeted at children from birth to five with special needs.

Even though states do not administer federally funded Head Start programs, 13 states[25] supplement Head Start grantees in their states by extending the day, offering quality enhancements, or adding seats (Friedman-Krauss et al., 2024).

In addition, there are also temporary funding sources like the COVID-19 relief funds (CARES, ARP, Governor's Emergency Education Relief Fund) and the Preschool Development Grants Birth through Five that some states have used to increase access to or enhance the quality of their Pre-K programs.

Coordination of State Policy for Pre-K

Given the multiple agencies that may have authority and oversight for programs and public funding before kindergarten entry, some states have formally established early care and education advisory committees. Though most may influence policy, they are typically advisory and do not have authority/oversight of programs. About half of states have a formal ECE collaborative/advisory committee to align and coordinate ECE services across ages and agencies (Education Commission of the States, 2020). Additionally, in some states, such as Kentucky, Illinois, and Rhode Island, the governor has established an office of early learning in the governor's office to coordinate policy and funding across state agencies. Some state boards of education (SBOEs) also have authority over Pre-K (National Association of State Boards of Education, 2022), and many are increasingly providing leadership on Pre-K policy (Regenstein, 2023). For example, the Maryland State Board of Education[26] monitors, advises, and makes recommendations on education policy specifically outlined in its *Strategic Plan, the Blueprint for Maryland's Future*,[27] which has a strong focus on early childhood education.

K–12 System Actors[28]

Public K–12 schools serve approximately 49.4 million students, making it essential to understand how the system can address equitable STEM

---

[25]The 13 states that supplement their state's Head Start programs are Alabama, Arkansas, Connecticut, Maine, Maryland, Massachusetts, Minnesota, New Jersey, Oklahoma, Oregon, Pennsylvania, Rhode Island, and Wisconsin.

[26]See https://marylandpublicschools.org/stateboard/Pages/default-2023.aspx

[27]See https://blueprint.marylandpublicschools.org/

[28]Portions of this text were drawn from the commissioned paper by Woulfin and colleagues (2024).

educational opportunities for all students. Within the K–12 public education system, governors, state legislators, and state education officials from the SEA and SBOE, all play a critical role in shaping STEM initiatives and their successful implementation. State-level actors can prioritize the need for STEM innovations and reform efforts within their sphere of influence through policies, programs, and publicity. These actors also are critical in ensuring successful implementation of innovative STEM education through statewide coordination, funding, and evaluation (Zinth & Goetz, 2016).

Chief State School Officers (CSSO)

CSSOs are tasked with effectively leading the regulatory, administrative, and operational needs of schools. Notably, there exists variability in the titles and method of selections for their state education leader. Throughout the 50 states and territories, these leaders are referred to as commissioners or secretaries of education, or state superintendents of schools or public instruction. In 12 states, the CSSO is elected, while in the remaining 38, they are appointed by the governor, the SBOE, or a board of regents. CSSOs have much influence in the uptake of STEM innovations within the SEA and, increasingly, as public figures. As public leaders of education, CSSOs can bring significant attention to STEM innovations. For instance, a CSSO may visit schools to highlight innovative programs or engage with other districts or outside partners to facilitate partnerships associated with STEM initiatives. These activities elevate the importance of STEM innovation efforts, encouraging or motivating shifts in practice.

State Board of Education (SBOE)

The SBOE plays an important role in establishing statewide goals and supervision for a state's public education system. The SBOE shapes STEM teaching and learning by adopting education regulations for state standards, assessments, curriculum, instructional materials and graduation requirements. Just as the selection and organization of CSSOs differs from state to state, so does the SBOE. Members of the SBOE may be elected or appointed and often have political and business ties within the state that can influence their actions and interests. The nature of members' selection to the SBOE may influence their relationship to other state policy actors including the governor, CSSO, and members of the state legislature. The SBOE may adopt a unified set of legislative priorities with varying levels of influence and respond to the requirements of state legislative action that fall within its statutory authority (see Education Commission of the States, 2020). For example, in Washington state, the legislature created the STEM pilot program to invest in access to laboratory space to support the SBOE-adopted graduation requirement of three science credits, two of which must be laboratory sciences (Noahr, Black, & Rogers, 2016). Actions by the SBOE can also bring attention to issues such as gender gaps in STEM and reviewing state standards and curricula on STEM (Young, VanGronigen, & Reynolds, 2019). SBOE may also recognize a state definition for STEM, or craft strategic plans to accomplish goals for state STEM education.

State Educational Administrators

State administrators also modulate STEM innovation efforts vis-a-vis the development and administration of grant programs. Many SEAs receive both federal and private grants targeting STEM innovations that they, in turn, award to LEAs. These grants not only provide critical resource support for LEAs, but also signal what and how schools prioritize STEM innovations. In other cases, SEAs might support STEM innovations by awarding grants to organizations outside of the LEA. In Indiana, the Higher Education Commission awarded $10 million in grants to different organizations, including colleges and universities, to recruit and retain STEM teachers (Indiana Commission for Higher Education, 2023). Whereas many state initiatives for supporting STEM innovations are funded through grants or partnerships with private foundations and corporations, some SEAs have begun to design, implement, and fund initiatives to support science achievement (Pruitt & Wallace, 2012).

Although the decision on the adoption and implementation of curriculum is often left to the LEA, state-level actors are increasingly enacting policy to shape local decisions. State legislatures, SBOE, and SEAs all influence LEAs by identifying and incentivizing the adoption of curriculum and high-quality instructional materials (HQIM) that align with the state education standards and academic goals. Some states, like Louisiana, have created rubrics to help LEAs identify HQIM and provide benefits for those who adopt materials designated as quality (Doan et al., 2022). These benefits include financial incentives and professional learning opportunities to strengthen teachers' implementation of high-quality materials. Coordination among state actors supports a coherent instructional system of aligned learning standards, curriculum, HQIM, and teacher professional learning opportunities necessary to successful implementation of STEM education (Cherbow at al., 2020).

State administrators' roles and responsibilities linked to assessment policies and programs can also shape STEM initiatives. Specifically, state educational administrators implement assessments that are aligned to their state standards, as federally required by ESSA. In mathematics, assessments occur annually for third through eighth grade students, while ESSA only requires students to be assessed in science three times, once in each of the 3–5, 6–9, and 10–12 grade-bands. Results of assessments, along with school quality indicators, are publicly reported annually through a state report card. In high school, states choose to administer assessments as an end-of-course requirement or as specific biology, chemistry, or physical science tests. In Massachusetts, state leaders adopted a Science and Technology/Engineering test design that covers earth and space science, life science, physical science, and technology/engineering, which aligns with the state's adopted STE curriculum framework (Massachusetts Department of Education, 2024). Some states that have adopted NGSS standards administer an assessment aligned to these standards.

Finally, state administrators also support innovations in STEM education by recognizing programs that support STEM achievement. North Carolina created its STEM Schools of Distinction program to recognize schools dedicated to providing quality STEM programs (North Carolina Department of Public Instruction, 2024). Some states prioritize programs to recognize exemplary STEM students and facilitate opportunities to extend their STEM education through community programming and funding for postsecondary degree attainment. In Florida, the Sunshine State Scholars Programs recognizes exemplary STEM students and rewards students with both scholarships and unique STEM experiences to further their learning (Florida Department of Education, 2024). This program is supported through partnerships between the Florida Department of Education and private corporations, foundations, universities, and the Florida Lottery. These recognition programs bring important attention to innovative strategies for STEM education while providing evidence-based programs with the knowledge and investments to further their impact.

LOCAL-LEVEL ACTORS[29]

Local-level actors within the K–12 system influence what happens within districts and schools. What follows is a discussion of the major players within each of these levels.

District

Educational systems vary considerably across dimensions—for example, across traditional public school districts and charter management organizations, or across localities (i.e., urban and suburban to rural contexts). Across diverse systems, district leaders play key roles in designing and implementing STEM innovations. Their activities range from framing ideas about and allocating funding for STEM programs and initiatives to

---

[29]Portions of this text were drawn from the commissioned paper by Woulfin and colleagues (2024).

recruiting and retaining STEM educators and staff and facilitating professional learning opportunities related to innovations.

Superintendents

The role of the superintendent has changed over the decades (Björk, Browne-Ferrigno, & Kowalski, 2014). Superintendents were once deemed to be teacher leaders who might have more closely supported STEM innovations through a more hands-on approach, but their scope has shifted to encompass larger, more complex political and operational responsibilities (Brunner, Grogan, & Bjork, 2002). Superintendents currently balance local interests with the challenges of political pressures as well as accountability-based reforms emanating from the state and federal levels (Bredeson & Kose, 2007). There has been documentation that the high pace of the work and increased demands associated with this shift in scope has led to turnover and ongoing instability in school district leadership (White, 2023).

For over 30 years, the focus on large-scale educational reforms has linked superintendents with these reform movements (Björk et al., 2014). As the face of the district, superintendents set a vision for the district and communicate this with the public, advocating on behalf of the community. Yet, amid demands for increased accountability, superintendents must also comply with legislative requirements. Superintendents typically champion reform efforts but must ensure any proposed innovations fit the district's needs and priorities. Thus, superintendents operate as political actors and may promote STEM innovations by framing them to appeal to district educators, families, and community members.

Superintendents are also responsible for overseeing the day-to-day operations of the district and may further support STEM initiatives by facilitating the hiring of proper personnel and setting goals for student outcomes. Depending on factors such as a district's size, location, and organizational structure, specific central office STEM leadership roles as well as titles within districts may differ. More specific day-to-day tasks such as hiring, payroll, and resource distribution, are routinely delegated to a designated cabinet member or department of the district's central office. Thus, while superintendents are broadly responsible for district operations touching upon STEM innovation efforts, in reality, they primarily act as CEOs, while central office staff are responsible for keeping the district running—and designing and enacting STEM improvement and reform efforts.

District Leaders

School districts carry out the directives of the superintendent, the school board, the county office of education, and the state and federal agencies at play (Björk, 2005). Thus, district administrators hold multiple responsibilities related to setting and enforcing district policies, interpreting state and federal educational legislation, and ensuring that STEM initiatives are in alignment with this legislation.

District leaders play essential roles in the implementation of STEM innovations (Johnson & Chrispeels, 2010). For district-specific STEM initiatives, district leaders craft policies, guidelines, and programs from the ground up. In many cases, the policy-in-progress would be passed through multiple central office departments (i.e., the Office of Innovation, Office of Teaching and Learning, and Technology Departments) to ensure it fits the district requirements within each department and aligns with state and local curriculum standards. For larger-scale STEM initiatives, district leaders take steps for adopting the innovation to their district. Similarly, they help determine standards and develop or select appropriate curriculum and corresponding assessments to align with state curriculum standards and the intent of the proposed STEM innovation. They also support the implementation of STEM initiatives by setting professional learning requirements for educators and facilitating professional learning activities. Central office staff further manage the logistics of STEM innovation implementation by acquiring and distributing necessary materials, technology, and human capital to schools and classrooms (Lasky, 2004).

Larger-scale STEM innovations can be more difficult to fit to a district in a manner aligned with the intent of the organization who developed the STEM innovation. Each district has its own set of resources, policies, and challenges. Moreover, district administrators may interpret the intent or process of a STEM innovation differently than how it was created, leading to misalignments from implementation to outcomes. While a district's perceived failure to implement a STEM initiative with fidelity may give the appearance of resistance to innovation, it may also be due to the district's limited capacity to fully enact the innovation, either due to limited resources or local policymakers' limited understanding of the intent of the innovation (Spillane & Callahan, 2000). See Chapter 4 for more discussion of fidelity.

School Boards

School boards often hold the power to make final decisions related to adopting STEM innovations. They may receive policy proposals from the superintendent/central office leadership, or a proposed program or innovation from an outside organization or community member. Additionally, school boards are responsible for setting the district budget, which affects how much money can be spent, where it can be spent, and how it can be used to advance STEM innovation efforts. Moreover, financial constraints shape the implementation of these innovations by setting limitations on resources and personnel. Although school boards are tasked with allocating funds, they often do not have revenue-raising authority, so they seek approval from officials and depend on voter financing. School boards also hold regular public meetings to assess community priorities and public opinion. Historically, school board meetings are the primary venue in which parents and other interested parties in the community are invited to engage in the policymaking process (Björk, 2005). School boards thus act as both professional organizations (i.e., expected to support the superintendent and the district by enacting the "best" educational policies) and as representative bodies (i.e., tasked with responding to parent and community demands; Greene, 1992). When these roles conflict with one another, the process to implement a reform agenda or a particular innovation may lengthen as a policy undergoes several rounds of board review.

Some school boards are appointed by city or county officials, but most are elected by constituents. School board officials are largely elected in low-turnout and low-interest elections, with local school board elections typically reporting voter turnout no greater than 15 percent (Hartney & Flavin, 2011). Likely partially due to this low turnout, teacher unions—who otherwise have limited power in the policymaking process—are typically successful in campaigning on behalf of school board candidates (Moe, 2014).

Teacher Unions

A previous study on the political influence of teacher unions revealed that legislators overwhelmingly ranked their state's teacher union as the most active, effective, and powerful interest group in the state capitol (Hrebnar & Thomas, 2004). However, this perception may be due to their success in recruitment and organizational processes rather than any measurable political outcomes (Bascia, 2000).

A set of critics claim that teacher unions impede STEM innovation because unions prioritize the wellbeing and security of their member educators above all else. However, unions often only appear hypercritical of innovations because teachers are often relegated to the periphery of policymaking and reform (Poole, 1999). Unions and their members are rarely invited to early conversations about new initiatives, and typically learn of them when the public does (Cowan & Strunk, 2014). Consequently, they are forced to quickly shift their attention and resources to supporting their member educators through the implementation process.

Unions may challenge innovative STEM initiatives over concerns of process, philosophy, and student outcomes, or over concerns regarding the content of the initiative or related implementation factors and conditions. Unions may also appear to be critical of STEM innovations that require a larger or more specialized labor force, or additional labor from educators—particularly in the absence of additional support in the forms of compensation, training, and adequate hiring of proper personnel to comprehensively support implementation.

Despite a lack of agency in the development of most initiatives, educators are at the front lines of implementing STEM innovations in the classroom. Though unions may be vocally critical of a STEM initiative, in the long run, they are likely to support these efforts by creating, housing, and connecting teachers with resources (Bascia, 2000; Poole, 1999), such as professional learning opportunities (Bredeson, 2001). Some unions may even appoint specialized committees to participate in decisions about technology purchasing to support STEM innovations (Kochan, 2022). Unions may also be likely to support new innovations by proactively participating in reform movements—lobbying for provisions to protect workforce conditions alongside the implementation of a curricular innovation or broader school reform effort (Poole, 1999). By supporting educational initiatives in this way, unions may gain a modest amount of access to the political process, enabling them to advocate for the safeguarding of teachers' rights in the face of educational change.

Schools

Principals

At the school level, principals make sense of policy directives from state and district leaders and employ a variety of leadership styles to manage the micropolitical processes of implementation among campus instructional staff (Donaldson & Woulfin, 2018; Horsford, Scott, & Anderson, 2019). Drawing on multiple competencies, including their understanding of state and local policies, discipline-specific STEM content knowledge, and capacities for leadership (Geiger et al., 2023), principals lead STEM policy implementation by framing and prioritizing STEM instruction, engaging and supporting staff to adopt STEM initiatives, buffering staff against onerous or intrusive reform elements, and fostering STEM-supportive school cultures and climates (Falloon et al., 2021).

As campus instructional leaders, principals frame, prioritize, and communicate expectations about teaching and learning to instructional staff (Terosky, 2016). Yet researchers have noted that principals' diverse interpretations of STEM instruction differentially shape their messaging about STEM initiatives. Sterrett and colleagues (2018) observed that principals expressed a variety of understandings about the purpose and quality of STEM instruction, which influenced their approaches for providing feedback to teachers and planning teacher professional learning. Interestingly, research has shown that principals do often share a common understanding of STEM education's core elements, but even when this is the case, differences in their sensemaking about their leadership roles for STEM can lead to divergent messaging about curriculum, pedagogy, and student learning environments (Holmlund, Lessig, & Slavit, 2018; Lochmiller, 2016). And because some principals possess limited understandings of STEM subjects and high-quality STEM instructional practices (Lochmiller, 2015; McNeill, Lowenhaupt, & Katsch-Singer, 2018), they might lack critical expertise in framing or prioritizing implementation of STEM innovations and reform efforts (Allen & Heredia, 2021).

Principals engage in numerous tasks to supervise and support STEM educators, including observing and providing feedback on classroom instruction (Rigby et al., 2017), setting campus budgets and schedules (Ringstaff & Sandholtz, 2018), buffering teachers from onerous or disruptive directives (Wenner & Settlage, 2015), and ensuring access to STEM programs, materials, and resources (Falloon et al., 2021). Principals who foster collaborative approaches to supporting educators tend to experience greater success in sustaining STEM innovations, as these models draw on teacher leadership and expertise to inform understandings of high-quality STEM instruction (Kubasko, Rhodes, & Sterrett, 2019; Sterrett et al., 2020).

Campus principals also influence STEM innovations through their efforts to shape school cultures and climates (Fullan, 2023). Specifically, when principals foster school cultures that prioritize relational trust, collaboration, and teacher and student risk-taking, they bolster the capacity of instructional staff to overcome the challenges that typically accompany the implementation of STEM innovations (Falloon et al., 2021; Lesseig et al., 2019; Waters & Orange, 2022).

Instructional Coaches

In addition to principals, instructional coaches, teacher leaders, and department chairs hold agency to shape the nature and outcomes of STEM innovations. These school-based instructional leaders influence teachers and their STEM instruction (Matsumura et al., 2010; Russell et al., 2020; Woulfin, Strunk, & Jones, 2023). There is mounting evidence that coaching can improve student outcomes in various content areas and for various outcomes (Kraft, Blazar, & Hogan, 2018).

Carrying out an educative role, coaches can develop teachers' capacity to teach in ways aligned with STEM innovations (Coburn & Woulfin, 2012; Sarrell, Zelkowski, & Livers, 2024). Efficacious educative coaching practices include conducting robust, targeted conversations about curriculum, pedagogy, and students; setting improvement goals; and delivering evidence-based feedback on teachers' STEM instruction (Russell et al., 2020). Gibbons and colleagues (2017) highlight how coaches build the collective capacity of teachers by facilitating professional learning routines addressing the principles and practices of ambitious mathematics instruction. Coaches' educative work occurs with individual teachers as well as groups of teachers. Moreover, as demonstrated by Sarrell and colleagues (2024), coaches play key roles in designing mathematics professional learning systems at the district and school levels.

By translating and mediating policy messages, coaches also play a political role. Based on their knowledge, prior experiences, and local conditions, coaches make sense of messages regarding STEM in varied ways (Spillane, Reiser, & Reimer, 2002). For example, coaches make sense of math assessment guidelines and NGSS-aligned instructional materials. Such interpretations influence coaches' strategic communication, or framing, of STEM innovations. In turn, this framing affects how teachers, leaders, and other actors develop understandings of how and why to implement specific STEM innovations.

Importantly, coaches apply their agency to amplify particular ideas about STEM innovations, while downplaying others (Benford & Snow, 2000; Coburn, 2006). Their persuasive communication about innovations can influence how teachers and other individuals implement STEM instructional improvement efforts. For example, a math coach can point to problematic inequities in students' math formative assessment results while facilitating a grade-level team meeting. Or a STEM coach can elevate the benefits of using lesson plans from their district's NGSS-aligned science curriculum while giving feedback to a novice teacher. In both examples, coaches are highlighting certain aspects of a STEM innovation while downplaying others to advance particular types of change. Notably, coaches engage in framing STEM innovations in facilitating professional learning opportunities for teachers and may thus promote the uptake and sustained adoption of STEM innovations.

Teachers

Teachers interpret and respond to STEM innovations in varied ways. Based upon individual knowledge and experiences as well as collective learning opportunities, teachers make sense of messages about STEM innovation that influence implementation (Spillane, Reiser, & Reimer, 2002). In many districts and schools, teachers hold considerable discretion for what occurs day-by-day, or moment-by-moment, inside classrooms (NASEM, 2020). Even when provided a common curriculum or instructional framework (e.g., mathematics HQIM as designated by a state), teachers make many decisions about how to translate, or enact, the curriculum to meet student needs and fit local conditions (Hall & Hampden-Thompson, 2022; Lowell, Fogelman, & McNeill, 2024). The policy environment, however, affects educators' degree of discretion (Penuel et al., 2009). In particular, accountability policies that tightly monitor mathematics and English language arts standardized test scores constrain teachers' agency, oftentimes narrowing their attention toward tested subjects or seeking to raise test scores to meet particular targets (Berliner, 2011; Booher-Jennings, 2005; Milner, 2013).

Collaborative spaces and networks play roles in promoting teacher agency to enact STEM innovations. First, professional learning communities (PLCs) provide time and routines for educators to share ideas about STEM teaching and learning, and to gain insights on how to refine their classroom practices (Mesa & Pringle, 2019; Townley, 2020); however, it is worth pointing out that how PLC time is allocated depends on school leadership. As discussed earlier, instructional leaders, such as coaches or department chairs, can facilitate PLC sessions, encouraging reflection, transparent communication, and sharing of resources and tools. Further, when teachers engage in PLCs, they form networks that enable the sharing of other ideas related to STEM instructional improvement. Building collective capacity matters for the degree to which teachers tinker or work strategically (Coburn, 2001), and supports the development of teachers' professional agency for implementing and sustaining STEM innovations (Balgopal, 2020; Bonner, Diehl, & Trachtman, 2020).

Teachers also influence the implementation of STEM innovations through their enactment of teacher leadership practices. STEM teachers who develop leader identities not only experience a stronger sense of self-efficacy, but also develop supportive networks with colleagues to expand their collective instructional capacity (Park et al., 2024; Quaisley et al., 2023). When teachers develop a strengthened sense of self-efficacy, they also increase their ability to advocate for STEM education policies and improved teaching and learning conditions in their schools (Velasco, Hite, & Milbourne, 2022).

REGIONAL ACTORS

It is also vital to attend to many of the regional actors who shape the design and enactment of STEM innovations. From textbook publishers, professional learning providers, and professional societies to philanthropic foundations and industry partners, a broad array of regional actors are involved in steering and modulating innovations seeking to alter the quality of STEM teaching and learning (Hodge et al., 2019; Rowan, 2006). The sections below describe a STEM ecosystems approach to fostering connection between regional actors and those at the center of the education system; the special role of families and communities as regional actors; and the many other forms of connection that can grow among actors within the broader learning environment.

STEM Ecosystems

The STEM ecosystems approach has gained significant traction in a variety of states (see Chapter 5 for a broader discussion). The collective regional actors listed above, along with other actors within the educational system described in this chapter, have been characterized, as noted earlier, within a STEM learning ecology. The STEM learning *ecosystem* concept differs from the concept of STEM learning *ecologies*. While both focus on the interrelationship of multiple components of a learning environment, a description of *STEM learning ecologies*, positions the child at the center, *STEM learning ecosystems* concept, on the other hand, underpins and drives the formation of an intentional community of practice, which it situates at the center of the learning environment. The intentional formation of partnerships—including and especially with regional actors—is a defining part of a STEM learning ecosystem.

Definitions of STEM learning ecosystems focus on a multi-sectored constituency including formal and informal learning settings; suggest collaborative interactions and adaptability; identify purpose; and imply both tactical and strategic approached to achieving desired outcomes; and these learning ecosystems are meant to be sustained.

The STEM Funders Network along with its partners, the Afterschool Alliance, and the Teaching Institute for Exemplary STEM (TIES; See Box 2-6), define STEM ecosystems in this way:

> A STEM learning ecosystem encompasses schools, community settings such as after-school and summer programs, science centers and museums, and informal experiences at home and in a variety of environments that together constitute a rich array of learning opportunities for young people. A learning ecosystem harnesses the unique contributions of all these different settings in symbiosis to deliver STEM learning for all children. Designed pathways enable young people to become engaged, knowledgeable and skilled in the STEM disciplines as they progress through childhood into adolescence and early adulthood. (Traill & Traphagen, 2014, p. 2)

The STEM Funders Network, an affiliation of grant makers seeking to "create equitable access to STEM learning experiences across the continuum for historically marginalized groups, such as underserved populations and under-resourced communities,"[30] set the formalized STEM ecosystem concept in motion in 2015 through a Communities of Practice initiative that aimed "to establish 100 STEM Ecosystems by 2020, bringing together school districts, afterschool providers, institutions of higher education,

---

[30] See https://stemfundersnetwork.org/who-we-are/

> **BOX 2-6**
> **Teaching Institute for Exemplary STEM (TIES)**
>
> TIES partners with communities globally to create STEM learning ecosystems. This includes partnering with private sectors to optimize investments as well as helping to guide school districts to achieve their vision for STEM. TIES is guided by the engineering design process in that every project has cycles of iteration and collaboration that consider the problem; identifying and imaging solutions; planning, creating, testing and evaluating; to improve and communicate the results. Each project progresses through four phases: (a) listen and learning, (b) design, (c) implementation, and (d) sustainability and transition.
>
> SOURCE: Adapted from https://www.tiesteach.org/about-ties/

cultural institutions, businesses, and families to provide engaging, high-quality STEM learning opportunities."[31]

The STEM ecosystems concept gained prominence at the federal level with inclusion in the White House OSTP STEM Education Strategic Plan (National Science and Technology Council, Committee on STEM Education, National Science & Technology Council, the White House, 2018, p. 10), which not only defines what STEM ecosystems are, but also identifies their many and varied actors. Increasingly, the STEM ecosystem concept has been used as an organizer of action around STEM learning at the state, regional, and local levels. State-sun STEM ecosystems can perform a number of different functions, as characterized by the example in Box 2-7.

There is substantial variability in efforts that seek to coordinate STEM learning across the various layers and actors within the STEM ecosystem. Some are designed to press on multiple levers given their positioning within state government and their available funding (e.g., Iowa and Alabama), whereas others are designed to push on levers at the family/community level (e.g., STEM NOLA).[32] Chapter 5 provides a more detailed discussion of these examples.

Families and Communities

Families and communities themselves are also key regional and local actors throughout all levels of the landscape. Human learning is *life-long* (learning occurs throughout life), *life-wide* (learning occurs across a range of activities one participates across home, schools, community

---

[31] See https://overdeck.org/portfolios/spotlight/stem-funders-network-2/
[32] See personal communications on December 7, 2023.

> **BOX 2-7**
> **State STEM Ecosystems Functions**
>
> State STEM ecosystems are programs that supports STEM learning across the dynamic interaction among individual learners, diverse settings where learning occurs, and the community and culture in which they are embedded (NRC, 2015). They can be used to help manage complex systems in a relatively local environment through a variety of different actions. Some of these functions include the following:
>
> - Map the elements and/or relationships within the system
> - Coalesce community relationships to invite a broader sense of belonging
> - Facilitate communication and activity across cultural spaces
> - Monitor the health of the system
> - Engage in keystone capacity building to cascade knowledge across the system
> - Understand the local conditions to support system resilience
> - Sort and filter innovations in relation to their capacity to achieve agreeable outcomes
> - Leverage actions that place filtered opportunities and resources in proximity to intended users across formal and informal learning settings
> - Facilitate localized adaptation of innovations to promote implementation
> - Generate localized innovations

organization), and *life-deep* (learning cultivates particular values and social beliefs that impact how one acts in the world; Banks et al., 2007, pp. 12–13). Over the lifecourse, humans spend about only 18.5 percent of their waking hours in K–12 schools. A vast majority of their time is spent outside of school settings, learning new ideas, languages, and participating in new practices on outside-of-school time settings (Banks et al., 2007). As such learning begins with the lives of learners, and family members are key partners with deep expertise regardless of their preparation in formal STEM education (NASEM, 2024b). These are numerous examples of co-designing with family members, community members, researchers, and educators in which participants bring together diverse forms of expertise to provide more nuanced support across multiple forms of learning such as rich sensemaking repertoires, everyday practices, linguistic resources, family histories, and community values, in support of curriculum, teacher learning, and children's learning in STEM (e.g., Booker & Goldman, 2016; Gomez, Kyza, & Mancevice, 2018; Ishimaru & Bang, 2022; Tzou et al., 2019). Families and communities play important roles in and bring key expertise to the landscape of STEM learning to support districts and school leaders (NASEM, 2024b).

Connections across Actors

In many ways, regional actors have set the stage, or laid the groundwork, for major STEM innovation efforts. First, STEM education organizations and professional societies, including NGSS Lead States, National Governors Association, and Council of Chief State School Officers have played crucial roles in drafting content standards and instructional frameworks related to Pre-K–12 mathematics and science. In the case of science standards development, NGSS Lead States emphasized their partnership with other regional actors (e.g., National Science Teachers Association, higher education faculty, scientists, business leaders)—while underscoring "no federal funds were used to develop the standards." Turning to mathematics reform efforts, a set of regional actors with the financial support of the Carnegie Corporation of New York drafted Common Core State Standards for Mathematics (Garland, 2014). Thus, they shaped the direction of early-2010s math instructional reform efforts. This included partnering with curriculum designers to produce Common Core–aligned textbooks (Hodge et al., 2019).

Second, professional learning providers shape educators' access to ideas about—and learning opportunities regarding—STEM innovations. Many educational systems and schools contract with professional learning providers to assist with facilitating professional learning for teachers as well as leaders. These providers often facilitate curriculum-linked workshops to build educator capacity, which may apply reform-oriented principles (Penuel et al., 2007). Hodge and colleagues (2019) issue the reminder that professional learning providers tend to follow supply-demand needs. In this manner, professional learning providers reinforce the approaches from curricula.

Together, the various regional actors help to support the implementation of STEM education innovations by helping to build individual and organizational capacity within the more formal Pre-K–12 education system.

SUMMARY

This chapter presented an overview of what is known about the formal Pre-K–12 education system. Overall, despite the variability in the purpose of the different actors, they play important roles in helping STEM education innovations to take shape and to scale. Each of the multiple, nested levels of the education system contain regulations, ideas, and resources related to STEM education innovations. And the various actors, positioned across the multiple levels of the education system, face different institutional and organization conditions as they deploy their agency while enacting innovations. These actors not only engage in different responsibilities but hold also different levels of power and authority for motivating the implementation of various Pre-K–12 STEM education innovations. Chapter 8 takes up these issues more.

Moreover, the formal Pre-K context is different from the formal K–12 education system and there is not clear alignment or coherence of policies, standards, and teaching practices from Pre-K into the K–12 system. Each state designs its own Pre-K system through authorizing legislation and funding, and determines eligibility, quality standards, and monitoring. Because of this, the governance is highly variable and fragmented. A few states and districts have developed a scalable and sustainable approach to integrating STEM fields through curriculum, professional preparation, and professional development of Pre-K teachers and administrators.

REFERENCES

Allen, C. D., & Heredia, S. C. (2021). Reframing organizational contexts from barriers to levers for teacher learning in science education reform. *Journal of Science Teacher Education, 32*(2), 148–166.

Balgopal, M. M. (2020). STEM teacher agency: A case study of initiating and implementing curricular reform. *Science Education, 104*(4), 762–785.

Banks, J., Au, K., Ball, A. F., Bell, P., Gordon, E., Gutierrez, K., Brice-Heath, S., Lee, C. D., Mahiri, J., Nasir, N., Valdes, G., & Zhou, M. (2007). *Learning in and out of school in diverse environments: Life-long, life-wide, life-deep*. The LIFE Center (University of Washington, Stanford University and SRI) & the Center for Multicultural Education, University of Washington.

Barnett, W. S., & Kasmin, R. (2018, January). Fully funding Pre-K through K-12 funding formulas. *State Education Standard, 18*(1), 22–28.

Bascia, N. (2000). The other side of the equation: Professional development and the organizational capacity of teacher unions. *Educational Policy, 14*(3), 385–404.

Benford, R. D., & Snow, D. A. (2000). Framing processes and social movements: An overview and assessment. *Annual Review of Sociology, 26*(1), 611–639.

Berliner, D. (2011). Rational responses to high stakes testing: The case of curriculum narrowing and the harm that follows. *Cambridge Journal of Education, 41*(3), 287–302.

Björk, L. G. (2005). Superintendent-board relations: An historical overview of the dynamics of change and sources of conflict and collaboration. In G. J. Petersen & L. D. Fusarelli (Eds.), *The district superintendent and school board relations: Trends in policy development and implementation* (pp. 1–22). Information Age.

Björk, L. G., Browne-Ferrigno, T., & Kowalski, T. J. (2014) The superintendent and educational reform in the United States of America. *Leadership and Policy in Schools, 13*(4), 444–465, https://doi.org/10.1080/15700763.2014.945656

Bonner, S. M., Diehl, K., & Trachtman, R. (2020). Teacher belief and agency development in bringing change to scale. *Journal of Educational Change, 21*(2), 363–384.

Booher-Jennings, J. (2005). Below the bubble: "Educational triage" and the Texas accountability system. *American Educational Research Journal, 42*(2), 231–268.

Booker, A., & Goldman, S. V. (2016). Participatory design research as a practice for systemic repair: Doing hand-in-hand math research with families. *Cognition and Instruction, 34*(3), 223–235.

Bredeson, P. V. (2001). Union contracts and teacher professional development. *Education Policy Analysis Archives, 9*, 26–26.

Bredeson, P. V., & Kose, B. W. (2007). Responding to the education reform agenda: A study of school superintendents' instructional leadership. *Education Policy Analysis Archives, 15*(5).

Brunner, C. C., Grogan, M., & Björk, L. G. (2002). Shifts in the discourse defining the superintendency: Historical and current foundations of the position. In J. Murphy (Ed.), *The educational leadership challenge: Redefining leadership for the 21st century* (pp. 211–238). University of Chicago Press.

Carlson, E., Daley, T., Bitterman, A., Heinzen, H., Keller, B., Markowitz, J., & Riley, J. (2009). *Early school transitions and the social behavior of children with disabilities: Selected findings from the Pre-Elementary Education Longitudinal Study. Wave 3 overview report from the Pre-Elementary Education Longitudinal Study (PEELS)* (Report No. NCSER 2009-3016). National Center for Special Education Research.

Cherbow, K., McKinley, M. T., McNeill, K. L., & Lowenhaupt, R. (2020). An analysis of science instruction for the science practices: Examining coherence across system levels and components in current systems of science education in K-8 schools. *Science Education, 104*(3), 446–478. https://doi.org/10.1002/sce.21573

Coburn, C. E. (2001). Collective sensemaking about reading: How teachers mediate reading policy in their professional communities. *Educational Evaluation and Policy Analysis, 23*(2), 145–170.

———. (2006). Framing the problem of reading instruction: Using frame analysis to uncover the microprocesses of policy implementation. *American Educational Research Journal, 43*(3), 343–349.

Coburn, C. E., & Woulfin, S. L. (2012). Reading coaches and the relationship between policy and practice. *Reading Research Quarterly, 47*(1), 5–30.

Connors-Tadros, L., Northey, K., Frede, E., Hodges, K. & Jost, T. (2021). *Effective state offices of early learning: Structural features, enabling conditions, and key functions in four states*. National Institute for Early Education Research. https://nieer.org/research-library/effective-state-offices-early-learning

Connors-Tadros, L., & Weisenfeld, G. G. (2024). [An analysis of US Pre-K STEM educational policy]. Paper commissioned by the Committee on Pre-K–12 STEM Education Innovations. https://nap.nationalacademies.org/resource/27950/Analysis%20of%20US%20PreK%20STEM%20Educational%20Policy_Connors-Tadros%20Weisenfeld.pdf

Cowan, J., & Strunk, K. O. (2014, April). *How do teachers' unions influence education policy? What we know and what we need to learn* (Working Paper No. 42). Education Policy Center at Michigan State University

Doan, S., Kaufman, J. H., Woo, A., Tuma, A. P., Diliberti, M. K., & Lee, S. (2022). *How states are creating conditions for use of high-quality instructional materials in K–12 classrooms*. RAND Corporation.

Donaldson, M. L., & Woulfin, S. (2018). From tinkering to going "rogue": How principals use agency when enacting new teacher evaluation systems. *Educational Evaluation and Policy Analysis, 40*(4), 531–556.

Education Commission of the States. (2020, November). *K–12 governance: State board of education; What constitutional or statutory powers and duties does the state board have as it relates to education policy?* https://reports.ecs.org/comparisons/k-12-governance-state-board-of-education-01

Falloon, G., Stevenson, M., Beswick, K., Fraser, S., & Geiger, V. (2021). Building STEM in schools. *Educational Technology & Society, 24*(4), 110–122.

Florida Department of Education. (2024). *Sunshine state scholars: Florida high school STEM scholars*. https://www.fldoe.org/academics/sunshscholars/

Franchino, E., & Loewenberg, A. (2019, September 30). Federal spending on early care and education: Past, present, and future. EdCentral. *New America*. https://www.newamerica.org/education-policy/edcentral/federal-spending-early-care-and-education-past-present-and-future/

Friedman-Krauss, A., & Barnett, S. (2024). Opportunities and challenges for preschool expansion. *State Education Standard, 24*(2). National Association of State Boards of Education. https://www.nasbe.org/opportunities-and-challenges-for-preschool-expansion/

Friedman-Krauss, A., Garver, K., Nores, M., Li, Z., & Whitman, C. (2020). *Connecticut preschool special education needs assessment* (NIEER Technical Report). National Institute for Early Education Research.

Friedman-Krauss, A. H., Barnett, W. S., Hodges, K. S., Garver, K. A., Jost, T. M., Weisenfeld, G., & Duer, J. (2024). *The state of preschool 2023: State preschool yearbook.* National Institute for Early Education Research.

Fullan, M. (2023). *The principal 2.0: Three keys to maximizing impact.* John Wiley & Sons.

Garland, S. (2014). *The man behind Common Core Math.* https://www.npr.org/sections/ed/2014/12/29/371918272/the-man-behind-common-core-math

Geiger, V., Beswick, K., Fraser, S., & Holland-Twining, B. (2023). A model for principals' STEM leadership capability. *British Educational Research Journal, 49*(5), 900–924.

Gibbons, L. K., Kazemi, E., & Lewis, R. M. (2017). Developing collective capacity to improve mathematics instruction: Coaching as a lever for school-wide improvement. *The Journal of Mathematical Behavior, 46*, 231–250.

Gomez, K., Kyza, E.A., & Mancevice, N. (2018). Participatory design and the learning sciences. In F. Fischer, C. E. Hmelo-Silver, S. R. Goldman, & P. Reimann (Eds.), *International handbook of the learning sciences* (pp. 401–409). Routledge.

Greene, K. R. (1992). Models of school board policy-making. *Educational Administration Quarterly, 28*(2), 220–236. https://doi.org/10.1177/0013161X92028002004

Hall, M., & Hampden-Thompson, G. (2022). The teacher as street-level bureaucrat: Science teacher's discretionary decision-making in a time of reform. *International Journal of Science Education, 44*(6), 980–999.

Hartney, M., & Flavin, P. (2011). From the schoolhouse to the statehouse: Teacher union political activism and U.S. state education reform policy. *State Politics & Policy Quarterly, 11*(3), 251–268.

Hodge, E., Childs, J., & Au, W. (2020). Power, brokers, and agendas: New directions for the use of social network analysis in education policy. *Education Policy Analysis Archives, 28*(117).

Hodge, E. M., Salloum, S. J., & Benko, S. L. (2019). The changing ecology of the curriculum marketplace in the era of the Common Core State Standards. *Journal of Educational Change, 20*(4), 425–446.

Holmlund, T. D., Lesseig, K., & Slavit, D. (2018). Making sense of "STEM education" in K–12 contexts. *International Journal of STEM Education, 5*, 1–18.

Horsford, S. D., Scott, J. T., & Anderson, G. L. (2019). *The politics of education policy in an era of inequality.* Routledge.

Hrebnar, R. J., & Thomas, C. S. (2004). Interest groups in the states. In V. Gray & R. L. Hanson (Eds.), *Politics in the American states* (pp. 100–128). CQ Press.

Indiana Commission for Higher Education. (2023, August 8). *Over $10 Million in STEM teacher grants awarded to organizations and colleges: Grants support organizations preparing Hoosier educators in STEM subject areas.* https://www.in.gov/che/files/2023STEMGRANT.PR.pdf

Ishimaru, A. M., & Bang, M. (2022). Designing with families for just futures. *Journal of Family Diversity in Education, 4*(2), 130–140.

Johnson, P. E., & Chrispeels, J. H. (2010). Linking the central office and its schools for reform. *Educational Administration Quarterly, 46*(5), 738–775.

Kochan, T. A. (2022). Proactive union and teacher strategies for shaping technology in education. *New England Journal of Public Policy, 34*(1).

Kraft, M. A., Blazar, D., & Hogan, D. (2018). The effect of teacher coaching on instruction and achievement: A meta-analysis of the causal evidence. *Review of Educational Research, 88*(4), 547–588.

Kubasko, D., Rhodes, G., & Sterrett W. (2019). A case study approach to STEM supervision: A collaborative model for teaching and principal preparation. *Journal of Interdisciplinary Teacher Leadership, 4*(1).

Larimore, R. A. (2020). Preschool science education: A vision for the future. *Early Childhood Education Journal, 48*(6), 703–714.

Lasky, S. G. (2004). *Toward a policy framework for analyzing educational system effects*. The Center for Research on the Education of Students Placed at Risk.

Lesseig, K., Firestone, J., Morrison, J., Slavit, D., & Holmlund, T. (2019). An analysis of cultural influences on STEM schools: Similarities and differences across K–12 contexts. *International Journal of Science and Mathematics Education, 17*(3), 449–466.

Lochmiller, C. R. (2015). Exploring principal leadership for math and science. *Journal of School Leadership, 25*(1), 24–53.

———. (2016). Examining administrators' instructional feedback to high school math and science teachers. *Educational Administration Quarterly, 52*(1), 75–109.

Lowell, B. R., Fogelman, S. E., & McNeill, K. L. (2024). Organizational sensemaking during curriculum implementation: The dilemma of agency, role of collaboration, and importance of discipline-specific leadership. *Science Education*.

Massachusetts Department of Education. (2024). *Science and technology/engineering (STE) test design and development*. https://www.doe.mass.edu/mcas/tdd/sci.html

Matsumura, L. C., Garnier, H. E., Correnti, R., Junker, B., & DiPrima Bickel, D. (2010). Investigating the effectiveness of a comprehensive literacy coaching program in schools with high teacher mobility. *The Elementary School Journal, 111*(1), 35–62.

McNeill, K. L., Lowenhaupt, R. J., & Katsh-Singer, R. (2018). Instructional leadership in the era of the NGSS: Principals' understandings of science practices. *Science Education, 102*(3), 452–473.

Mesa, J. C., & Pringle, R. M. (2019). Change from within: Middle school science teachers leading professional learning communities. *Middle School Journal, 50*(5), 5–14.

Milner IV, H. R. (2013). Scripted and narrowed curriculum reform in urban schools. *Urban Education, 48*(2), 163–170.

Moe, T. M. (2014). Teacher unions and American education reform: The power of vested interests. In J. A. Jenkis & S. M. Milkis (Eds.), *The politics of major policy reform in postwar America*. Cambridge University Press.

Morgan, C. W., Cheatham, G. A., Lim, S., Amilivia, J. M., & Martinez, J. R. (2023). Enacting the social-relations approach: A relational framework for inclusive early childhood education. *Exceptionality, 31*(5), 362–378.

National Academies of Sciences, Engineering, and Medicine (NASEM). (2018). *Transforming the financing of early care and education*. The National Academies Press.

———. (2020). *Changing expectations for the K–12 teacher workforce: Policies, preservice education, professional development, and the workplace*. The National Academies Press.

———. (2023). *Closing the opportunity gap for young children*. The National Academies Press.

———. (2024a). *A new vision for high-quality preschool curriculum*. The National Academies Press.

———. (2024b). *Equity in K–12 STEM education: Framing decisions for the future*. The National Academies Press.

National Association of State Boards of Education. (2022). *A look at state education governance*. https://www.nasbe.org/state-education-governance/

National Research Council. (2012). *A framework for K–12 science education: Practices, crosscutting concepts, and core ideas*. The National Academies Press.

———. (2015). *Identifying and supporting productive STEM programs in out-of-school settings*. The National Academies Press.

National Science and Technology Council, Committee on STEM Education, National Science & Technology Council, the White House. (2018). *Charting a course for success: America's strategy for STEM education*. A Report by the Committee on STEM Education of the National Science & Technology Council. https://files.eric.ed.gov/fulltext/ED590474.pdf

Noahr, L., Black, S., & Rogers, J. (2016). *STEM Pilot Project Grant Program: Report to the legislature, December 2016.* Washington Office of Superintendent of Public Instruction.

North Carolina Department of Public Instruction. (2024, March 27) *Recognized North Carolina STEM schools of distinction.* https://www.dpi.nc.gov/recognized-nc-stem-schools-distinction

Park, B. Y., Campbell, T., Hanrahan, J., Dolma, T., Murray, E., Russell, J. Lisy, E., & Bai, Y. (2024). Teacher leadership within a districtwide STEM teacher professional network. *International Journal of Leadership in Education*, 1–31.

Parker, E., Diffy, L., & Atchison, B. (2018). *How states fund pre-k: A primer for policy makers.* Education Commission of the States.

Pelsue, B. (2017). When it comes to education, the federal government is in charge of...um, what? *Harvard Ed. Magazine.* https://www.gse.harvard.edu/news/ed/17/08/when-it-comes-educationfederal-government-charge-um-what

Penuel, W. R., Fishman, B. J., Yamaguchi, R., & Gallagher, L. P. (2007). What makes professional development effective? Strategies that foster curriculum implementation. *American Educational Research Journal*, 44(4), 921–958.

Penuel, W., Fishman, B. J., Gallagher, L. P., Korbak, C., & Lopez-Prado, B. (2009). Is alignment enough? Investigating the effects of state policies and professional development on science curriculum implementation. *Science Education*, 93(4), 656–677.

Piasta, S. B., Pelatti, C. Y., & Miller, H. L. (2014). Mathematics and science learning opportunities in preschool classrooms. *Early Education and Development*, 25(4), 445–468.

Poole, W. L. (1999). Teachers union involvement in educational policy making: Issues raised by an in-depth case. *Educational Policy*, 13(5), 698–725.

Pruitt, S. L., & Wallace, C. S. (2012). The effect of a state department of education teacher mentor initiative on science achievement. *Journal of Science Teacher Education*, 23(4), 367–385. http://www.jstor.org/stable/43156653

Quaisley, K., Smith, W. M., Criswell, B., Funk, R., & Hutchinson, A. (2023). From becoming to being: How STEM teachers develop leadership identities. *International Journal of Leadership in Education*, 1–28.

Regenstein, E. (January 2023). State boards and the governance of early childhood education. *State Education Standard*, 23(1). National Association of State Boards of Education. https://www.nasbe.org/state-boards-and-the-governance-of-early-childhood-education/

Rigby, J. G., Larbi-Cherif, A., Rosenquist, B. A., Sharpe, C. J., Cobb, P., & Smith, T. (2017). Administrator observation and feedback: Does it lead toward improvement in inquiry-oriented math instruction? *Educational Administration Quarterly*, 53(3), 475–516.

Ringstaff, C., & Sandholtz, J. H. (2018). From budgets to bus schedules: Contextual barriers and supports for science instruction in elementary schools. *Pedagogical Content Knowledge in STEM: Research to Practice*, 67–82.

Rowan, B. (2006). The school improvement industry in the United States: Why educational change is both pervasive and ineffectual. *The New Institutionalism in Education*, 67–86.

Russell, J. L., Correnti, R., Stein, M. K., Thomas, A., Bill, V., & Speranzo, L. (2020). Mathematics coaching for conceptual understanding: Promising evidence regarding the Tennessee math coaching model. *Educational Evaluation and Policy Analysis*, 42(3), 439–466.

Sarrell, A., Zelkowski, J., & Livers, S. (2024). The critical roles of a mathematics specialist in establishing effective, coordinated professional development systems. *Investigations in Mathematics Learning*, 1–20.

Spillane, J. P., & Callahan, K. A. (2000). Implementing state standards for science education: What district policy makers make of the hoopla. *Journal of Research in Science Teaching*, 37(5), 401–425.

Spillane, J. P., Reiser, B. J., & Reimer, T. (2002). Policy implementation and cognition: Reframing and refocusing implementation research. *Review of Educational Research*, 72(3), 387–431.

Sterrett, W., Rhodes, G., Kubasko, D., & Fischetti, J. (2018). A different "noticing": Examining principal perceptions of STEM instruction. *American Journal of Educational Science*, 4(4), 180–187.

Sterrett, W., Rhodes, G., Reid-Griffin, A., Robinson, K. K., Hooker, S. D., & Ryder, A. J. (2020). Shaping the supervision narrative: Innovating teaching and leading to improve STEM instruction. *Journal of Educational Supervision*, 3(3), 59–74.

Terosky, A. L. (2016). Enacting instructional leadership: Perspectives and actions of public K–12 principals. *School Leadership & Management*, 36(3), 311–332.

Townley, A. L. (2020). Leveraging communities of practice as professional learning communities in science, technology, engineering, math (STEM) education. *Education Sciences*, 10(8), 190.

Traill, S., & Traphagen, K. (2014). *Assessing the impact of STEM learning ecosystems*. https://stemecosystems.org/wp-content/uploads/2015/11/Assessing_Impact_Logic_Model_Template_STEM_Ecosystems_Final.pdf

Tzou, C. T., Meixi, Suárez, E., Bell, P., LaBonte, D., Starks, E., & Bang, M. (2019). Storywork in STEM-Art: Making, materiality and robotics within everyday acts of Indigenous presence and resurgence. *Cognition and Instruction*, 37(3), 306–326. https://doi.org/10.1080/07370008.2019.1624547

U.S. Department of Education. (2024). *Serving children through Title 1, Part A of the Elementary and Secondary Education Act of 1965, as amended: Non regulatory guidance*. https://oese.ed.gov/files/2024/02/Title-I-Preschool-Early-Learning-Guidance-Revised-2023-FINAL.pdf

Velasco, R. C. L., Hite, R., & Milbourne, J. (2022). Exploring advocacy self-efficacy among K–12 STEM teacher leaders. *International Journal of Science and Mathematics Education*, 20(3), 435–457.

Wagner, M., Newman, L., Cameto, R., & Levine, P. (2006). *The academic achievement and functional performance of youth with disabilities. A report from the National Longitudinal Transition Study-2 (NLTS2)* (Report No. NCSER 2006-3000). Online Submission.

Walsh, B., Smith, L. & Mercado, K. (2023, January). *Integrated efficient early care and education systems, a state-by-state analysis revisited*. Bipartisan Policy Center. https://bipartisanpolicy.org/download/?file=/wp-content/uploads/2023/01/BPC_State-Governance-Report-1.25.23.pdf

Waters, C. C., & Orange, A. (2022). STEM-driven school culture: Pillars of a transformative STEM approach. *Journal of Pedagogical Research*, 6(2), 72–90.

Wenner, J. A., & Settlage, J. (2015). School leader enactments of the structure/agency dialectic via buffering. *Journal of Research in Science Teaching*, 52(4), 503–515.

White, R. S. (2023). Ceilings made of glass and leaving en masse? Examining superintendent gender gaps and turnover over time across the United States. *Educational Researcher*, 52(5), 272–285.

Woulfin, S. L., Strunk, K. O., & Jones, B. (2023). Studying implementation: How researchers and practitioners can gain clarity on the theory of change of education policies. In L. Cohen-Vogel, J. Scott & P. Youngs (Eds.), *AERA Handbook of education policy research* (Vol. 2). AERA.

Woulfin, S. R., Dawer, D., McKenzie, L., & Pernetti, M. (2024). [The ecosystem of actors influencing the implementation of STEM innovations]. Paper commissioned by the Committee on Pre-K–12 STEM Education Innovations. https://nap.nationalacademies.org/resource/27950/Ecosystems%20of%20Actors%20Influencing%20the%20Implementation%20of%20STEM%20Innovations_Woulfin%20Dawer%20McKenzie%20Pernetti.pdf

Young, M. D., VanGronigen, B. A., & Reynolds, A. L. (2019). State boards of education: Lesser known policy actors. *Educational Policy*, 33(1), 205–233.

Zinth, J., & Goetz, T. (2016). *A state policymaker's STEM playbook. Promising practices*. Education Commission of the States.

ANNEX 2-1: TRACKED CoSTEM FEDERAL PRE-K–12 STEM EDUCATION PROGRAMS AND INVESTMENTS

TABLE 2A-1 CoSTEM Federal STEM Education Programs and Investments Directly or Indirectly Impacting Pre-K–12

Agency and Subagency	Programs*	Keyword Descriptions	2022–2024 Combined Estimated Investment Directly Impacting Pre-K–12	Total 2022–2024 Combined Estimated Investment Indirectly Impacting Pre-K–12
Corporation for National and Community Service under AmeriCorps	• NCCC • National Partnership for Student Success • State and National Competitive and Formula • VISTA	Public-private partnership; high-impact tutoring and mentoring; STEM literacy; Mathematics	0M	368.7M
Department of Commerce under the National Institute of Standards and Technology	• Summer Institute for Middle School Science Teachers	Internship; professional development	0.8M	0.8M
Department of Commerce under the National Oceanic and Atmospheric Administration	• Bay Watershed Education and Training • Environmental Literacy Program • NOAA Teacher at Sea Program • National Sea Grant College Program • Ocean Exploration Education and Internships	Aquaponics; aquaculture; competitive grants; informal education; instructional materials development; online learning; professional development	25.7M	43.6M

(*continued*)

TABLE 2A-1 Continued

Agency and Subagency	Programs*	Keyword Descriptions	2022–2024 Combined Estimated Investment Directly Impacting Pre-K–12	Total 2022–2024 Combined Estimated Investment Indirectly Impacting Pre-K–12
Department of Defense under the Air Force	• **K–12 STEM Outreach Program** • **LEGACY**	Direct classroom instruction; instructional materials development; online education; professional development; tutoring; mentoring	15.5M	15.5M
Department of Defense under the Deputy Assistant Secretary of the Army	• Army Educational Outreach Program	K–12 student competition; camp; enrichment; hands-on, minds-on activities; Title 1 schools	0M	33M
Department of Defense under the Under Secretary of Defense for Personnel and Readiness	• STARBASE	Direct classroom instruction; instructional material development; online education; professional development	0M	92M
Department of Defense under the National Security Agency	• **GenCyber**	Pre-service teacher activities	Not Collected	Not Collected
Department of Defense under the Missile Defense Agency	• Inspiring Generations with New Ideas to Transform Education (IGNITE)	Authentic STEM learning experiences	0M	1.1M
Department of Defense under the Defense Threat Reduction Agency	• **Joint Science and Technology Institute**	Authentic STEM research experiences	2M	2M

Department of Defense under the Under Secretary of Defense of Research and Engineering	• National Defense Education Program STEM Education and Outreach	Direct classroom instruction; instructional material development; online education; professional development; teacher pre-service activities	0M	87.5M
Department of Defense under the Office of Naval Research	• **Science and Engineering Apprenticeship Program SEAP**	Internships or traineeships	2.4M	2.4M
Department of Defense and the Smithsonian Institution		Computational thinking; resources development; upskilling teachers; grades 3 and 4; rural schools; military bases		
Department of Energy Under the Office of Energy Efficiency and Renewable Energy	• Advanced Vehicle Technology Competitions • Algae Technology Educational Consortium • BETO STEM Activity • **Bioenergy Research and Education Bridge Program** • Collegiate Wind Competition • Frontier Observatory for Research in Geothermal Energy • Geothermal Energy STEM Activities • Hydrogen, and Fuel Cell STEM Activities • Solar STEM Activities • Water Power STEM/Workforce	Direct classroom instruction, outreach, mentoring, professional development, authentic STEM experiences, IM development, online education, fellowships, internships, STEM learning program, outreach, professional development	1.7M	59.3M

(continued)

77

TABLE 2A-1 Continued

Agency and Subagency	Programs*	Keyword Descriptions	2022–2024 Combined Estimated Investment Directly Impacting Pre-K-12	Total 2022–2024 Combined Estimated Investment Indirectly Impacting Pre-K-12
Department of Energy under Indian Energy Policy and Programs	• Alaska Resource Education Energy Education and Outreach	Direct classroom instruction, outreach, mentoring, professional development, authentic STEM experiences, IM development, online education, fellowships, internships, STEM learning program, outreach, professional development	0M	1.8M
Department of Energy under the Office of Science	• National Science Bowl	Academic competition	9M	9M
Department of Transportation under the Federal Highway Administration	• National Summer Transportation Institute	Authentic STEM experiences	0M	8.1M
Department of Transportation under the Federal Railroad Administration	• Encouraging Interest in Railroad Careers through STEM Education • Making Railroading a Career of Choice through STEM Education	Outreach	0.2M	2.4M
Department of Interior under the U.S. Geological Survey	• Secondary Transition to Employment Program	LEA partnership; cognitive disabilities; job skills	Not Collected	Not Collected

Department of Labor	• Cybersecurity Apprenticeship Sprint and Advanced Manufacturing Workforce Spring	Workforce development program model development; hiring	0M	0M
Department of Education under the Institute of Education Sciences	• **Regional Education Laboratories** • **Research in Special Education** • **Research, Development, and Dissemination**	Training or professional development, teacher in-service activities, research aimed at improving STEM education, research aimed at improving opportunities and supporting the full participation of talent in STEM fields and careers	267.7M	267.7M
Department of Education under the Office of Elementary and Secondary Education	• **Education Innovation and Research** • **Out of School Time Career Pathway**	Competitive discretionary research grants to support evidence-based STEM interventions to enhance student academic achievement and teacher efficacy To SEAS in partnership with 21st Century Community Learning Centers grantees, including at least one rural LEA to offer students work-based learning experiences and industry recognized credentials, internships, and apprenticeships	172.8M	172.8M
Department of Education under the Office of Postsecondary Education	• **Teacher Loan Forgiveness**	Loan forgiveness for K–12 educators	291.1M	291.1M

(*continued*)

TABLE 2A-1 Continued

Agency and Subagency	Programs*	Keyword Descriptions	2022–2024 Combined Estimated Investment Directly Impacting Pre-K-12	Total 2022–2024 Combined Estimated Investment Indirectly Impacting Pre-K-12
Environmental Protection Agency under the Office of the Administrator	• Environmental Education Grant Program • **National Environmental Education and Training Program**	Competitive grants to support design or dissemination of practices, methods, or techniques that promote environmental education; Direct classroom instruction, outreach, mentoring, professional development, authentic STEM experiences, IM development, online education, fellowships, internships, STEM learning program, outreach, professional development	6.7M	16.7M
Department of Health and Human Services under the National Institutes of Health	• National Cancer Institute Youth Enjoy Science Research Education Program • Research Supplements in Promote Diversity in Health-Related Research • **Science Education Partnership Award** • Student Intramural Research Training Award Program • Summer Research Education Experience Program • Short-Term Research Experience Program to Unlock Potential	Direct classroom instruction, instructional materials development, online education resources sites, fellowship internships or traineeships, stem learning, authentic STEM experiences, research aimed at improving opportunities and supporting the full participation of talent in the STEM fields and careers	98.1M	557.1M

National Aeronautics and Space Administration under the Office of STEM Engagement	• Minority University Research and Education Project • National Space Grant College and Fellowship Project • NextGen STEM	Fellowships, internships or traineeships, STEM learning program, outreach, training or professional development, institutional support for infrastructure, instructional material development, online education, authentic learning experiences, teacher pre-service activities, research aimed at improving STEM education, research aimed at improving opportunities and support the full participation of talent in STEM fields and careers, loan forgiveness	53.2M	359.3M
National Aeronautics and Space Administration under the Science Mission Directorates	• Global Learning and Observations to Benefit the Environment Program • Robotics Alliance Project • Science Activation Program	Citizen science, authentic STEM learning experiences; Instructional material development, online education resource sites, outreach, mentoring, teacher in-service activities,	0M	200.3M
National Aeronautics and Space Administration under the Space Technology Mission Directorate	• NASA's TechRise Student Challenge	Instructional material development, online education resource sites, outreach, mentoring, teacher in-service activities, authentic STEM experiences, 6–12 student challenge and suborbital flight opportunity	6.8M	6.8

(*continued*)

TABLE 2A-1 Continued

Agency and Subagency	Programs*	Keyword Descriptions	2022–2024 Combined Estimated Investment Directly Impacting Pre-K–12	Total 2022–2024 Combined Estimated Investment Indirectly Impacting Pre-K–12
National Science Foundation	• Eddie Bernice Johnson Inclusion across the Nation of Communities of Learners of Underrepresented Discoverers in Engineering and Science Initiatives • Research Experiences for Teachers	Instructional material development; Online education resource sites; Fellowships; Internships or Traineeships; STEM learning program; Outreach; Mentoring; Training or Professional development; Institutional support for leaderships; Teacher in-service activities; Research aimed at improving STEM education; Research aimed at improving opportunities and supporting the full participation of talent in STEM fields and careers; Research aimed at improving STEM education	34.1M	142.6M

National Science Foundation under the Directorate for STEM Education	<ul><li>Advanced Technological Education</li><li>Advancing Informal STEM Learning</li><li>Cybercorps: Scholarship for Service</li><li>**Discovery Research Pre-K-12**</li><li>EDU Core Research Program</li><li>Excellence Awards in Science and Engineering</li><li>**Innovative Technology Experiences for Students and Teachers**</li><li>NSF Research Traineeships</li><li>**Robert Noyce Teacher Scholarship Program**</li><li>**CS for All: Research and RPPs**</li><li>**STEM Teacher Corps**</li></ul>	Direct classroom instruction; Instructional material development; Online education resource sites; Fellowships, Internships or Traineeships; STEM learning program; Outreach; Tutoring; Mentoring; Training or Professional development; Institutional support for leaderships; Teacher pre-service activities; Teacher in-service activities; Research aimed at improving STEM education; Research aimed at improving opportunities and supporting the full participation of talent in STEM fields and careers; Other authentic STEM experiences	780.3M 1955.5M

(*continued*)

TABLE 2A-1 Continued

Agency and Subagency	Programs*	Keyword Descriptions	2022–2024 Combined Estimated Investment Directly Impacting Pre-K-12	Total 2022–2024 Combined Estimated Investment Indirectly Impacting Pre-K-12
National Science Foundation under the Directorate for Engineering	• Research Experience and Mentoring	Direct classroom instruction; Instructional material development; Online education resource sites; Fellowships; Internships or Traineeships; STEM learning program; Outreach; Tutoring; Mentoring; Training or Professional development; Institutional support for leaderships; Teacher pre-service activities; Teacher in-service activities; Research aimed at improving STEM education; Research aimed at improving opportunities and supporting the full participation of talent in STEM fields and careers; Other authentic STEM experiences	0M	3M

Smithsonian Institution	• STEM Informal Education and Instruction	Direct classroom instruction; Instructional material development; Online education resource sites; Fellowships; Internships or Traineeships; STEM learning program; Outreach; Tutoring; Mentoring; Training or Professional development; Institutional support for leaderships; Teacher pre-service activities; Teacher in-service activities; Research aimed at improving STEM education; Research aimed at improving opportunities and supporting the full participation of talent in STEM fields and careers; Other authentic STEM experiences	17.1M	17.1M
United States Department of Agriculture under the National Institute of Food and Agriculture	• 4-H Science and 4-H Youth Development Program • Agriculture in the Classroom	Direct classroom instruction; Instructional material development; Online education resource sites; Outreach; Tutoring; Mentoring; Training or Professional development; Institutional support for leaderships; authentic STEM learning experiences	Not Collected	Not Collected

NOTE: *Programs primarily for Pre-K–12 are bolded.
SOURCE: White House Office of Science and Technology Policy https://www.whitehouse.gov/wp-content/uploads/2024/04/2023-CoSTEM-Progress-Report.pdf

3

History of Federal and National STEM Education Improvement Efforts

A focus on science, technology, engineering, and mathematics (STEM) education is not new.[1] Since the 1950s, there has been increasing emphasis on building a skilled STEM workforce with various federal and national initiatives designed to spur improvements in K–12 STEM education. As these efforts continued and evolved, an emphasis on expanding and improving STEM education persisted (e.g., American Association for the Advancement of Science [AAAS], 1990, 1993; Council on Competitiveness, 2005; National Governors Association, 2007; National Science Board, 2007; President's Council of Advisors on Science and Technology [PCAST], 2012). Over time, the goals for STEM education have expanded beyond primarily acting in service of economic prosperity (including workforce development) to also include national security, cultural enrichment, and civic engagement. These expanded goals have led to increasing calls to document and understand how to increase students' performance and persistence in STEM fields more broadly (National Academy of Engineering [NAE] & National Research Council [NRC], 2014; NRC, 2011, 2013; PCAST, 2010).

Historically, as highlighted in Chapter 2, the U.S. federal government plays an influential role in education as the control of education is at the state and local levels (Rippner, 2015). Even today, the federal government exerts limited control over schooling, with few direct throughlines to communities and classrooms (Bowman, 2017). Yet researchers and practitioners point

---

[1]Although we are using the word STEM throughout this chapter, it is worth noting that the term did not come into play until 1990 (see Chapter 1 and Raup, 2019).

to multiple ways that federal legislation, guidance, and leadership affect local systems and activities. Several important drivers within the education system have been targeted in the work associated with improving STEM education, including the creation of standards documents, professional development networks, and curricula (NAE & NRC, 2014), all of which have increased attention to the teaching and learning of these subjects.

This chapter provides an overview of the history of federal and national attempts to improve K–12 STEM education, starting with the launch of Sputnik through the more recent wave of reforms.[2] The discussion is organized in four sections marking important milestones, sometimes linked to landmark legislative shifts; these sections include:

- 1958–1983: Launch of Sputnik to *A Nation at Risk*
- 1983–2001: From *A Nation at Risk* to No Child Left Behind
- 2001–2015: No Child Left Behind to Every Student Succeeds Act
- 2015–Present: The Current State of STEM Education

Each section describes the intended shifts and goals for K–12 education more broadly in STEM education in particular,[3] including a discussion of some of the levers (i.e., policies for standards, assessments, and accountability; curriculum; professional learning; and state/district systemic capacity building) as appropriate, and, when possible, the evidence of impact for the initiatives.

LAUNCH OF SPUTNIK TO *A NATION AT RISK* (1958–1983)

Although national security is not typically seen as a primary objective of public education, the launch of Sputnik during the Cold War accelerated a significant educational response that had begun at the start of the Cold War. The United States Congress enacted what can now be seen as the inaugural significant shift in STEM education, known as the National Defense Education Act (NDEA) of 1958, and continued with a new wave of reforms through the Elementary and Secondary Education Act (ESEA) of 1965.

The NDEA of 1958, which was managed by the U.S. Department of Education (ED; created in 1867), spurred several important initiatives to enhance

---

[2]The committee primarily focuses on K–12 as many of the legislative shifts that have an impact most related to STEM education are in that arena. There have been a number of notable moves in early childhood, but the focus has not been on STEM education in the same way.

[3]It is worth noting that most of the legislative shifts primarily call out science and mathematics, particularly for K–12. Engineering only entered the mainstream discourse in K–12 with *A Framework for Science Education* (NRC, 2012). There were a few states that had engineering in their standards a few years prior (Massachusetts including engineering with science standards in 2003), but implementation was limited.

STEM education in the United States, particularly in science and mathematics, by providing funding for STEM education at all levels, including fellowships for boosting the number of skilled engineers and scientists. There were ten major provisions within NDEA. Title VII of this act also facilitated the use of emerging technologies, promoting the development and use of educational television and other media to enhance STEM teaching and learning in and outside the classroom (Flattau et al., 2006). Title III is most closely related to the committee's statement of task. It provided states with funds to strengthen mathematics, science, and foreign language instruction, which included better equipment and materials, along with professional development[4] for teachers (Jolly, 2009). Congress funded Title III at $70 million over a four-year period (1958–1962), with an additional $5 million to be provided for supervisory and related services (P.L. 85-864).

A distinguishing characteristic of this reform movement was a focus on collaborative efforts between teachers and researchers, as seen in the provisions in Title III that focused on instruction. Rather than being passive recipients of content and strategies, teachers were treated as fundamental contributors to the process and funded accordingly or otherwise supported (Dow, 1997). As a result, teacher professional learning was intended to ensure that educators would implement up-to-date curricular resources in their own classrooms, stay current with the advancement in STEM, and adopt new teaching methodologies.

Flattau and colleagues (2006) conducted a review of NDEA. Their analysis revealed that Title III programs reached nearly every state and local agency in the country and expanded the number of specialists working for educational agencies. State surveys conducted in the 1960s suggested that better equipment and teacher education contributed to students' increased interest in mathematics and science; however, the surveys also indicated that states did not have a satisfactory way to evaluate their programs (Gaarder, 1966).

The Elementary and Secondary Education Act (ESEA) of 1965 was the federal government's first foray into public K–12 education and specifically authorized the federal government to equalize educational opportunities of all children by directing federal education dollars to the most disadvantaged children living in poverty (Paul, 2016). ESEA was enacted after the Civil Rights Act and the same year as the Voting Rights Act, serving "as a vehicle to promote federal, state, and local cooperation, support students' civil rights, and expand access to quality educational opportunities" (DeBray et al., 2023). The legislation strengthened the federal government's ability to help states' efforts both to address racial discrimination in public education and to provide technical assistance and support to districts seeking to desegregate public schools.

---

[4] As a reminder, we are using the language in federal legislation.

The shift in federal categorical programs (seen in both NDEA and ESEA) necessitated the creation of federal and state administrative capacities to oversee the administration of the programs and ensure state compliance (McGuinn, 2015; Paul, 2016). ESEA offered new grants to districts serving low-income students, federal grants for textbooks and library books, funding for special education centers, and scholarships for low-income college students. Additionally, the law provided federal grants to state educational agencies to improve the quality of elementary and secondary education.

Title I is a program created by ED as part of ESEA and is designed to distribute funding to schools and school districts with a high percentage of students from low-income families; this accounts for 5/6ths of the total funds authorized by ESEA (Paul, 2016). The other programs included:

- Title II, supporting school libraries and textbook acquisition for both private and public schools, preparing and training teachers, and funding of preschool programs
- Title III, mandating educational programming even when school was not in session
- Title IV, funding educational research and training
- Title V, supplementing grants to state departments

Disseminating Educational Innovations

A part of Title IV funding was the authorization of the establishment of a network of large-scale labs that have a focus on basic research and the development and dissemination of educational innovations. This network is run out of the U.S. Department of Education's Regional Educational Laboratory (REL) program which is administered through the Institute of Education Science (IES) National Center for Education Evaluation and Regional Assistance (NCEE).[5] Although the goals for the program have changed over time (see Box 3-1), the RELs have collaborated with school districts, state departments of education, and other education stakeholders to help generate and apply evidence, with the goal of improving learner outcomes.

The work of the REL program, as described in Chapter 2, is intended to complement other ED programs. In particular, the RELs coordinate with the Comprehensive Centers[6] and the Equity Assistance Centers[7] by conducting rigorous applied research and development work and integrating and

---

[5] The text for this section is derived from https://ies.ed.gov/ncee/rel/About
[6] For more information see https://compcenternetwork.org/
[7] For more information see https://oese.ed.gov/offices/office-of-formula-grants/program-and-grantee-support-services/training-and-advisory-services-equity-assistance-centers/

> **BOX 3-1**
> **History of Goals for the Regional Educational Laboratory (REL) Program**
>
> What follows is a timeline of the change in goals for the REL program, which began in 1965.
>
> **1965–1985:** pursue broad goal of general education improvement
>
> **Beginning 1985:** enhance impact by identifying school and classroom improvement
>
> **1990–1995:** focus on education of at-risk children
>
> **1995–2000:** promote excellence and equity for all students and scale up reform to encompass all schools, all levels of educational administration, all programmatic areas, and diverse social contexts
>
> **2000–2005:** create procedural knowledge of best practices for transforming low-performing schools into high-performing learning communities and promote use of such knowledge
>
> **2006–2011:** provide technical assistance based on highest-quality evidence as defined by scientifically valid research principles; expected to engage in high quality, rigorous research to address effectiveness of programs, policies, and/or practices for improving educational outcomes
>
> **2012–2017:** address disconnect between researchers and practitioners through researcher-practitioner partnerships known as research alliances
>
> **2017–2022:** build on and extend recent history of high-quality research, genuine partnership, and effective communication
>
> SOURCE: Based on https://ies.ed.gov/ncee/rel/About

building on that research and development work with high-quality training, coaching, technical support, and dissemination to ultimately improve learner outcomes.

Emphasis on Curriculum Development

In responding to the legislative shifts described above, there were significant investments in National Science Foundation (NSF)-funded curriculum projects (through Instructional Materials Development [IMD] grants) such as the Physical Science Study Committee (PSSC),[8] the Biological Sciences Curriculum Study (BSCS),[9] the Chemical Education Material Study

---
[8] See https://archivesspace.mit.edu/repositories/2/resources/1118
[9] See https://bscs.org/about/our-story/

(CHEM Study),[10] the Earth Science Curriculum Project (ESCP),[11] and the School Mathematics Study Group (SMSG).[12] Whereas the science curricula prioritized inquiry-based learning approaches and emphasized conceptual understanding of science over rote memorization of facts, changes on the mathematics side introduced new teaching approaches and resources, with an emphasis on a deeper understanding of mathematics concepts and problem-solving skills. The IMD grants required curriculum developers to forge partnerships with major publishing companies to ensure scale and sustainability of NSF's investments.[13]

Additional development efforts in new math and science curricula included Project 2061, led by AAAS, which focused on reforming K–12 science education. Project 2061 emphasized more integrated interdisciplinary curricula that connected scientific concepts across disciplines and grade levels, moving away from rote memorization towards deeper understanding.[14] Elementary Science Study (ESS) also emerged during this period, with a focus on hands-on, inquiry-based learning that included kits with science materials, along with teacher and student guides. However, especially at the secondary grades, these national curricular investments in the sciences resulted in the siloing of subjects and curriculum by discipline, leading to a lack of interdisciplinary integration and collaboration in STEM education (Yee & Kirst, 1994). Meanwhile, over time, ESS faced funding challenges: it launched with substantial funding through ESEA, which allowed for the development and scaling of this curriculum, but as federal funding priorities shifted and resources became scarcer, sustaining the program, both in the material resources and teacher education, was not feasible.

Development of the National Assessment of Educational Progress

Alongside NDEA and ESEA, the 1960s also saw an increased interest in data-gathering. During the early 1960s, the U.S. Commissioner of Education recognized the need for a national assessment that could provide data regarding students' knowledge, skills, and abilities.[15] The assessments first took place in 1969, known as the National Assessment of Educational Progress (NAEP), and focused on citizenship, science, and writing. In 1986, the NAEP was revised to develop new assessments and long-term trend

---

[10]See https://archives.sciencehistory.org/repositories/3/resources/124
[11]See https://scholarworks.uni.edu/cgi/viewcontent.cgi?article=2640&context=istj
[12]See https://dbpedia.org/page/School_Mathematics_Study_Group
[13]Many of these early funded curricular efforts (e.g., FOSS, STC) are still in use today and are being updated to meet the evolving demands of standards.
[14]See https://www.aaas.org/programs/project-2061
[15]For reference, see https://nces.ed.gov/nationsreportcard/about/timeline.aspx

assessments in reading, mathematics, and science. The NAEP is still in use today and has changed to align with evolving standards and understandings of how people learn in addition to ensuring the efficiency of its processes and credibility of results.

Changing the Landscape of Special Education

The Individuals with Disabilities Act (IDEA), which was passed in 1975, changed the landscape of special education in the United States. ED created IDEA in response to a need for a structured special education system with the main goal of offering a free and appropriate public education in the least restrictive environment. Through the enactment of this legislation, schools could no longer marginalize students with disabilities. For states to receive funding, they must develop policies and submit a detailed plan that focuses on creating a free and appropriate public education; the amount of funding awarded is based on the number of children with disabilities. A key component of IDEA is that guardians serve as advocates for their child's rights and needs. However, it is worth noting that despite the intention by Congress to ensure that all disabled children have meaningful access to educational opportunities, Black students, students of color, and student from low-income, less-resourced communities continue to be underserved (Davis, 2021).

FROM *A NATION AT RISK* TO NO CHILD LEFT BEHIND (1983–2001)[16]

In 1983, NCEE released the report *A Nation at Risk*. The report called for reform to public school education to address the inadequate quality of American education. The report made several recommendations, including the following:

1. All students seeking a high school diploma have a foundation in the "five new basics" (e.g., four courses in English, three in mathematics, three in science, three in social studies, 0.5 credit in computer science)
2. Schools adopt more "rigorous and measurable standards" and higher expectations for student performance and conduct
3. Schools devote more time to teaching the new basics (e.g., longer school days, longer school year, more efficient use of school day)

---

[16] Portions of this text were derived from https://www2.ed.gov/pubs/IASA/newsletters/profdev/pt2.html#:~:text=The%20Eisenhower%20Program%20authorizes%20support,learning%20in%20mathematics%20and%20science

4. Improvement to teacher quality including higher standards for teacher preparation programs, competitive teacher salaries, 11-month contracts, differentiated career ladders, allocation of resources to teacher-shortage areas, incentives for drawing highly qualified applicants into the profession, and mentoring programs for novice teachers (Park, 2022)

This report drew attention to the importance of education policy and served to provide the impetus for a number of comprehensive school improvement measures, including the academic-standards movement and a focus on school accountability (Weiss, 2003).

The decade following *A Nation at Risk* saw changes to legislation in response to the 1993 National Assessment of ESEA Title I (Paul, 2016). Improving America's Schools Act (IASA; which reauthorized ESEA) and Goals 2000: Educate America Acts[17] of 1994 codified national education goals and offered grants to states that committed themselves to specific plans for systemic reform of K–12 education. IASA attempted to coordinate federal resources and policies with the preexisting efforts at the state and local levels to improve instruction for all students through three major changes to Title I: (a) adding math and reading/language arts standards to be used to assess student progress and provide accountability; (b) reducing the threshold for schools to implement schoolwide programs from 75 percent poverty to 50 percent and giving schools a longer time to use federal funding from multiple programs to dispense funds at a school wide level; and (c) giving more local control overall so that federal officials and states could waive federal requirements that interfered with school improvements.

Taken together, these shifts elevated the need for public school reform by focusing on the need for standards, addressing teacher professional learning needs, supporting state-wide initiatives, developing leaders, enhancing informal science education programs, and expanding educational technology.

Standards-Based Reform Efforts

IASA and Goals 2000 called for the development of national standards in core subjects and encouraged states and localities to adopt these standards and align their curricula accordingly. States and districts responded to this policy environment by undertaking a variety of curricular and structural reforms, including raising graduation requirements, offering more advanced courses, and adopting new textbooks to improve the quality of instruction

---

[17]The Goals 2000: Educate America Act, P.L. 103-227, became law on March 31, 1994.

(Hamilton, Stecher, & Yuan, 2008). Massell (1994) analyzed many of these efforts and concluded that they failed to produce widespread improvement in part because of lack of coherence and failure to communicate a common understanding of what was expected to be taught. This led to conversations about further systemic reform efforts that included standards for what students were expected to learn; assessment and teacher training aligned to the standards; and restructured governance (Smith & O'Day, 1991).

From this period, frameworks like the National Council of Teachers of Mathematics Standards and the National Science Education Standards emerged, providing clear guidelines for what students should know and be able to do at each grade level (NRC, 1996).[18] By the early 2000s, every state in the United States had adopted a system of standards and assessments and was using this system as an accountability mechanism to promote school improvement; however, fewer than one-half were in full compliance with IASA standards (Hamilton, Stecher, & Yuan, 2008). With the passage of the No Child Left Behind Act in 2001 (NCLB, described in more detail in the next section), which mandated states to develop standards and aligned assessments in reading and math, the federal government assumed an increased role in stimulating this nationwide reform effort.

Policy researchers (McDonnell & Weatherford, 2016) have noted that the political dynamics at play when federal legislation or policy is drafted and enacted around issues like standards and accountability systems are different from the political dynamics that emerge when states and local education agencies attempt to interpret and implement the policies or comply with federal mandates. Drafting and passing federal legislation, for example, usually occurs within a relatively compact timeframe with a limited number of national actors in a well-defined decision-making venue. Implementation, in contrast, entails decisions and actions involving many more actors in a large variety of contexts (each individual state as well as LEAs) over a much longer period of time. Different sets of interest groups are likely to organize and mobilize during the extended implementation phase. Understanding and anticipating the political aspects of implementation can have significant implications for the long-term sustainability of reform efforts.

Professional Development Opportunities

Improved teaching and learning were central in both IASA and Goals 2000. Both provided new opportunities for enhancing teachers'

---

[18]These standards framework documents influenced curricula development and adoption across the country and laid the groundwork for the most recent iterations of standards-based reform initiatives including the Common Core State Standards as well as the Framework for K–12 Science Education (NRC, 2012) and Next Generation Science Standards (NGSS).

skills to enable all students to reach high academic standards. ED played a central role in creating professional development opportunities for school staff through the Eisenhower Professional Development Program (Title II of ESEA). In particular, this program authorized support for professional development for teachers in core academic areas but emphasized improving teaching and learning in mathematics and science. To receive funding, states had to show plans that illustrated their goals in helping teachers receive sustained, high-quality professional development tied to high content standards (as well as their performance indicators and timelines for meeting program goals). The legislation also emphasized the flexible and creative uses of materials. For example, professional development resources could be combined to address school-wide professional development needs as opposed to narrowly defined needs.

A Focus on Systemic Initiatives

The NSF's systemic initiatives (1990–2008) promoted education reform in math and science through cooperative working arrangements or partnerships among SEAs, colleges and universities, and business and citizen groups. These initiatives included the Statewide Systemic Initiative (SSI), which begun in 1990, the Urban Systemic Initiative (USI) in 1993, and the Rural Systemic Initiative (RSI) in 1994, and targeted curriculum, instruction, assessment, professional development for teachers, and state policies as areas of potential reform. These initiatives focused more broadly on a collective of schools/districts within a geographically-defined region. They afforded some autonomy and could "nudge" the schools, school districts, and communities in the defined geographic region into alignment toward achieving desired study outcomes in mathematics and science.

Statewide Systemic Initiatives

In 1990, NSF created the SSI Program. Funded projects were to align various parts of the system to produce comprehensive, coordinated, and sustained change.[19] This approach was to address perceived limitations of past reform efforts, such as targeting isolated components of the system

---

[19]The facets to be considered as part of systemic reform included "curriculum learning goals; content, instructional materials, and practice; assessment; teacher recruitment and preparation; professional development of teachers, administrators, and others" and "organizational structure and decision making, allocation of resources, articulation within the system, and accountability" (Heck & Weiss, 2005, p. 1).

(as previously addressed) or multi-pronged reform efforts that were tied too closely with a single individual or funding source (Heck & Weiss, 2005). Thus, this initiative aimed to implement comprehensive reforms at state and local levels through the promotion of high-quality, standards-based STEM curricula by focusing on developing and implementing high-quality standards, curriculum, assessment, and professional development (see Figure 3-1). Each SSI needed to articulate a clear and shared vision while devising ways to scale up interventions, develop new leaders and stable sources of funding, and tend to the politics associated with large-scale education reform (Heck & Weiss, 2005).

From 1991 to 1998, NSF funded 26 SSIs in amounts up to $2 million per year for five years. A subset (4) of the SSIs terminated early, and several others (8) received funding for an additional five-year phase (8). A review of the program conducted by SRI in 1998 revealed that while each SSI was able to coordinate efforts affecting a number of different components of the education system, the most successful had very ambitious and comprehensive plans and were able to carry them out effectively to achieve significant impact (Zucker & Shields, 1998). Those initiatives that were less successful had designs that were too narrow and/or experienced problems with implementation, quality control, or management. Even in the most successful of SSIs, the impacts were uneven and were unable to go to scale. As such, SSIs provided a mechanism for scaling up STEM improvements but could not fully solve the problem (Zucker & Shields, 1998).

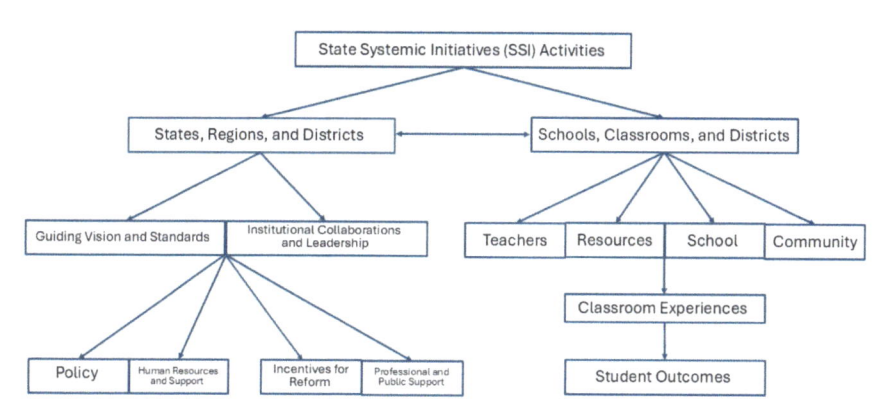

FIGURE 3-1 Statewide Systems Initiatives (SSI) activities.
SOURCE: Adapted from Zucker & Shields, 1998, https://www.nsf.gov/pubs/1998/nsf98147/nsf98147.pdf. The conduct of this study and preparation of this report were sponsored by the National Science Foundation, Directorate for Education and Human Resources, Division of Research, Evaluation and Communication, under Contract No. SED-9255371.

Urban Systemic Initiatives

Beginning in 1993, NSF initiated the USIs, which focused on the largest cities with the greatest numbers of students living in poverty. Through 1996, a total of 21 urban sites received funding in four yearly cohorts with each site receiving a five-year award of $15 million dollars. A study by Borman and colleagues (2002) revealed that mathematics achievement in the schools studied improved, reducing the achievement gap as compared to relatively affluent, predominantly White schools. Changes in school culture brought about by the activity of the USIs led to changes related to improved student outcomes; when teachers viewed themselves as learners and believed their students could achieve, improved student outcomes were likely.

Rural Systemic Initiatives

The RSIs were launched in 1994 with more than $140 million invested through 2008 in 30 RSIs to improve mathematics and science education in rural areas within the United States. RSIs sought to raise educational standards within rural schools and to address challenges associated with poverty, economic deprivation, geographic isolation, teacher turnover, and lack of resources in order to enhance the quality of life for rural residents (Harmon & Smith, 2012). A review of the RSI projects revealed three challenges that RSIs were able to respond to: leadership capacity, teacher recruitment and retention, and policy actions.

Leadership Development

The National Academy of Sciences and the Smithsonian Institution founded the National Science Resources Center (NSRC)—now called the Smithsonian Science Education Center (SSEC)—in 1985. In 1990, NSRC secured an NSF IMD grant to develop curriculum called Science & Technology for Children (STC), in collaboration with a major curriculum publisher who marketed and distributed the STC kits and teachers' materials to states, districts, and schools. The Smithsonian Institution then went on to develop an influential leadership development program. The Leadership and Assistance for Science Education Reform (LASER) model, funded by NSF in 1994, was developed by the Smithsonian Science Education Center (formerly NSRC until 2010, when the Smithsonian took over the Center full-time) to create a framework for systemic reform using STC and other similar materials. LASER is a systemic approach to science learning and teaching based on five infrastructure pillars: research-based curriculum, differentiated professional development, administrative and community

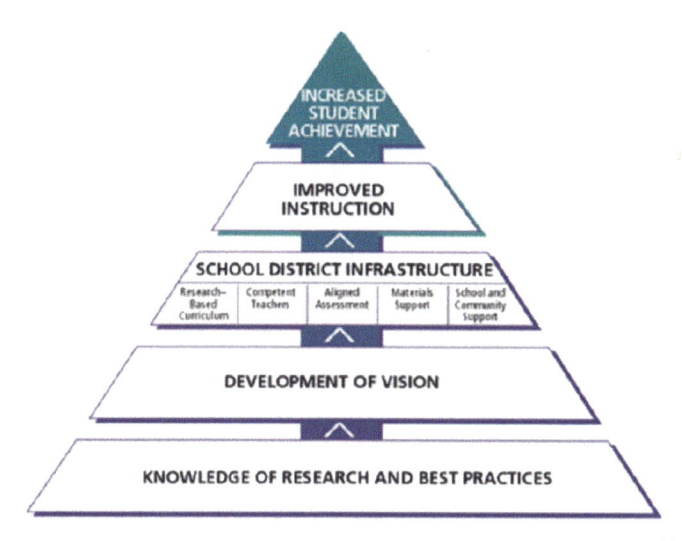

FIGURE 3-2 Leadership and Assistance for Science Education Reform (LASER) model.
SOURCE: Smithsonian Science Education Center, https://ssec.si.edu/laser-model.

support, materials support, and assessment. The SSEC designs leadership development programs and resources to move leaders representing education, government, and business through a strategic process of science education reform.[20] This process is aligned with the SSEC's theory of action (see Figure 3-2). The LASER model is still active today and has been validated through a 5-year study funded by the ED's Investing in Innovation (i3) program (Zoblotsky et al., 2017).

Informal Science Education[21]

NSF played a pivotal role in transforming science education through substantial funding that supported the expansion of science centers. The NSF's Informal Science Education program, active from 1983 to 2012, aimed to enhance public understanding of science and technology, provide lifelong learning opportunities, support nontraditional educational environments, and encourage collaboration among institutions. The program

---

[20] See https://www.si.edu/newsdesk/factsheets/smithsonian-science-education-center

[21] For more information about the emergence of informal learning environments, see the 2009 National Academies report on *Learning science in informal environments: People, places, and pursuits.*

was instrumental in driving innovation in science education methods and tools, leveraging emerging technologies and interactive experiences to engage the public meaningfully (NRC, 2009). Notably, initiatives like the Nanoscale Informal Science Education Network (NISEnet) exemplified these goals by fostering public awareness and engagement in nanoscale science. NISEnet connected science museums, research centers, and educational institutions, creating engaging and accessible science education experiences that have left a lasting impact on public understanding of STEM (St. John et al., 2009).

Educational Technology

Federal initiatives have played a pivotal role in integrating new technologies into Pre-K–12 STEM learning. These efforts have seen remarkable advancements, promising benefits, and significant challenges. The seeds of this transformation were planted in the late 1950s and early 1960s when NSF began funding groundbreaking curricula such as BSCS, Chemical Systems, and CHEM. These programs introduced high school students to innovative educational tools like videos and specialized classroom apparatus. For younger students, kits like FOSS revolutionized science instruction by bringing hands-on learning into elementary classrooms. These early efforts laid the foundation for a new era of educational technology.

Fast-forward to 1997, when NSF recognized the increasing overlap between learning concepts and emerging technologies. This realization led to the creation of the Learning and Intelligent Systems (LIS) program. The LIS program funded 25 research projects and three Learning Technologies Centers to explore how new computer and communication technologies could enhance learning and teaching. The program focused on integrating theoretical research with practical experiments, developing tools for real-world application, and advancing our understanding of learning processes.

Building on this momentum, NSF launched the Advanced Learning Technologies (ALTs) centers in 2005. These centers aimed to drive innovations in STEM education through extensive research and development. The ALTs facilitated institutional commitments and field-building activities, although the program ended after five years, limiting its long-term impact. As these initiatives unfolded, the benefits of educational technologies became increasingly apparent. Tools like PhET Simulations supported innovative classroom instruction by providing interactive and engaging science learning experiences (see the compendium in Appendix C for a detailed description). Technology also fostered digital literacy, offering students and teachers diverse learning experiences that encouraged critical thinking about the role of technology in society. Over time, students have gained access to vast digital resources, enabling hands-on learning and real-world problem-solving (see Chapter 6 for more discussion).

Moreover, the Education Sciences Reform Act of 2002 noted the importance of technology and specified that the role of technology in education be one of the primary foci of IES's work (NASEM, 2022). IES competed Education Technology as a separate topic from 2008 to 2020, but not in 2021 or 2022—with the rationale that education technology plays a central role across all topic areas. For more discussion on this topic, see the 2022 National Academies report *The Future of Education Research at IES: Advancing an Equity-Oriented Science*.

NO CHILD LEFT BEHIND TO THE EVERY STUDENT SUCCEEDS ACT (2001–2015)

No Child Left Behind (NCLB) Act, passed into public law in 2001, was a re-authorization of ESEA and marked a number of critical changes in the federal education policy landscape by significantly increasing the role of states in holding schools responsible for the academic progress of all students. The core of NCLB was to improve student achievement through annual standardized assessments of student learning, thereby quantifying education progress and making schools accountable for student performance. Specifically, NCLB required that all U.S. public schools test and report student achievement in mathematics and English language arts annually in grades 3–8 and once in high school; science testing was required once in each grade span (i.e., elementary, middle, and high school). Additionally, schools were required to report results for the student population overall as well as for specific subgroups of students (i.e., English learners, students in special education, students from low-income families, and students from racial/ethnic minoritized groups). If schools missed their state's annual achievement targets for two or more years—either for all students or for a particular subgroup—it led to a cascade of increasingly serious sanctions (e.g., allow students to transfer, offer free tutoring, state intervention).

NCLB, in addition to requiring standards, closing achievement gaps, assessments, and data collection, also required that every classroom have a "highly qualified" teacher. By "highly qualified" it meant that every teacher should hold a bachelor's degree, have state licensure or certification, and demonstrate knowledge of the subject that they teach. When assessing teachers' ability to demonstrate knowledge, states had latitude in that determination. As such, there was variability across states in the tests used as well as the determination of what constituted a passing score (Birman et al., 2007). Furthermore, the law required that these highly qualified teachers be evenly distributed among wealthier schools and those with high concentrations of poverty.

> **BOX 3-2**
> **Race to the Top (RTTT) Program**
>
> The overall aims of the RTTT program were to:
>
> - Encourage and reward states that created the conditions for education innovation and reform
> - Achieve significant improvement in student achievements and outcomes
> - Close achievement gaps
> - Improve high school graduation rates
> - Ensure that students were prepared for success in college and careers
>
> This entailed implementing plans in four areas of educational reform:
>
> - Adopting suitable standards and assessments
> - Building data systems to measure student progress and inform teachers and principals how teaching could be improved
> - Recruiting, developing, rewarding, and retaining effective teachers and principals
> - Turning around the lowest-achieving schools
>
> SOURCE: Taken from the Economic Policy Institute, https://www.epi.org/publication/race-to-the-top-goals

By 2009, there remained continued concern about the low levels of educational attainment in schools and the potential impact on the U.S. global economy. To stimulate the economy—including education—the American Recovery and Reinvestment Act (2009) was passed. One part of this legislation was a competitive grant program named RTTT; see Box 3-2 for an overview of the aims and plans for educational reform. RTTT was launched and administered through the U.S. Department of Education and was the key player in assisting states in writing their applications by offering technical assistance.

Accountability and High-Stakes Assessment

NCLB ushered in a new era of high-stakes assessment in mathematics (and science), which established and solidified accountability systems. This was achieved in two primary ways through the National Assessment of Educational Progress Authorization Act in the Education Sciences Reform Act of 2002.[22] First, NAEP was required to conduct national and state

---
[22] P.L. 107-279 Title III, section 303.

assessments at least once every two years in reading and mathematics in grades 4 and 8. Second, for states and local education agencies to receive Title I funding, plans needed to include intent to participate in the biennial state NAEP assessment.

State accountability systems provided transparent data for instructional improvement, made visible the learning gaps across equity groups, and encouraged innovations in assessment practices. However, most states relied heavily on assessments that were affordable, efficient, and easily standardized: these are generally easy-to-score multiple-choice and short open-ended questions that assess recall of facts. And assessments that are used as benchmarks of progress, and even those embedded in curriculum, often use basic and efficient paper-and-pencil formats (NRC, 2001). This led to national and state assessment programs exploring new directions in assessment. In particular, two multistate consortia received grants under the RTTT assessment program to develop assessments aligned to standards: the Partnership for Assessment of Readiness for College and Careers (PARCC) and the Smarter Balanced Assessment Consortium (SBAC; Olson, 2020).

With the movement over the past two decades toward setting challenging academic standards and measuring students' progress in meeting those standards, educational assessment has played a greater role in decision making. This has led to questions concerning whether current large-scale assessment practices are yielding the most useful kinds of information for informing and improving education. Meanwhile, classroom assessments, which have the potential to more directly enhance instruction and learning, are not being used to their fullest potential. As a result, there is a need to consider the purpose and goals of the assessment (e.g., is a given assessment intended to evaluate individual students' progress? Teacher effectiveness? Evaluation of a curriculum or program? School- or district-level performance? Effectiveness of a policy?). Given this variability in purposes and goals and variability in assessment modalities and strategies, a 2001 National Academies report acknowledged that it is important to strive for alignment between the assessment purpose/goal and modality/strategy (NRC, 2001). More recent studies have gone on to conclude that developing assessment programs that meet the goals of the changing standards presents complex conceptual, technical, and practical challenges, including cost and efficiency, obtaining reliable results from new assessment types, and developing tasks that are equitable for students across a wide range of demographic characteristics (NRC, 2014).

Despite providing more transparency in student learning, the provisions of NCLB also had unintended consequences. The intense focus on math assessments led to a narrowing of the curriculum, with teachers often feeling pressured to "teach to the test," disproportionately impacting schools that were not meeting state standards (Au, 2007; Cawelti, 2006; Olson, 2020; Ravitch, 2010). Science learning became even more deprioritized, especially when schools did not meet the accountability measures set forth by NCLB. As a result, instructional time and resources were frequently diverted from science to focus on improving math and reading scores, further marginalizing science education (Blank, 2013). Although ESSA eased some of the high stakes associated with NCLB and RTTT, the increased focus on student performance and achievement have fundamentally altered STEM education. Overall, high stakes assessments still have disproportionate influence; assessments are frequently used beyond their intended purposes; and high-quality, well-conceived assessment is expensive and difficult to do at scale.

Focus on Teacher Quality[23]

RTTT also focused on increasing teacher quality and achieving equity in teacher distribution but went beyond teacher quality as defined in NCLB to include a focus on teacher effectiveness. It did this by giving higher scores to proposals that included teacher performance evaluations based on student achievement. States responded by creating educator evaluation systems that considered student achievement data alongside teacher observations and other sources of evidence of student learning. These teacher evaluations systems had direct consequences for teachers (NASEM, 2020). Federal initiatives have notably improved teacher quality through targeted professional development and support. Programs like the Noyce Scholarship have successfully recruited talented STEM professionals into teaching.[24] Enhanced collaboration through initiatives like Mathematics and Science Partnerships (MSP) and Centers for Learning and Teaching (CLT), as discussed below, has led to innovative teacher training and professional development approaches.

Centers for Learning and Teaching

In recent history, the NSF's investment in the CLT program was designed to support innovation in STEM educator development and practice. The 12 projects awarded between 2000 and 2003 focused on advanced preparation for STEM educators and meaningful partnerships among education entities, including universities, school systems, and informal

---
[23]This section was developed based on NASEM, 2020.
[24]See https://www.nsfnoyce.org/

education organizations. The program aimed to renew and diversify the cadre of leaders in STEM education, increase the number of K–16 educators capable of providing high-quality STEM instruction and assessment, and conduct research into nationally important STEM education issues, such as the nature of learning, effective teaching strategies, and the outcomes of reform policies.

The CLTs introduced into the NSF education directorate the center model of five-year funding with the potential for renewal for a full ten-year program that research units at NSF use to drive advancement in a field. The various topics and partnerships present in the center awards were beneficial for advancing implementable STEM education innovation in a field characterized by many different and incoherent programs and initiatives. Unfortunately, the program ended after the first five years, and there was no opportunity to support the renewal option. This national disinvestment in supporting STEM teacher development shifts responsibility for support to the states, often resulting in uneven and inequitable opportunities for teachers to sustain their learning.

Mathematics and Science Partnerships (MSP) Program

From 2002 to 2016, the MSP program aimed to improve student achievement in math and science by enhancing teachers' content knowledge and teaching skills. The program was reauthorized as part of the America COMPETES Act of 2007 and provided additional appropriations in the American Recovery and Reinvestment Act of 2009. The NSF MSP coordinated efforts with ED's MSP program. MSP fostered valuable partnerships between K–12 schools and higher education institutions (see Figure 3-3). As described by Yin (2008), more than 140 MSP projects had been funded, which led to observed impacts in partnership-driven work; teacher quality, quantity, and diversity; challenging courses and curricula; impacts on students; evidence-based design and outcomes; and institutional change and sustainability.

In 2014, NSF merged the MSP program with the Computing Education for the 21st Century and relaunched it as the Science, Technology, Engineering, Mathematics, including Computing Partnerships (STEM+C) program. Moreover, in 2015 with the passage of ESSA, ED's MSP program authority was repealed and a new block grant program was established—the Student Success and Academic Enrichment Grants program (Title IV block grants). Although this includes STEM education activities, given the structure and style of the program, funding for STEM is indistinguishable from funding for other authorized activities (Granovskiy, 2018).

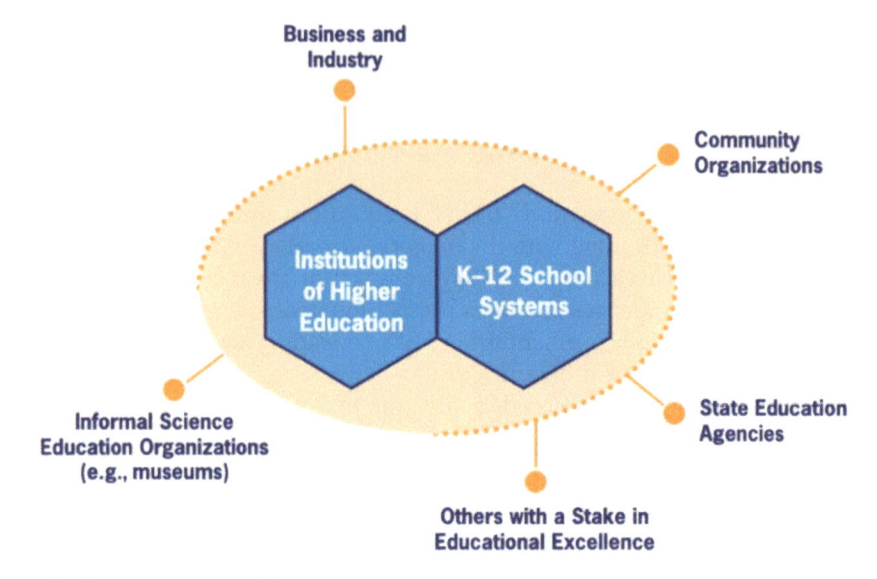

FIGURE 3-3 MSP model.
SOURCE: https://www.nsf.gov/pubs/2010/nsf10046/nsf10046.pdf

Robert Noyce Teacher Scholarship Program[25]

The Robert Noyce Teacher Scholarship Program, established in 2002, has been another key initiative. It aims to recruit STEM professionals and recent graduates to become K–12 teachers, particularly in high-need school districts. The program consists of four tracks: (a) Robert Noyce Teacher Scholarships and Stipends; (b) NSF Teaching Fellowships; (c) NSF Master Teaching Fellowships; and (d) Noyce Research. Through these programs, NSF encourages partnerships between two-year and four-year institutions. While the program has attracted many talented individuals, it struggles with limited funding and needs ongoing support and mentorship to improve retention rates.

Teacher Quality Partnership Grants[26]

The Teacher Quality Partnership Grants, initiated in 2008 and authorized in Title II of the Higher Education Act, focus on improving the quality of new teachers through innovative preparation programs that

---

[25] See https://www.nsfnoyce.org/
[26] See https://oese.ed.gov/offices/office-of-discretionary-grants-support-services/effective-educator-development-programs/teacher-quality-partnership/about-us/ and https://aacte.org/federal-policy-and-legislation/teacher-quality-partnership-grants/

emphasize clinical experience and partnerships between universities and school districts. The program is funded out of ED's Office of Innovation and Improvement. These grants have supported the development of residency programs that align closely with schools and district's needs. In the current funding cycle, the competition includes four competitive priorities: (a) increasing educator diversity; (b) supporting a diverse educator workforce and professional growth to strengthen student learning; (c) meeting student social, emotional, and academic needs; and (d) promoting equity in student access to educational resources and opportunities. Although some research has suggested improvement in the quality and retention of teachers and in the quality of students' learning experiences and achievement; scaling these programs has been difficult due to varying levels of commitment among partner institutions and the need for sustained funding.

FROM EVERY STUDENT SUCCEEDS ACT TO NOW: THE CURRENT STATE OF STEM EDUCATION (2015–PRESENT)

ESSA of 2015 established federal responsibility for investing in education, reinforced access to high-quality education for all students, maintained an expectation of state accountability to its lowest performing schools, and prioritized evidence-based and place-based local innovations. ESSA employs a logic model that holds that state-level measurement of disaggregated student achievement data based on progress toward common academic standards, and state-level accountability systems designed to funnel funds and technical assistance toward schools with lowest achievement together lead to more consistent opportunities to learn across school contexts, even as schools and districts maintain autonomy over decisions closest to teaching and learning. Specific to STEM subjects, the law requires state standards and aligned assessments in both math and science, while the federal government only requires states to include student progress toward math proficiency in their accountability systems. ESSA makes no specific mention of computer science or engineering education.

The passage of ESSA reframed conversations about how federal funding and accountability could be leveraged to promote more equitable systems of education for all students. It eased some of the high stakes associated with NCLB's accountability requirements and RTTT's educator evaluation systems, which had increased focus on student performance and achievement. Specifically, it offered states more flexibility in their assessment systems, including expanding assessment formats to include performance assessments. And, unlike the RTTT competitive grant program, which cemented the outsized role of summative assessment in asking states to use data from state assessments to evaluate teacher effectiveness and guide educational decisions, ESSA relaxed these requirements.

However, relaxing these requirements lead to less clarity for states in the planning process to know what needs to be included for approval, resulting in fragmentation (Olson, 2020). For example, ESSA contains statutory language requiring state plans to be "ambitious," but the law and ED's regulations do not define what is meant by ambitious (McGuinn, 2019). Additionally, although states continue to assess students annually, there is increased latitude in using alternative assessments rather than standardized end-of-year tests; declines in the usage of assessments aligned to the Common Core State Standards (i.e., PARCC and SBAC) have also been noted (McGuinn, 2019). There has also been growing interest in states designing assessment systems that better reflect and support the daily work of students and teachers in classrooms (Olson, 2020). Through these efforts, additional research could aid in providing better ongoing information about student progress while giving teachers more guidance on how to adjust instruction.[27]

The role of technology in assessment is not new, but this has accelerated since NCLB (see Chapter 6 for more discussion of the emerging frontiers and artificial intelligence). The use of technology-based assessments can lead to:

- obtaining finer-grained, continuous data on individual students' learning behavior and progress while learning is taking place;
- generating very large datasets from many students to model learning in specific domains;
- being fully embedded in ongoing learning (including the use of active assessments as a form of learning);
- being used adaptively to customize learning for individual students; and
- allowing modes of presentation and interaction that can get beyond standardized multiple choice tests and be adapted for students with learning differences.

However, there is still progress to be made in this area to realize the potential of technology-based assessments.

SUMMARY

Overall, it is clear that there has been a long history of education reforms that have had impact on the teaching and learning of STEM disciplines in the United States. Early initiatives like NDEA and ESEA made

---

[27]Some states that have been part of these innovations include Georgia, Louisiana, Massachusetts, New Hampshire, and North Carolina.

significant advancements in leveraging science and mathematics curricular resources to improve STEM education at scale. From there, NCLB and ESSA ushered in the standards-based reform movement, which attempted to promote widespread changes in curriculum, teaching, and assessment practices. The passage of NCLB marked critical changes to the federal education policy landscape and significantly increased the role of states in holding states and schools responsible for the academic progress of all students. Throughout the different efforts, attention has been paid to different levers in the system: standards, curriculum, professional development, building capacity within leaders and state systems, as well as assessment and accountability.

However, across all the different pushes, while there have been pockets of success and real change to systems, there have also been unintended consequences and failures to sustain momentum and progress by withdrawing or diverting funding. Curricular resources showed promise as a key tool for instructional improvement, but their potential to drive transformative and sustained improvement in STEM learning is limited without continuous, long-term funding and easy-to-manage distribution channels (see Chapter 6). Standards and accountability in assessments had the potential to lead to impact on student learning but focus on high-stakes assessments in mathematics (and English language arts) resulted in a narrowing of curriculum and teachers feeling pressured to "teach to the test." Moreover, this shift also resulted in changes in the prioritization of STEM content, with increased emphasis on mathematics and deprioritization of science and engineering (as observed in reduced instructional time and resources). Lastly, although federal initiatives have advanced integrating educational technologies in STEM education, enhancing learning experiences and fostering digital literacy, work is still needed to address challenges in professional development, infrastructure, and prioritizing education goals over technological novelty.

REFERENCES

American Association for the Advancement of Science (AAAS). (1990). *Science for all Americans*. Oxford University Press.
———. (1993). *Project 2061: Benchmarks for science literacy*. Oxford University Press.
Au, W. (2007). High-stakes testing and curricular control: A qualitative metasynthesis. *Educational Researcher*, 36(5), 258–267.
Birman, B., Le Floch, K. C., Klekotka, A., Ludwig, M., Taylor, J., Walters, K., Wayne, A., Yoon, K.-S., Vernez, G., Garet, M. S., & O'Day, J. (2007). *Evaluating teacher quality under No Child Left Behind: Research summary*. RAND Corporation. https://www.rand.org/content/dam/rand/pubs/research_briefs/2007/
Blank, R. K. (2013). Science instructional time is declining in elementary schools: What are the implications for student achievement and closing the gap? *Science Education*, 97(6), 830–847.

Borman, K., Boydston, T., Kang, E., Katzenmeyer, W. G., Kersiant, G., Lee, R., Mehta, N., & Moriarty, K. O. (2002). *Assessing the impact of the National Science Foundation's urban systematic initiative on student achievement: Closing the gap in four USI sites*. National Science Foundation.
Bowman, K. L. (2017). The failure of education federalism. *University of Michigan Journal of Law Reform*, 51, 1.
Cawelti, G. (2006). The side effects of NCLB. *Educational Leadership*, 64(3), 64.
Council on Competitiveness. (2005). *Innovate America*. www.compete.org/images/uploads/File/PDF%20Files/NII_Innovate_America.pdf
Davis, L. (2021). How the Individuals with Disabilities Education Act fails minority students. *Michigan Journal of Race & Law*, 26. https://mjrl.org/2021/02/18/how-the-individuals-with-disabilities-education-act-fails-minority-students/#:~:text=Under%20the%20Individuals%20with%20Disabilities,the%20disabled%20student.%5Bv%5D
DeBray, E., Finnigan, K. S., George, J., & Scott, J. T. (2023). Re-centering civil rights in the reauthorization of ESEA: An equitable, ecological, evidence-based framework. *Education Policy Analysis Archives*, 31(95), n95.
Dow, P. (1997). *The Sputnik-inspired reforms of the 60's*. http://www.nationalacademies.org/sputnik/dow2.htm
Flattau, P. E., Bracken, J., Van Atta, R., Bandeh-Ahmadi, A., de la Cruz, R., & Sullivan, K. (2006). *The National Defense Education Act of 1958: Selected outcomes*. Science and Technology Policy Institute.
Gaarder, A. B. (1966). *Improving instruction in the public schools through Title III of the NDEA* (Vol. 29065). U.S. Department of Health, Education, and Welfare, Office of Education.
Granovskiy, B. (2018). *Science, technology, engineering, and mathematics (STEM) education: An overview* (CRS Report No. R45223, Version 4). Congressional Research Service.
Hamilton, L. S., Stecher, B. M., & Yuan, K. (2008). *Standards-based reform in the United States: History, research, and future directions*. Center on Education Policy.
Harmon, H. L., & Smith, K. C. (2012). *Legacy of the rural systemic initiatives: Innovation, leadership, teacher development, and lessons learned*. Edvantia.
Heck, D. J., & Weiss, I. R. (2005). *Strategic leadership for education reform: Lessons from the statewide systemic initiatives program* (CPRE Policy Brief No. RB-41). Consortium for Policy Research in Education.
Jolly, J. L. (2009). Historical perspectives: The National Defense Education Act, current STEM initiative, and the gifted. *Gifted Child Today*, 32(2), 50–53.
Massell, D. (1994). Three challenges for national content standards. *Education and Urban Society*, 26(2), 185–195.
McDonnell, L. M., & Weatherford, M. S. (2016). Recognizing the political in implementation research. *Educational Researcher*, 45(4), 233–242.
McGuinn, P. (2015). Schooling the state: ESEA and the evolution of the US Department of Education. *The Russell Sage Foundation Journal of the Social Sciences*, 1(3), 77–94.
———. (2019). Assessing state ESSA plans: Innovation or retreat? *Phi Delta Kappan*, 101(2), 8–13.
National Academies of Sciences, Engineering, and Medicine (NASEM). (2020). *Changing expectations for the K–12 teacher workforce: Policies, preservice education, professional development, and the workplace*. The National Academies Press.
———. (2022). *The future of education research at IES: Advancing an equity-oriented science*. The National Academies Press.
National Academy of Engineering, & National Research Council. (2014). *STEM integration in K–12 education: Status, prospects, and an agenda for research*. The National Academies Press. https://doi.org/10.17226/18612

National Commission on Excellence in Education. (1983). A nation at risk: The imperative for educational reform. *The Elementary School Journal, 84*(2), 113–130.
National Governors Association. (2007). *Innovation America: A final report*. www.nga.org/files/live/sites/NGA/files/pdf/0707INNOVATIONFINAL.PDF
National Research Council (NRC). (1996). *National science education standards*. The National Academies Press. https://doi.org/10.17226/4962
———. (2001). *Classroom assessment and the National Science Education Standards*. The National Academies Press.
———. (2009). *Learning science in informal environments: People, places, and pursuits*. The National Academies Press. https://doi.org/10.17226/12190
———. (2011). *Successful K–12 STEM education: Identifying effective approaches in science, technology, engineering, and mathematics*. The National Academies Press. https://doi.org/10.17226/13158
———. (2012). *A framework for K–12 science education: Practices, crosscutting concepts, and core ideas*. The National Academies Press.
———. (2013). *Monitoring progress toward successful K–12 STEM education: A nation advancing?* The National Academies Press. https://doi.org/10.17226/13509
———. (2014). *Developing assessments for the Next Generation Science Standards*. The National Academies Press.
National Science Board. (2007). *National action plan for addressing the critical needs of the U.S. science, technology, engineering and mathematics education system*. www.nsf.gov/nsb/documents/2007/stem_action.pdf
Olson, L. (2020). A shifting landscape for state testing. *State Education Standard, 20*(3), 7.
Park, J. (2022). A nation at risk. *EdWeek*. https://www.edweek.org/policy-politics/a-nation-at-risk/2004/09
Paul, C. A. (2016). Elementary and Secondary Education Act of 1965. *Social Welfare History Project*.
President's Council of Advisors on Science and Technology. (2010). *Prepare and inspire: K–12 education in science, technology, engineering, and math (STEM) for America's future*. President's Council of Advisors on Science and Technology. http://www.whitehouse.gov/sites/default/files/microsites/ostp/pcast-stem-ed-final.pdf
———. (2012). *Report to the president. Engage to excel: Producing one million additional college graduates with degrees in science, technology, engineering and mathematics*. www.whitehouse.gov/sites/default/files/microsites/ostp/pcast-engage-to-excel-final_feb.pdf
Raupp, A. B. (2019, August 4). STEM education's lost decade and tenor: Contemporary insights into a popular, global movement. *Medium*. https://medium.com/datadriveninvestor/stem-educations-lost-decade-and-tenor-3f741bd728e6
Ravitch, D. (2010). *The death and life of the great American school system: How testing and choice are undermining education*. Basic Books
Rippner, J. A. (2015). *The American education policy landscape*. Routledge.
Smith, M. S., & O'Day, J. (1991). Educational equality: 1966 and now. In D. A. Verstegen & J. G. Ward (Eds.), *Spheres of justice in education*. Harper Collins.
St John, M., Helms, J., Castori, P., Hirabayashi, J., Lopez, L. & Phillips, M. (2009). Overview of the NISE network evaluation. *Inverness Research*.
Weiss, T. H. (2003). *Scientists researching teaching: Reforming science education and transforming practice*. University of Massachusetts Amherst.
Yee, G., & Kirst, M. (1994). Lessons from the new science curriculum of the 1950s and 1960s. *Education and Urban Society, 26*(2), 158–171.
Yin, R. K. (2008). The math and science partnership program evaluation: Overview of the first two years. *Peabody Journal of Education, 83*(4), 486–508.

Zoblotsky, T., Bertz, C. Gallagher, B., & Alberg, M. (2017). *The LASER Model: A systemic and sustainable approach for achieving high standards in science education: SSEC i3 validation final report of confirmatory and exploratory analyses.* The University of Memphis, Center for Research in Educational Policy. Summative report prepared for Smithsonian Science Education Center.

Zucker, A. A., & Shields, P. M. (1998). *A report on the evaluation of the National Science Foundation's Statewide Systemic Initiatives Program.* https://www.nsf.gov/pubs/1998/nsf98147/nsf98147.pdf

4

Approaches to Scaling and Sustaining Innovations

With this chapter, we turn to a detailed consideration of one of the key concepts in this report: scale. As such, this chapter has two goals. The first goal is to put forth a multidimensional framework for conceptualizing scale, adapted from Coburn (2003), and which informs the chapters that follow. This framework articulates four dimensions of scale: spread, depth, sustainability, and shift in ownership. As discussed above in Chapter 1 and elaborated more extensively below, most assessments of scale focus primarily on the spread of the innovation, yet considerations of the depth of implementation of the innovation, sustainability, and shifts in ownership are critical to making sense of why an innovation may (or may not) successfully scale (Coburn, 2003).

The second goal of this chapter is to discuss, in broad strokes, affordances and challenges of approaches to scaling innovations with respect to the four dimensions of scale, and for which there is empirical evidence demonstrating their impact. The committee discusses (a) pathways to scaling an existing innovation in new contexts in which implementation is tightly prescribed (i.e., a focus on fidelity of implementation), and (b) pathways where principled adaptation of the innovation is expected and desired as it is implemented in new contexts (i.e., a focus on integrity of implementation). The committee then discusses (c) approaches in which researchers and educators (and sometimes youth, family, and/or community members) collaboratively design innovations and their implementation, with attention to scale and sustainability. The committee offers a discussion of the affordances and limitations of each approach.

Some notes on terminology support this discussion. As described in Chapter 1, each innovation involves interested and affected parties, among which the committee distinguishes: designers (those who design the innovation); enactors (those who directly enact the innovation); enablers (those who support the enactors, through funding, providing leadership and/or professional development, etc.); and beneficiaries (those whose interests the innovation is meant to directly serve). As discussed further below, some persons play more than one role in the initial design, enactment, and/or scaling of an innovation. The committee refers to the potential of an innovation to be "scaled" as its "scalability." In what follows, "scalability" will be distinguished from whether "scale" (or particular dimensions of scale) has been "achieved" in relation to a given innovation. Of course, what counts as "achieving" scale is always relative to the intended goals of an innovation, the intended beneficiaries, and the context within which it is enacted, as well as a given time period.

In addition, although the committee decided that it is important to conceptualize sustainability as a dimension of scale, throughout the report, the language of "scale and sustainability" is used. This choice of language is deliberate. One reason is that the language of "sustained implementation" is in the committee's task statement. The second reason is that, in the everyday language of policy and practice, assessments of whether an innovation has "scaled" are often made absent attention to whether the innovation is sustained. Bringing attention to "scale and sustainability" is intended to underscore the importance of considering not just the spread, or reach, of an innovation, but also its lifespan, especially given trends of educator turnover in educational contexts.

The chapter begins with a discussion of the four dimensions of scale, as adapted from Coburn, that inform our analysis in the chapters that follow. We then turn to three approaches to scaling up—fidelity of implementation; principled adaptation; and collaborative design and implementation—and examine the affordances and challenges of each. Throughout this review of implementation approaches, we also discuss a common assessment sequence and how it unfolds when applied to each approach.

CONCEPTUALIZING SCALE AS MULTIDIMENSIONAL

The term "scale" means many things to many people. People who design and implement innovations, including educators and researchers, as well as policymakers and members of the science, technology, engineering, and mathematics (STEM) professions, conceptualize scale in diverse ways, and use various criteria to assess whether, and in what ways, an innovation has "scaled" (e.g., Morel et al., 2019). Most discussions of scale focus solely on increasing the number of enactors, beneficiaries, and/or contexts in which an innovation is enacted (Coburn, 2003). As Coburn (2003) cautioned, however, focusing only on increasing numbers "says nothing about the nature of the change envisioned or the degree to which schools and teachers have the knowledge and authority to continue to grow the [innovation] over time" (p. 4). Moreover, focusing on numbers alone in an assessment of scale often precludes researchers and educators from attending to critical factors that may explain whether an innovation scales up successfully, and why or why not.

Adapting Coburn's (2003) framework for conceptualizing scale along four "interrelated dimensions" (p. 3) has allowed the committee to bring a fuller sense of scale to the issues above. In addition to the spread of the innovation, the committee views the three other dimensions articulated by Coburn—depth of change to enactors' current beliefs, knowledge, and practice, the sustainability of the innovation, and ownership of the innovation—as critical dimensions to consider in efforts to "scale" an innovation. Not all efforts to scale an innovation will explicitly attend to each of these dimensions, nor will they give equal weight or priority to the dimensions on which they focus. As detailed in Chapter 8, conceptualizing scale along these dimensions has implications for the identification of critical conditions that enable or act as barriers to the scalability of an innovation and how to assess or measure the extent to which an innovation has "scaled."

In conceptualizing these dimensions, Coburn (2003) focused on the scaling of classroom instructional reforms.[1] As such, implementation and scaling of an innovation was primarily conceived of in terms of classrooms, as embedded in schools, as embedded in school districts. The focus of this committee is not limited to classroom instructional innovations; we consider Pre-K–12 classroom, school, and district innovations, as well as innovations focused on afterschool and community settings, and innovations intended to scale at the state level and across regions. Spread, depth, sustainability, and ownership are important to consider, in designing for and assessing scale in these alternative contexts as well.

Dimension 1: Spread

Typically, in the literature, "spread" refers to the expansion or diffusion of an innovation, to more contexts and/or larger numbers of participants. As noted above, spread is the most common way of conceptualizing scale. Traditionally, scale was identified with spread, expressed as a *number*—the number of sites (schools, districts) to which the innovation has expanded

---

[1] The committee recognizes that not all instructional reforms are innovations; however, there are a number that are designed that would meet the definition of "innovation" provided in Chapter 1. The committee strives to delineate these concepts as much as possible.

(geographic spread); or the number of people (teachers, students) affected (demographic spread; Coburn, 2003, p. 7). Demographic spread might also reflect increasing diversity of the affected population, even in the absence of geographic spread.

In setting goals for the spread of an innovation, and when assessing spread, it is critical to consider the specific populations and communities for which an innovation is designed and appropriate. For instance, Advancing Indigenous People in STEM (AISES) is a nonprofit indigenous organization "founded in 1977 by American Indian scientists, engineers, and educators" that aims to substantially increase "the representation of Indigenous peoples in STEM studies and careers."[2] They provide, among other supports, culturally relevant curriculum programs for Pre-K–12 Indigenous students in computer science and coding, and mentorship and networking opportunities for Indigenous college and university students. AISES organizes its activities via regionally based chapters across the United States and North America, and is guided by eight "Advisory Councils," which include Tribal Nations Advisory Councils, a Council of Elders, as well as Councils of Indigenous Peoples in Industry. In relation to spread, then, AISES focuses on reaching a particular population, whereas other STEM-focused organizations might focus on different or broader populations. As such, goals for spread and assessing progress of spread will necessarily vary.

Of course, an exclusive focus on numbers of sites and/or people says nothing about the nature of the innovation (*what* is spread), whether the "what" is implemented in a superficial or deep manner, or whether the innovation is sustained, especially as enablers and enactors come and go. These critical issues are the focus of dimensions of scale discussed below: *depth*, *sustainability*, and *ownership*.

Dimension 2: Depth

A second, critical dimension of scale concerns the nature of change to the enactor's current practice that is intended or implied by the innovation, and the depth of the change that is implemented. The implementation and scaling of some innovations aim at integrating minor changes into educators' and learners' existing practice, whereas others entail substantial change to educators' and learners' usual practice. As Coburn (2003) argues, getting clear on the nature and the quality of the change that is intended matters in being able to both support and assess the scaling of the innovation.

Innovations requiring minor changes to educators' current practices might include, for example, the provision of a new platform students can use to practice math skills. Implementing the platform may require some

---

[2] See https://aises.org/about/

technology "know-how" but it likely does not entail substantial change to teachers' current beliefs about students, or assumptions about teaching and learning. For example, a classroom teacher may decide to incorporate an online tool for math homework assignments and formative assessments that is compatible with curriculum already in use and can be easily integrated with the school's existing learning management system (e.g., ASSISTments[3]).

In contrast, implementing innovations that "[go] beyond surface structures or procedures" typically necessitate "deep change" to educators' assumptions about teaching, learning, and subject matter, norms of interaction between teachers and students, and pedagogical principles (Coburn, 2003, p. 4; see also Brown, 1992). For example, consider the implementation of a new curriculum designed to engage students to use science and engineering concepts to make sense of scientific phenomena. In many contexts, for many science teachers, learning to engage students in phenomena-focused learning requires substantial shifts in how they currently teach, and it requires new content as well as pedagogical knowledge regarding the integration of scientific, mathematical, and engineering concepts (Reiser et al., 2017). It also likely requires new forms of collaboration among science teachers and teacher educators (Reiser et al., 2017).

The committee considers *depth* in terms of the extent to which the innovation is intended to create or entails substantial shifts to what Elmore (1996) terms the "core of educational practice" (p. 2). When assessing depth, it is important to distinguish the *depth of intended change* from the *depth of achieved change*. For example, in cases where the intended change requires substantial shifts in current educators' current assumptions, knowledge, and practices, how "deep" is the implementation? In enacting the innovation, have educators shifted longstanding beliefs about their learners? Have they deepened their knowledge of and practice in eliciting and responding to students' current ideas and reasoning, in order to advance the learning of each student? Or, have educators enacted features of the innovation in superficial ways, where, for example, materials or "sentence stems" may be visible in instruction, but the focus of discourse remains on "the right format," rather than the substance of what students are reasoning about?

Coburn (2003) anticipated that "some may argue that [. . .] components of depth are more appropriate for principle-based reforms" than those that are more narrowly focused on discrete aspects of teaching or learning (p. 5). Coburn cautioned, however, that "most [innovations], even those that are *not* explicitly principle-based, 'carry' sets of ideas about what constitutes appropriate [teaching and learning]," for example, about the "nature of subject matter, valued student outcomes, how students

---

[3] See https://new.assistments.org/

learn" and so forth (p. 5). Therefore, even in cases in which the intended shift in enactors' current practices appear minor, it is important to attend to the depth with which the innovation is enacted, when assessing scale. Attention to depth, no matter the nature of the intended change, highlights how critical it is to consider not just *whether* new materials, or a new pedagogy, or new tools are present in a setting, but *how* they are being used as the innovation is implemented and scaled.

Attention to depth also has important implications for the study of scaling STEM innovations. Although studies of scale often include some assessment regarding the implementation of innovations, oftentimes those assessment focus on surface-level indications of adoption (e.g., number of users, presence of materials, time spent using the materials; Coburn, 2003). Conceptualizing depth as critical to understanding and assessing scale implies a need to both develop and use measures that attend to educators' assumptions about STEM teaching and learning as well as students' capabilities, content-specific knowledge, and their developing forms of practice. As Coburn (2003) argues, "The increased emphasis on depth as a key element of scale calls into question the degree to which [. . .] implementation can be assessed using survey methods alone" (p. 5).

Dimension 3: Sustainability

A third, interrelated dimension of scale concerns the sustainability of innovations, that is, whether the innovation endures over time in the original and new contexts when the initial circumstances, such as funding, run their course (Coburn et al., 2012; Datnow, Hubbard, & Mehan, 2002; Scheirer, 2005). Coburn (2003) underscored, "Most discussions address issues of sustainability and scale separately, obscuring the way that scale, in fact, depends upon sustainability" (p. 6). Sustaining an innovation requires attention to spread and depth of change in the practice of both those who have been there for a long period of time and those who are new, while being responsive to changes in the contexts in which the innovation is enacted (McLaughlin & Mitra, 2001).

Gersten and colleagues (2000) bring attention to how considerations regarding the sustainability of innovations will vary, depending, in part, on the nature of change implied by the innovation. For example, for innovations that target substantial changes in the instructional core, teachers' willingness to consider new pedagogical approaches is a critical consideration for sustainability. In contrast, innovations that focus on structural changes to schooling (e.g., changes in how often courses meet) may require specific considerations related to the school culture, as well as district and state policies.

Although sustainability of innovations is fundamental to scale, few studies explicitly address it in their conceptualizations or research designs to examine scale (Coburn et al., 2012; Gersten, Chard, & Baker, 2000; Hargreaves & Goodson, 2006). Most studies related to scale-up efforts of innovations focus on the first few years of implementation and fail to attend to their sustainability after the implementation period, when start-up resources and supports have officially ended (Coburn, 2003). Part of the challenge is that sustainability is about what occurs *after* the work on the design and initial implementation of an innovation have been completed. Often, research funding for that work has ended, and researchers move on to a different set of problems (Fishman et al., 2011). Few studies have attempted to interrogate the sustainability of the program after initial scale-up efforts (though, see Zoblotsky et al., 2017 for a three-year follow-up study of the LASER program described in Chapter 3).

Whereas many studies fail to attend to the sustainability of innovations, there is growing attention by funders and enactors of various STEM education innovations to what happens after the initial funding for the innovations end. For example, Fishman and colleagues (2011) followed up with teachers after their participation in a randomized trial where they were introduced to a technology-infused mathematics curriculum. Via a teacher survey, Fishman et al. explored factors related to the continued use of the curriculum in ways that were congruent with the developers' intent. Their findings revealed disparities in terms of the settings in which the use of the curriculum was sustained. Namely, the higher the socioeconomic status of student populations, and the greater the students' performance with respect to conceptually rich mathematics prior to using these materials, the more likely teachers were to continue using the materials. Teachers' perceptions of coherence, or "how well the professional development matched the teacher's goals for professional development, the existing reform ideas within the school, and whether the professional development was followed up with activities that built upon what was already learned," were also found to be related to sustained use of materials (p. 341). These findings suggest that sustaining innovations requires ongoing attention to enactors' assumptions and current practices (i.e., depth of change), issues of equity in implementation, and how an innovation can be coherently integrated into the broader system within which it is intended to work.

There is ample evidence showing that sustaining innovations is challenging due to various factors such as competing priorities in school and districts, limited resources, and teachers' social relations and turnover (e.g., Bryk et al., 2010; Gersten, Chard, & Baker, 2000; Klingner et al., 1999). As stated by Datnow and colleagues (2002), "Forces at the state, in districts, design teams, the school and classrooms all interact to shape the longevity of reform" (p. 135). Based on five years of research in schools that engaged in one of three theory-based innovations, McLaughlin and Mitra (2001) identified five essential factors that shape sustainability. These include (a) access to sufficient resources, (b) knowledge of the first principles of the innovation, (c) a supportive community of practice, (d) a knowledgeable and supportive principal, and (e) a compatible district context. All in all, these studies demonstrate how sustainability of innovations maybe a central challenge to bring innovations to scale. We return to these points in Chapter 8.

Dimension 4: Ownership

A fourth dimension of scale includes attention to the broadening and deepening of ownership of the innovation. As an innovation is implemented and scaled in a particular context, there is typically a set of enablers, who are tasked with guiding the implementation effort. Oftentimes, the enablers of the innovation are distinct from the original designers. For example, district leaders may be tasked with implementing a new STEM curriculum that was designed and tested in distant districts. In some cases, the initial designers or "authors" of the innovation may be centrally involved in implementation; this is especially true in cases where the innovation was designed by members of the community itself or in cases in which local educators and researchers co-designed the innovation in the local context. In either case, a critical component of taking an innovation to scale entails creating conditions to deepen, expand, and/or shift knowledge and authority of the innovation. Broad, local ownership among enactors supports deep implementation and sustainability of an innovation. Enactors can anticipate challenges to implementation and inform contextually specific decision making regarding what would support deep implementation. Broad ownership among enactors can result in a professional community that, in turn, invites and supports new "users" (McLaughlin & Mitra, 2001; Rogers et al., 2009).

Coburn (2003) cautioned that discussions of ownership often focus on "buy-in" rather than "a shift in knowledge of and authority for the reform" (p. 8), especially in relation to initial adoption of an innovation of instructional materials or a technology. Instead of focusing on "teachers' buy-in," it is more productive, long term, to foster teachers' ownership of the instructional sequences to enable them to take increasing responsibility in improving the sequences, based on enactment in their classrooms (Cobb & Jackson, 2015). It is rare to find explicit discussion of shift in ownership in research on the implementation and scaling of innovations. Yet, there are studies that provide insights into what this transition in ownership might entail. For example, McLaughlin and Mitra (2001) analyzed the sustainability and spread (and challenges therein) of three classroom innovation efforts that were initially designed by university researchers; each of the innovations targeted deep change in classroom practice.[4] Given that the innovations were initiated "from the outside," questions of ownership were critical, particularly once the funding and university-based support ended. In one of the projects, attention to the transfer of ownership was an explicit focus of the last year of the funded project. University researchers engaged in multiple intentional conversations with school and district leadership to discuss and plan how leaders and teachers could continue to deepen an understanding of the principles of the reform absent the presence of the university team; their goal was that "teachers [could] develop the confidence to make their own decisions related to project activities" (p. 320).

As another example, consider the design and scaling of the National Science Foundation (NSF)-funded River City "multi-user virtual environment curriculum designed to enhance engagement and learning in middle school science" (Clarke & Dede, 2009, p. 354).[5] Drawing on design-based research methods, Clarke and Dede (2009) detailed how the research team intentionally designed for spread, depth of implementation, sustainability, and shift in ownership. Specific to shift in ownership, Clarke and Dede underscored the importance of strong relationships with teachers, who they involved as "co-evaluators" and "co-designers" throughout their multi-year design, implementation, and scaling efforts (p. 362). For example, teachers who had implemented River City in a prior phase supported the onboarding of new teachers, in new sites. In addition, the research team continued to elicit feedback from implementers, new and old, to inform changes and elaborations to the curriculum.

As part of designing for sustainability and shift in ownership, Dede (2006) suggests the *evolution* of the innovation as a key dimension of scale. Evolution refers to

> when the adopters of an innovation revise it and adapt it in such a way that it is influential in reshaping the thinking of its designers. This in turn creates a community of practice between adopters and designers whereby the evolution evolves. [. . .] Evolution is more than providing teachers with ownership; it is incorporating their ownership into the evolution of the curriculum. Evolution is really a product of depth, spread, and shift. (Clarke & Dede, 2009, p. 354)

As an example of evolution, Clarke and Dede detail how their team's thinking about the design and facilitation of professional development evolved, as ownership of the innovation shifted from a "train the trainer

---

[4]The Jasper component included a math focus, the Fostering Communities of Learners is about literacy, discourse, and metacognitive reasoning as applied to many different topics, and the CSILE component could involve various content. Therefore, the degree to which the components focused on STEM varied.

[5]See https://muve.gse.harvard.edu/

model" to monthly webinars focused on "just in time training." Writing primarily from the perspective of researchers designing innovations for scalability, Clarke and Dede (2009; see also Dede, 2006) proposed the addition of "evolution" of the innovation as a fifth dimension to Coburn's (2003) four dimensions of scale (spread, depth, sustainability, ownership). The committee elected to treat attention to the evolution of the innovation as an important aspect of fostering sustainability and shift in ownership, given the broad scope of innovations and origins of their development within the committee's charge.

Summary: Four, Interrelated Dimensions of Scale

These four dimensions of scale—spread, depth, sustainability, and ownership—are not independent (Coburn, 2003). Indeed, they are intertwined in complex ways. If the innovation involves superficial or minor changes to enactors' current practice, its adoption and assimilation by practitioners may perhaps be easily achieved. That said, superficial change is inherently fragile. If, on the other hand, the innovation entails substantial change to enactors' current practices, then the depth of implementation and expansion of ownership among enactors is a formidable challenge that demands time and substantial professional resources to accomplish. It is a change of culture. But, once achieved, it provides a foundation for sustainability, at least in the particular context for which the innovation was designed.

In Elmore's (1996) view, depth is the enemy of spread, at least of geographic spread to new contexts. Elmore writes: "The closer an innovation gets to the core of schooling, the less likely it is that it will influence teaching and learning on a large scale" (p. 4). As elaborated in Chapter 7, this is because sustaining innovations that entail substantial changes to "business as usual" entails concerted and coordinated changes in the broader educational system (e.g., leadership, accountability relations). As Coburn (2003) stated, "[T]he more ambitious [an innovation], the more challenging it may be to simultaneously achieve spread, sustainability, and depth" (p. 9).

SCALING INNOVATIONS

Just as there are multiple meanings of "scale," there are various ways by which enactors and researchers go about "scaling" or "scaling up" an innovation (e.g., Elmore, 1996; Morel et al., 2019). "Scaling an innovation" typically refers to how various actors plan for, work to achieve, and assess the implementation of innovations in broader contexts and/or with broader populations, than those for which it was initially designed and enacted (Dede, 2006). In some cases, the innovation's designers are researchers who may or may not be members of the communities in which the innovation is being implemented and scaled. Further, researchers who study the scaling of the innovation may or may not be the initial designers of the innovation. More recently, there has been growing attention to the value of educators (and sometimes youth, families, and community members) and researchers co-designing innovations in local contexts, with intentional consideration of implementation, scale, and sustainability as part of the innovation's initial design (e.g., Bryk et al., 2015; Penuel et al., 2011; Peurach et al., 2022; Roschelle, Mazziotti, & Means, 2021).

In what follows, the committee presents an overview, in broad strokes, of three approaches to scaling innovations: (a) *focus on fidelity of implementation:* scaling innovations in which implementation is tightly prescribed (i.e., a focus on fidelity of implementation), (b) *principled adaptation:* scaling innovations, where principled adaptation of the innovation is expected and desired (i.e., a focus on integrity of implementation), and (c) *collaborative design:* approaches in which researchers and educators collaboratively design innovations and their implementation, with deliberate attention to scale and sustainability. (Co-design approaches tend to reflect adaptation approaches to scaling.) Throughout, the committee discusses the affordances and challenges with the different approaches, with respect to concerns for spread, depth, sustainability, and ownership.

Two points are useful to keep in mind. First, approaches to scaling an innovation "may shift over time within the lifecycle of an innovation" (Morel et al., 2019, p. 370). For example, as the innovation is spread to new populations and new contexts, the various interested and affected parties shift, which often necessitates changes in who is involved in the scaling process and how it is being approached. Second, this discussion of approaches to scaling innovations is not exhaustive. For example, Morel and colleagues (2019) describes *reinvention* as another approach to scaling, in which researchers and designers "expect that innovations undergo radical transformation" as they are used in various contexts, for example open-source digital media platforms (p. 372). The committee did not report on reinvention, given difficulty in finding empirical evidence of the impact of STEM innovations reflecting such an approach to scale.

Focus on Fidelity of Implementation: Scaling in Tightly Prescribed Ways

One approach to scaling an innovation reflects the assumption that to claim an innovation has successfully scaled, enactors must implement the innovation in tightly prescribed ways, in contexts other than those in which it was initially designed and effective in service of a specific set of learning goals for the beneficiaries. Morel and colleagues (2019) described this approach to scale as replication: "an innovation is considered at scale if it is widespread, implemented with fidelity, and produces expected outcomes" (p. 371).

The concept of fidelity of implementation originated in public health and has been used in educational evaluation and intervention research for four decades or so (Gage, MacSuga-Gage, & Detrich, 2020; O'Donnell, 2008). Gage and colleagues (2020) described "fidelity of implementation" through an analogy from the medical field:

> A patient is diagnosed with strep throat and his or her doctor prescribes an antibiotic. The instructions inform the patient to take one pill twice daily for 10 days. The patient takes both doses of antibiotic on the first day, but only one on the second and third days. Remembering again, the patient takes two doses on the fourth and fifth days, but then stops taking the antibiotic. By the end of 10 days, the patient returns to the doctor, complaining that the medicine did not work. Upon review, the doctor discovers that the patient only took 8 of the 20 prescribed antibiotic pills, or, put differently, the patient implemented the intervention with 40% fidelity. The reason for the patient's lack of improvement was not that the intervention failed but that it was not implemented as prescribed. (p. 1)

"Fidelity" has been defined in different ways, and it is multidimensional (Gage, MacSuga, & Detrich, 2020; van Dijk, Lane, & Gage, 2023). Drawing on earlier work by Dane and Schneider (1998), van Dijk and colleagues (2023) defined key features of fidelity of implementation, which include (a) adherence (i.e., the degree to which all elements of an innovation were implemented); (b) dosage (i.e., time and/or frequency of use); (c) quality (i.e., how well the aspects of innovation were delivered); (d) differentiation (i.e., how the innovation is distinct from another condition); and (e) responsiveness (i.e., how the students respond to intervention). Attention to each of these dimensions is not essential for an intervention to be considered as implemented with fidelity. Rather, decisions about what features to attend to in conceptualizing and assessing fidelity of implementation need to be made in relation to an explicit program theory of change and improvement (O'Donnell, 2008).

By and large, federal agencies have encouraged studies of scaling that aim for "tight" implementation of an innovation in increasingly varied contexts, sequenced as follows (Roschelle, Mazziotti, & Means, 2021). *Pilot studies* focus on the "feasibility of an intervention that has [. . .] been implemented" and evaluated "under highly controlled conditions", and aim to answer the question, "Is the theory undergirding the intervention effective?" (Thomas et al., 2018, p. 319). *Efficacy studies* "[assess] the extent to which a successfully piloted intervention produces the desired outcomes under less controlled conditions," but where the designer is still "actively involved in implementing and evaluating the program" (Thomas et al., 2018, p. 319; see also O'Donnell, 2008). As described by Thomas and colleagues (2018), the guiding question is

"Can the intervention work outside of the laboratory or a few carefully selected sites under conditions that enable high-quality implementation?" (p. 319). Once an innovation has been shown to result in the desired outcomes, a next stage is to study the *effectiveness* of the innovation in a wider range of settings, where the designer is less involved in the implementation. The guiding question of effectiveness studies is: "Does the program work under conditions that approximate those under which the intervention would be delivered on a broader scale?" (Thomas et al., 2018, pp. 319–320). Assuming the implementation of the innovation continues to result in the desired outcomes, *scale-up studies* focus on the implementation of the innovation in new contexts, typically with increasing numbers of and heterogeneity of participants and/or sites (e.g., at a state level; Roschelle, Mazziotti, & Means, 2021; Thomas et al., 2018). See Box 4-1 for an example of an innovation that was tested and evaluated via a sequence of pilot, efficacy, effectiveness, and scale-up studies.

Conceptualizing and assessing fidelity of implementation is emphasized in each of these types of studies. When paired with an explicit theory of change, fidelity of implementation can help researchers identify faults in the innovation as designed (i.e., in the theory of change and its assumptions), and how variation in implementation impacts outcomes, for better and worse. Especially for innovations that target deep change to the instructional core, however, the relationship between "fidelity" and outcomes is often not clear in efficacy, effectiveness, and scale-up studies (O'Donnell, 2008; Penuel & Fishman, 2012). Teaching and learning take part in complex systems (e.g., classroom, school, district), and it is often difficult to "distinguish between the effects caused by the materials and the effects caused by the teachers' interactions with the materials" (O'Donnell, 2008, p. 44).

Moreover, it is easier to assess fidelity of implementation in relation to highly prescribed innovations, in that the boundaries of what counts as "low" and "high" implementation, and its impact on student outcomes, can, in theory, be distinguished. Yet, highly prescribed innovations are often much harder to "fit" into existing classroom, school, and district environments.

> Highly scripted, packaged programs provide a means to control implementation—which is ideal for teasing apart causality—but these can lead to an entire intervention being discarded when it does not fit well into the school environment. This creates an inherent tension between implementation and usefulness. The interventions most implementable with fidelity are heavily scripted and require specific supports, yet these requirements may not be feasible or desirable in many school environments (Coburn, 2003). (NASEM, 2022, pp. 67–68)

In addition, as highly prescribed innovations that have originated from "outside" the system are implemented and spread, attention to local resources

> **BOX 4-1**
> **Pre-K Mathematics**
>
> The *Pre-K Mathematics* supplementary mathematics curriculum for Pre-K children, "especially those from families experiencing economic hardship" is an example of an innovation that was tested and evaluated via a sequence of pilot, efficacy, effectiveness, and scale-up studies (Thomas et al., 2018, p. 328). Across the sequence of studies, the curriculum was implemented in increasingly diverse contexts, with positive effects on mathematics achievement (What Works Clearinghouse, 2023). The scale-up study took place across the state of California, "in public pre-K and Head Start programs in urban, suburban, and rural areas with large proportions of low-income families from diverse racial/ethnic backgrounds" (p. 330). Although the curriculum remained fairly stable across the studies, as reported in Thomas et al. (2018), the curriculum designers intentionally sought to learn what they might improve about the curriculum from each of the studies. For example, the designers learned that some activities took too long for the allocated time period, so "they altered the curriculum schedule" accordingly (p. 330). The designers predicted "that the quality of program delivery is likely to suffer at larger scales, due to less developer control over the implementation of the intervention" (Thomas et al., 2018, p. 331). Across the sequence of studies, in some sites, the curriculum's project staff "trained teachers and coached them," whereas in other sites they used a "train-the-trainer" model (p. 331). In the Statewide Scale-Up Study, fidelity of implementation was assessed as follows: a "local trainer" observed the teacher leading a small-group math activity and provided feedback about "any departures from fidelity" (p. 337). In addition, the trainer used a classroom observation tool to "record the type of mathematical content, number of children present, and the duration of the activity" (p. 337).
>
> Overall, the Statewide Scale-Up Study resulted in positive impacts on children's mathematics achievement that were consistent with those found in earlier studies; and the researchers found that "these effects did not demonstrably differ by the racial/ethnic background or pretest performance of children, or by the urbanicity of the settings" (p. 349). The researchers, however, also found that "scale-up is associated with smaller effect sizes—as studies got larger, more heterogeneous, less controlled, and used less well-aligned outcome measures, effect sizes tended to decrease" (p. 349). As a result, it is valuable to pair attention to implementation as part of the initial design work.

and expertise in a system is often minimal—which makes ownership and sustainability difficult. Further, the expectation of fidelity of implementation, especially in the earlier stages with limited contexts and participants, means that "implementation is highly monitored so that high fidelity is achieved" (NASEM, 2022, p. 78). As a result, challenges of implementation that are important for deep implementation of the innovation in additional contexts, as well as sustainability, "are not discovered until later studies with larger samples (Farley-Ripple et al., 2018; Finnigan & Daly, 2016)" (NASEM, 2022, p. 79).

As Penuel and Fishman (2012) argue, "an overemphasis on fidelity means giving less consideration to the ways that curriculum developers and professional development leaders could focus their efforts on helping teachers make productive adaptations of materials by being responsive to students" (p. 284).

As indicated above, until recently, federal agencies' grant funding structures for the design, study, and scale of STEM teaching and learning innovations have by and large reflected a phased logic, from pilot to efficacy to effectiveness to scale-up, paired with a focus on "tight" fidelity of implementation throughout the phases (cf. Penuel & Fishman, 2012). The National Academies's (2022) report, *The Future of Education Research at IES: Advancing an Equity-Oriented Science,* however, argues for the need to revise this logic. As discussed in subsequent chapters, the report calls for researchers to focus on "adaptation" of the intervention in "heterogenous environments that an intervention may be implemented within" (NASEM, 2022, p. 79). Careful study of adaptation in heterogenous environments from the start will allow researchers to "determin[e] barriers and facilitators (Tabak et al., 2012) and effective implementation strategies" that can support the scaling and sustainability of the intervention in additional contexts (NASEM, 2022, p. 79). Accordingly, the report calls for Institute of Education Sciences (IES), in particular, to shift from "Design and Development" studies to "Development and Adaptation" studies and to shift from "Efficacy" (i.e., replication) and "Effectiveness" studies to "Impact and Heterogeneity" studies. These suggested shifts reflect the value of making implementation of innovations, in relation to student learning outcomes, worthy of study in its own right:

> [. . . T]he success of interventions is driven in large part by their implementation. *It is also clear that understanding implementation needs to go beyond simply determining if a given intervention is implemented with fidelity.* Rather, there is increasing recognition that the process of implementation itself is worthy of study if education research is to provide sufficient guidance on how to improve student outcomes. (NASEM, 2022, p. 27, emphasis added)

Principled Adaptation

As indicated in the National Academies' (2022) call for a focus on *adaptation* of interventions, a second approach to scaling an innovation not only tolerates but also expects that there will be principled adaptations to the innovation as it is scaled, that is, as it is used and modified by new enactors, in new contexts. Scholars have described this approach to implementation and scale as "mutual adaptation," whereby enactors modify their current practices in order to implement the innovation, while also making adaptations to the innovation to make it "useable in their context"

(Russell et al., 2020, p. 156). Typically, designers articulate the desired learning goals associated with the implementation of the innovation as well as some core principles, both of which set expectations for the enactment of the innovation. But enactors are expected, and even encouraged, to adapt the innovation in response to their local contexts and needs (Means & Penuel, 2005; Penuel et al., 2011; Roschelle, Mazziotti, & Means, 2021). From this perspective, "[l]ocal actors know their context and can use this knowledge to effectively adapt innovations. Local conditions cannot be 'designed away,' but are key to successful outcomes" (Morel et al., 2019, p. 371).

From a mutual adaptation perspective, researchers tend to focus on what LeMahieu (2011) termed "integrity of implementation," rather than fidelity of implementation.[6] LeMahieu described the difference as follows: Fidelity of implementation suggests that enactors should "do exactly what [the designers] say to do," whereas integrity of implementation suggest that enactors should "do what matters most and works best while accommodating local needs and circumstances."[7] From an integrity of implementation perspective, as an innovation is scaled, data are generated and analyzed to examine the ways in which core principles associated with the innovation are maintained or perhaps evolved, whether the intended learning goals are met, and why or why not. Determinations need to be made regarding what adaptations preserve the integrity of the innovation, and which do not, and why.

Within adaptation approaches, there are differences in who is involved in the design process, and how much they are involved (e.g., how much enactors are part of the design itself). In some cases, like the Tennessee Math Coaching Project discussed in Box 4-2, the initial designers were primarily researchers and professional development providers; they generated the coaching model, and iterated upon it based on prior research on the impact of earlier iterations of the model on the quality of coaching and teaching in a limited set of districts (Stein et al., 2022), prior to scaling it across numerous districts in Tennessee (Russell et al., 2020). In other cases, as elaborated in the co-design section below, educators (the enactors), and beneficiaries (e.g., students, families) are more integrally involved in the design of the innovation from the start (Morel et al., 2019).

Innovations that invite principled, mutual adaptation, such as the example discussed in Box 4-2, can support deep and sustained implementation,

---

[6]LeMahieu (2011) distinguishes "fidelity of implementation" from "integrity of implementation." As indicated in O'Donnell (2008), however, researchers investigating fidelity of implementation sometimes treat the term "integrity" as synonymous with "fidelity."

[7]See https://www.carnegiefoundation.org/blog/what-we-need-in-education-is-more-integrity-and-less-fidelity-of-implementation/

BOX 4-2
Tennessee Math Coaching Project

There is increasing evidence that content-focused coaching in mathematics can support instructional improvement; however, "attempts to spread and scale coaching programs have resulted in variable outcomes, in part because coaching is highly context dependent" (Russell et al., 2020, p. 150). The Tennessee Math Coaching Project deliberately set out to study the *mutual adaptation* of a proven coaching model as it was implemented by 32 coaches in 21 school districts across the state (Russell et al., 2020). The core principles of the innovation (derived from earlier empirical studies of coaching that resulted in improvements to teaching and student learning) included specific "coaching practices" and a "coaching routine" in which coaches were expected to press and support teachers to identify specific mathematical goals, and to engage in deep and specific discussion of teaching in relation to artifacts of student learning. As Russell and colleagues (2020) described, as the model was spread to schools and districts across the state, they intended for enactors (in this case, coaches) and enablers (in this case, school and district leaders) to adapt the model in relation to "diverse organizational contexts" (p. 157). For example, the designers and researchers anticipated adaptations in relation to school- and district-level variation regarding the "selection of training of coaches," how coaches work is organized in schools (e.g., how much time they work with teachers, whether they are asked to perform additional duties), coaches' relationship with school principals (e.g., whether principals "endorse [. . .] coaches as sources of expertise"), and how school and district leaders "[frame] the purpose and goals of coaching" (p. 157). The designers and researchers also anticipated adaptations with respect to what they termed "diverse relational contexts," or how coaches adapted "their work with teachers based on their impression of the teacher's openness to coaching" (p. 157).

Adopting methods associated with continuous improvement and improvement science (e.g., Bryk et al., 2015), the researchers organized iterative cycles of inquiry in which they collected and analyzed quantitative and qualitative data to assess the coaches' enactment of the coaching practices and routines, in relation to teaching and learning outcomes, and to identify how the coaches adapted the model, why, and to what effect (Russell et al., 2020, p. 176). In doing so, they identified "which adaptations preserve (or violate) the *integrity* of the coaching model" (p. 176; emphasis added). Further, they used this knowledge to inform the professional learning of the coaches, so that the coaches deepened their understanding of the critical elements of the coaching model and were better equipped to anticipate challenges that would compromise the effectiveness of the model. On the basis of the cycles of inquiry, the team was in a position to offer interested states a comprehensive and empirically tested model for supporting the implementation of high-quality mathematics coaching at the scale of a state. The model includes "evidence-based coaching practices" that lead to the improvement of teaching; "an approach to train coaches to enact the coaching framework"; and "guidance for schools, districts, and states on how to organize and support a coaching program" (p. 150).

given that enactors and enablers adapt the given innovation in response to the needs, resources, and challenges of the specific context in which it is being implemented. Moreover, providing agency to local enactors and enablers to make principled adaptations to the innovation can enable a shift in ownership of the innovation.

Yet, there are tensions and challenges in implementing and scaling innovations characterized by principled and mutual adaptation. One tension concerns specifying and communicating the underlying principles of the innovation such that others can make sense of them deeply enough, to engage in adaptation without losing sight of the underlying assumptions and logic of the innovation (Brown & Campione, 1996). Kirschner and Polman (2013) addressed this tension directly in their respective design of innovations— methods of supporting "critical civic inquiry (CCI)" among youth and teachers, tied to disciplinary content, including science (Kirschner et al.)—and the teaching of science journalism to enable high school students' scientific literacy engagement in science. In both cases, the innovations were intended to be adapted in principled ways in new contexts and sustained. To facilitate principled adaptation, the teams developed what they term "signature tools," which "instantiate certain core goals of the intervention while also acting as 'thinking devices' that actors can adopt, adapt, modify, and borrow in locally appropriate ways" (p. 232). In the case of CCI, the team "formulated parameters for CCI projects that would provide consistency while also being flexible enough to accommodate local adaptation" (p. 228). CCI projects are expected to "focus on a problem experienced by students *at the school*, selected *by students*, and examined through the *lens of educational equity*" (p. 228; emphasis in original). The team therefore developed two signature tools to enable the CCI projects to maintain a focus on educational equity and school-based action, that is, CCI's core principles, knowing that the focus of CCI projects would necessarily vary in local contexts. In the case of SciJourn, the team developed "science literacy standards" and "standards for article writing," which teachers used to anchor various science journalism activities that fit with their local contexts. In both cases, consistent with Clarke and Dede's (2009) emphasis on evolution of the innovation, the teams deliberately set out to learn from the adaptations that the enactors made, in service of improving their innovations.

A second, related challenge to adaptation concerns the "looseness" regarding what counts as core principles to adhere to in adaptation. As an innovation that has "proven" effective in one context is adapted in another, there is always a risk that it might be altered in such a way that it no longer results in the desired outcomes. Without careful study of adaptations, as well as the impact of the innovation on the intended outcomes for beneficiaries, it is difficult to identify what makes for "lethal mutations" (Haertel, personal communication, 1984, as cited in Brown &

Campione, 1996, p. 292), therefore making it difficult to inform others' implementation efforts in new contexts. The committee returns to this issue in Chapters 7 and 8.

Collaborative Design: Attending to Scale and Sustainability

Over the past two decades, there has been increasing attention, as well as federal and philanthropic support, for researchers, educators, and sometimes youth and/or families, to *co-design*, implement, and evaluate innovations in local contexts, in response to "problems, needs, and opportunities" (Russell & Penuel, 2022, p.1). To be clear, not all cases in which researchers and educators collaboratively design innovations attend to issues of implementation, scale, and sustainability. In this section, the committee focuses on co-design approaches that squarely focus on implementation, scale, and sustainability. In particular, the committee features design-based implementation research (DBIR) and networked improvement communities (NICs), given the evidence base.[8] Co-design approaches focused on scale tend to reflect commitments to principled adaptation, as described above. A hallmark of DBIR and NICs is engagement in cycles of "continuous improvement;" that is, collaborators articulate theories of improvement, and engage in cycles of inquiry, in which "design and evaluation activities are tightly coordinated with one another, so that evidence from tests of innovations plays an integral role in informing design" and the evolving theory (Russell & Penuel, 2022, p. 5).

In addition, collaborators engaged in DBIR and NICs tend to take a "systemic perspective" (p. 5), meaning partners intentionally work to understand the broader system that has led to the problems they are working to address, and they understand that successfully addressing the problems will likely require concomitant changes in aspects of the system. In some cases, the collaboration results in a product that can be implemented and adapted in additional contexts. In other cases, however, the goal is not necessarily to produce a packaged product or model that can be implemented in other contexts, but rather to generate knowledge about ways to address a persistent problem of practice at scale, which can inform others' efforts to locally address a similar problem (Roschelle, Mazziotti, & Means, 2021).

Design-Based Implementation Research (DBIR)

DBIR is a kind of design research that involves the intentional design, implementation, and adaption of innovations as they go to scale (Fishman & Penuel, 2018; Penuel & Fishman, 2012). Different from other forms of

---
[8]It should be noted that this discussion was not meant to be exhaustive.

design research, DBIR focuses, from the start, on concerns of implementation and sustainability, including whether the innovation can be "adapted successfully to meet the needs of diverse learners across diverse settings, in both formal and informal education" (Fishman & Penuel, 2018, p. 393). Unlike conventional research focused on implementation, in DBIR, researchers do not observe implementation; instead, they actively seek to design for robust implementation, collect and analyze data on the implementation of the innovation, and use the analysis to improve and generate knowledge about what makes for productive implementation of the innovation. The projects often seek to address questions such as "What works when, how, and for whom?" "How do we improve this reform strategy to make it more sustainable?" and "What capacities does the system need to continue to improve?" (Penuel et al., 2011, p. 335). The dynamic, mutually engaged relationship among designers and enactors also provides new opportunities for recognizing and addressing issues of equity and responsiveness to local cultural contexts. Four key principles of DBIR include:

1. a focus on persistent problems of practice from multiple stakeholders' perspectives,
2. a commitment to iterative, collaborative design,
3. a concern with developing theory and knowledge related to both classroom learning and implementation through systematic inquiry, and
4. a concern with developing capacity for sustaining change in systems. (Fishman & Penuel, 2018, p. 393)

DBIR "challenges educational researchers and practitioners to transcend traditional research/practice barriers to facilitate the design of educational interventions that are effective, sustainable, and scalable" (p. 136). Underlying this call is an emphasis on research-practice partnerships, which reconfigures the roles of researchers and practitioners in design and implementation of innovations that can be scaled. This approach requires two-way and recursive relationships between research and practice (see Coburn & Stein, 2010), in contrast to "research and development as a linear process that leads from design by researchers to scale up by practitioners" (Penuel et al., 2011, p. 138). Collaboratively designed innovations are more likely to be usable since they are rooted in problems of practice and the needs of practitioners (Fishman et al., 2013). DBIR projects also typically include practitioners who work at multiple levels of a system (classroom, school, district), as well as community members, in order to ensure that community- and system-level concerns are attended to in the design of the innovation (Fishman et al., 2013). To understand these dynamics at a participatory and community-based level, designs can also center "processes of partnering as a primary object of analysis" when considering collaborations and power dynamics—especially when designing across multiple stakeholders including families, elders, teachers, and researchers (Bang & Vossoughi, 2016, p. 175). Box 4-3 provides an example of this approach.

Networked Improvement Communities (NICs)

Associated with continuous improvement research,[9] NICs offer a structure for practitioners, researchers, and designers to investigate and design strategies to pressing problems of practice at scale in diverse, local contexts (Roschelle, Mazziotti, & Means, 2021; Russell et al., 2017). The four essential characteristics of NICs are as follows:

1. [t]hey are focused on a well-specified common aim;
2. they are guided by a deep understanding of the problem, the system that produces it, and a shared working theory of how to improve it;
3. their work is disciplined by the rigor of improvement science; and
4. they are coordinated to accelerate the development, testing, and refinement of interventions, their rapid diffusion out into the field, and their effective integration into varied educational contexts (Bryk et al., 2015). (Russell et al., 2017, p. 3)

The use of the term "networked" to describe these communities is deliberate. Most pressing educational problems span multiple levels of a system (e.g., classroom, school, district) and often sectors (e.g., business community and education, health and education). As such, addressing a persistent problem at some scale likely entails engaging multiple role groups, and requires diverse forms of knowledge and expertise (Russell et al., 2017). Networks have the benefit of being able to engage diverse participants, and to spread knowledge across people, systems, and geographies that are often siloed. Moreover, it becomes possible to simultaneously test innovations in the multiple organizations participating in NICs, thereby accelerating learning about the particular innovation, in relation to context-specific resources and constraints. NICs in education have grown in number over the past decade or so, spurred by training and

---

[9]The IES Regional Educational Laboratory Program provides a toolkit for others looking to engage in continuous improvement: https://ies.ed.gov/ncee/rel/Products/Region/northeast/Publication/4005

BOX 4-3
Inquiry Hub Partnership

University of Colorado, Boulder researchers, as well as the nonprofit research organization BSCS Science Learning, engaged in a long-term partnership (Inquiry Hub) with educators in Denver Public Schools to design, test, and improve Biology curriculum materials. Other partners included Northwestern University's Next Gen Storylines team, and teachers in other states. The materials were "intended to help students gain a grasp of how to use science and engineering practices to explain phenomena that students find interesting and solve problems students perceive as relevant to themselves and their communities" (Penuel, 2019, p. 661). Importantly, the vision of science teaching and learning undergirding the materials represented a substantial shift from "business as usual."

It is not surprising then, that, as described by Penuel (2019), early in the classroom testing process, researchers found that the district's observation, evaluation, and feedback system was at odds with the instructional improvement efforts. Rather than treat the evaluation system as "outside the scope" of their work, from a design-based implementation research perspective, figuring out how to support teachers to navigate the system became a critical aspect of the partnership work. As Penuel (2019) described: "Our district partners insisted that we engage with the [evaluation] system and its processes rather than attempt to interfere with it. If we did create such a buffer, [. . .] we would only be creating a potential problem for sustaining implementation over the long haul" (p. 666). In response, the partnership created guides for observers regarding what they should expect to see as teachers were implementing the new Biology curriculum materials. They found, however, that guides were not enough to mitigate the challenges teachers faced as they were observed; so, as a next step, the partnership created a routine by which the district science specialist was able to conduct formal observations that reflected the intent of the new materials and their underlying vision of teaching and learning.

In addition to challenges with observation and feedback routines, researchers learned, based on classroom observations and student surveys, that teachers needed support to implement the materials in ways that advanced equity. The partnership designed a set of strategies (e.g., professional learning opportunities, routines for regularly eliciting and analyzing student feedback, generation of culturally relevant phenomena for students to investigate) to strengthen educators' commitments and practice in service of creating more inviting, inclusive science classrooms. In addition, the district "developed a cadre of leaders inside and outside the classroom who can recognize and support teachers in creating more inclusive cultures," which has enabled sustainability of the ongoing work (p. 670). As illustrated by the Inquiry Hub example, the attention to implementation, scale, and sustainability as part of the ongoing design work contrasts with "design research that develops and tests an innovation with no plan for how to support its implementation after the research ends" (p. 670). In this approach to scale, researchers and educators co-design an innovation that can fit better into an existing system—while also keeping an eye on the need to redesign aspects of the system (e.g., system-wide observation and feedback) to support underlying principles of the innovation.

funding from private foundations as well as federal agencies, including NSF and IES (Feygin et al., 2020; see Box 4-4).

Co-design efforts that explicitly focus on implementation and scale, such as the examples in Boxes 4-3 and 4-4, are poised to enable deep and sustained implementation in local contexts. This is because enactors (and sometimes beneficiaries) who have critical expertise regarding their local contexts and communities both anticipate and support teams to alter the design and implementation in response to particular resources, opportunities, and challenges. While an initial sense of ownership is built into co-design efforts, when the innovation spreads beyond those involved in the co-design, new enactors may not feel ownership of the innovation, or that the innovation is solving a problem they face. It is therefore necessary to continue to broaden and deepen ownership among enactors and enablers not initially included in the co-design efforts (Bryk et al., 2015). More generally, while there tends to be research on the impact of co-designed innovations on the intended outcomes, there is limited research on what happens when a co-designed product is implemented at scale in a context outside the one in which it was co-designed (Coburn & Penuel, 2016).

There are examples of co-design efforts that deliberately operate at a large scale (i.e., multiple districts, regions, etc.) from the start of the project, with explicit attention to enabling the spread of tools and knowledge focused on deep shifts to the instructional core (e.g., Cobb et al., 2018; Donovan, Wigdor, & Snow, 2003; Edelson et al., 2021). The development of Open SciEd instructional materials is a prime example (see also Seeding Innovations in Appendix C). As described in Edelson et al. (2021), Open SciEd was "launched in 2017 [. . .] as a collaboration of material developers, educational researchers, classroom educators, and educational leaders" (p. 780). Initially, it designed middle school science curriculum materials, paired with professional development materials, aimed at supporting deep shifts in science teaching and learning. Open SciEd has since gone on to create and field test curriculum in elementary and high school science as well, following similar co-design processes as they did with the middle school materials.[10]

Another affordance of co-design efforts is that they deliberately build in attention to equity and power relations as part of design and improvement processes (e.g., Peurach et al., 2022). Researchers and practitioners negotiate the problems of practice around which innovations are designed; and efforts are made to ensure that the people most affected by innovation are "at the table" as it is being designed, trialed, and improved. Recently, there have been some significant new efforts to co-create culturally equitable and responsive curriculum resources and programs through collaborative

---

[10] See https://digitalpromise.org/initiative/openscied-research-community/resources/

> **BOX 4-4**
> **Ambitious Science Teaching Networked**
> **Improvement Community**
>
> Between 2012–2017, the University of Washington Ambitious Science Teaching research team partnered with a team of educators in a moderately-sized district to support secondary science teachers' development of ambitious and equitable teaching practices, with a specific focus on supporting emergent bilingual students, as the district implemented the Next Generation Science Standards (Thompson et al., 2019). The initial research-practice partnership (RPP) included two schools; however, after the first year of the partnership, district leaders asked that the work be expanded to all schools. The RPP thus initiated a NIC (Bryk, Gomez, & Grunow, 2011), made up of each of the eight high school science professional learning communities (PLCs). All the district's secondary science teachers participated in the NIC, alongside science research-practice and emergent bilingual instructional coaches. This "all-comers" approach differs from most NICs, in which participants "opt in" and thus often includes some but not all members of a particular role group in a setting (Thompson et al., 2019).
> With financial support from the National Science Foundation and the district, the NIC established (a) "Studios," which were full-day job-embedded opportunities for PLCs to try out specific teaching practices in classrooms, analyze the impact of teaching on student learning, and set goals for future teaching; (b) "district science coaches who provided one-on-one coaching and facilitated Studios"; (c) "data meetings (in between Studios) where [PLCs] iterated on practices in relation to classroom data" and where teams would ask, "Which practices work? For whom? And under what conditions?"; (d) network-wide

networks that include families and community members as active partners. For example, the Learning in Places Collaborative,[11] with funding support from NSF, has been developing and studying new models for Pre-K–12 STEM learning that engage children through investigations in local outdoor settings and include indigenous ways of knowing that position people as a part of the natural world, rather than apart from it (Lees & Bang, 2022). Learning in Places also mobilizes knowledge, perspectives, and experiences shared by family and intergenerational community members and frames learning in the context of ethical decisions that affect the community in the present and the future. There is also ongoing work in early education spaces addressing similar issues (e.g., Dominguez et al., 2023; Kamdar et al., 2024; Lewis Presser et al., 2017; McWayne et al., 2021, 2022; Presser et al., 2019).

One challenge specific to co-design scaling approaches is that the current structure of the education system and expectations—especially for

---

[11] See https://learninginplaces.org

> meetings where PLCs would share common challenges and what they were learning across sites; and (e) "instructional walks" where principals would observe instruction with coaches (Thompson et al., 2019, p. 4). In year four, the RPP established a teacher leader cadre to "drive school-based improvement work and support sustainability" (p. 4). Grant funding ended in year four, and the district "assumed responsibility for funding Studios and the science coaching positions" (p. 4).
>
> Researchers conducted a retrospective analysis of how each of the PLCs launched its instructional improvement work, and how knowledge and tools varied and spread across the network, based on observational data of Studios and classroom instruction, as well as teachers' reflections and annual network surveys (Thompson et al., 2019). The researchers identified three patterns: (a) Local Practice Development, (b) Spread and Local Adaptation, and (c) Integrating New Practices. "PLCs with a common aim began with drafting and testing practices and tools (Local Practice Development)" (p. 18). In PLCs that struggled to initially develop a common aim and vision for improving science instruction, coaches and researchers intentionally shared practices and tools from other PLCs. As PLC teams tested these practices and tools from other PLCs, they began to identify localized problems of practice to focus on (Spread and Local Adaptation). Lastly, "[s]ome PLCs kept their baseline practice as a focus of inquiry, yet through examining data from students and developing theories of how students learned, they became dissatisfied with aspects of the practice and developed or adopted other network practices to address identified limitations (Integrating New Practices)" (p. 19). By identifying these launch patterns, researchers made visible the "messy middle" in RPPs (Penuel, 2019) where partners negotiate what and how to learn together and build structures to support their joint work.

teachers' work—is at odds with the time and space it takes to engage in ongoing cycles of design, implementation, and improvement of new practices, materials, and so forth (Cohen & Mehta, 2017). Teachers who participate in collaborative design and research projects are often self-selected and often engage in this work on top of their teaching. That said, there are examples, like the Ambitious Science Teaching NIC (Thompson et al., 2019) discussed in Box 4-4, in which researchers and system leaders collaborate to revise systems of professional learning and evaluation to enable broad participation.

Additionally, engaging in collaborative design, implementation, and scaling efforts requires new forms of expertise and of collaboration than is typical of STEM innovation design and research (Cohen-Vogel, Harrison, & Cohen-Vogel, 2022). It entails, for example, knowledge of systems, policy, leadership, and implementation alongside knowledge of STEM teaching and learning. Moreover, engaging in such efforts requires that "researchers develop new ways of working with practitioners that prioritize the development of trust, take schools' and districts' current improvement goals and strategies as a primary point of reference, and are sensitive to schools' and districts' capacities and constraints" (Cobb et al., 2013, p. 344). Similar issues with respect to building trust; creating time and space for full collaboration; and navigating alignment with existing goals, priorities, and routines arise for co-design projects that invite the participation of non-system actors, such as families and community members.

SUMMARY

Throughout this chapter, the committee demonstrated the importance of conceptualizing scale as multidimensional, especially when the innovation is aimed at engendering fundamental changes to STEM teaching and learning. We introduced Coburn's framework for thinking about scale, which includes four dimensions: spread, depth, sustainability, and shifts in ownership. Most research on and assessments of scale focus on spread, or increasing the number of enactors, beneficiaries, and/or contexts in which an innovation is enacted. The committee cautions against a blunt focus on spread for a couple of reasons. One reason is that some innovations are specifically tailored for particular populations and/or places. Another reason is a focus on spread alone does not support educators or researchers to know whether an innovation is resulting in the desired improvements and for whom, whether the innovation is sustained as enactors change, and why or why not. In addition to spread, it is critical to attend to how the innovation is implemented, or the extent to which the enactors adopt the innovation superficially or at some *depth*. Enacting an innovation with some depth typically entails substantial changes to enactors' current beliefs about teaching and learning, and about students, as well as enactors' content knowledge and practice. Moreover, it is critical to attend to the *sustainability* and *ownership* of the innovation, that is, whether the innovation endures over time in the original and new contexts when the initial circumstances, such as funding, change; and the conditions in which knowledge, authority, and ownership of the innovation are both broadened and deepened over time.

Assessments of scale often focus on surface-level indications of adoption (e.g., number of users, presence of materials, time spent using the materials), absent attention to depth, sustainability, and ownership. An important area for research on the scale of STEM innovations includes the development of measures, or ways of assessing, these additional dimensions of scale, especially when the innovations target substantial changes to the instructional core. Further, equity concerns are central in assessments of scale. For example, for whom is the innovation "working" and "not working," and why? Is there evidence that teachers view their students, particularly those who have not been served well in the current system, as capable and deserving of robust STEM instruction? Moreover, most studies of scaling up innovations focus on the first few years of implementation, without attention to what happens after additional resources and supports have officially ended. Incentives to both plan for and study issues of depth, sustainability, and ownership after initial implementation of an innovation are necessary, coupled with explicit attention to equity concerns.

Federal funding agencies have historically prioritized sequential studies of scaling innovations (pilot studies, efficacy studies, effectiveness studies, scale-up studies), whereby the innovation is implemented in tightly prescribed ways, in increasingly heterogenous sites and/or populations, and in service of a specified set of outcomes. "Fidelity of implementation" is prioritized. When paired with an explicit theory of change, fidelity of implementation can support researchers to identify faults in the innovation as designed (i.e., in the theory of change and its assumptions), and how variation in implementation impacts outcomes, for better and worse. Especially in cases in which the innovation targets changes to the instructional core, however, it is often difficult to tease apart issues with the innovation itself and aspects of the implementation context that negatively (or positively) impact implementation of the innovation. Moreover, a focus on fidelity of implementation often results in minimal attention to how educators might modify an innovation to make it work better in their context.

In response, more recent research on implementing STEM innovations at scale points to the value of approaches that invite principled, mutual adaptation. It is incumbent upon the designers to identify and communicate the core principles underlying the innovation. Then, as the innovation is scaled, researchers (and sometimes partner educators) generate and analyze data to examine the ways in which core principles associated with the innovation are maintained (what is sometimes referred to as "integrity of implementation") or evolve, whether the intended learning goals are met, and why or why not. Researchers deliberately study and learn from the adaptations enactors make as they implement the innovation, to both revise the innovation and so that they can inform enactors in other contexts regarding what features might support and serve as a barrier to implementation, and strategies for mitigating challenges.

Consistent with the principles of mutual adaptation approaches to scaling, there is growing evidence of the value of researchers and educators in communities collaboratively designing, implementing, and scaling innovations. In collaborative approaches (e.g., design-based implementation research, networked improvement communities) that explicitly take a systemic perspective, collaborators work to understand how various aspects of their local educational system (e.g., school leaders' expectations, hiring, time for teachers to collaborate) impact the challenge they are addressing, and they design and revise strategies to address those systemic challenges. An affordance of this approach is that concerns for implementation are part and parcel of the design of the innovation.

On the whole, there is growing evidence that approaches to scaling that invite principled, mutual adaptation, and those that are collaboratively designed, implemented, and scaled by researchers and educators, can enable deep and sustained implementation of STEM innovations. More documentation of the adaptations that enactors and enablers make and why, and the impact on teaching and learning outcomes, is needed to support implementation of promising innovations in new contexts. Attention to and documentation of how sustainability and shift in ownership are enabled—and if not, why not—is necessary in studies of scaling. Attention to developing the capacity of STEM researchers who have the requisite knowledge and mentored experience in engaging in research on STEM innovation, implementation, and scale is also needed. Further, time and resources are needed to support teachers (and leaders) to partner with researchers to design, implement, and study innovations.

REFERENCES

Bang, M., & Vossoughi, S. (2016). Participatory design research and educational justice: Studying learning and relations within social change making. *Cognition and Instruction, 34*(3), 173–193.

Brown, A. L. (1992). Design experiments: Theoretical and methodological challenges in creating complex interventions in classroom settings. *Journal of the Learning Sciences, 2*(2), 141–178.

Brown, A. L., & Campione, J. C. (1996). Psychological theory and the design of innovative learning environments: on procedures, principles, and systems. In L. Schauble & R. Glaser (Eds.), *Innovations in learning: New environments for education* (pp. 289–325). Lawrence Erlbaum Associates.

Bryk, A. S., Gomez, L. M., & Grunow, A. (2011). Getting ideas into action: Building networked improvement communities in education. In M. Hallinan (Ed.), *Frontiers in sociology of education* (pp. 127–162). Springer.

Bryk, A. S., Gomez, L. M., Grunow, A., & LeMahieu, P. G. (2015). *Learning to improve: How America's schools can get better at getting better.* Harvard Education Press.

Bryk, A. S., Sebring, P. B., Allensworth, E., Luppesco, S., & Easton, J. Q. (2010). *Organizing schools for improvement: Lessons from Chicago.* University of Chicago Press.

Clarke, J., & Dede, C. (2009). Design for scalabilty: A case study of the River City curriculum *Journal of Science Education and Technology, 18*(4), 353–365. https://www.jstor.org/stable/20627713

Cobb, P., & Jackson, K. (2015). Supporting teachers' use of research-based instructional sequences. *ZDM, 47*, 1027–1038.

Cobb, P., Jackson, K., Henrick, E., Smith, T., & MIST team. (2018). *Systems for Instructional Improvement: Creating coherence from the classroom to the district office.* Harvard Education Press.

Cobb, P., Jackson, K., Smith, T., Sorum, M., & Henrick, E. (2013). Design research with educational systems: Investigating and supporting improvements in the quality of mathematics teaching and learning at scale. In B. J. Fishman, W. R. Penuel, A.-R. Allen, & B. H. Cheng (Eds.), *Design based implementation research: Theories, methods, and exemplars. National Society for the Study of Education Yearbook* (Vol. 112, Issue 2, pp. 320–349). Teachers College.

Coburn, C. E. (2003). Rethinking scale: Moving beyond numbers to deep and lasting change. *Educational Researcher, 32*(6), 3–12.

Coburn, C. E., & Penuel, W. R. (2016). Research-practice partnerships in education: Outcomes, dynamics, and open questions. *Educational Researcher, 45*(1), 48–54. https://doi.org/10.3102/0013189X16631750

Coburn, C. E., Russell, J. L., Kaufman, J. H., & Stein, M. K. (2012). Supporting sustainability: Teachers' advice networks and ambitious instructional reform. *American Journal of Education, 119*(1), 137–182.

Coburn, C. E., & Stein, M. K. (Eds.). (2010). *Research and practice in education: Building alliances, bridging the divide.* Rowman & Littlefield.

Cohen, D. K., & Mehta, J. D. (2017). Why reform sometimes succeeds: Understanding the conditions that produce reforms that last. *American Educational Research Journal, 54*(4), 644–690.

Cohen-Vogel, L., Harrison, C., & Cohen-Vogel, D. (2022). On teams: Exploring variation in the social organization of improvement research in education. In D. J. Peurach, J. L. Russell, L. Cohen-Vogel, & W. R. Penuel (Eds.), *The foundational handbook on improvement research in education* (pp. 325–346). Rowman & Littlefield.

Dane, A. V., & Schneider, B. H. (1998). Program integrity in primary and early secondary prevention: Are implementation effects out of control? *Clinical Psychology Review, 18*(1), 23–45. https://doi.org/10.1016/S0272-7358(97)00043-3

Datnow, A., Hubbard, L., & Mehan, H. (2002). *Extending educational reform.* Taylor & Francis.

Dede, C. (2006). Evolving innovations beyond ideal settings to challenging contexts of practice. In R. K. Sawyer (Ed.), *The Cambridge handbook of the learning sciences* (pp. 551–566). Cambridge University Press.

Dominguez, X., Vidiksis, R., Leones, T., Kamdar, D., Presser, A. L., Bueno, M., & Orr, J. (2023). *Integrating science, mathematics, and engineering: Linking home and school learning for young learners.* Digital Promise.

Donovan, M. S., Wigdor, A. K., & Snow, C. E. (Eds.) (2003). *Strategic Education Research Partnership.* National Research Council.

Edelson, D. C., Reiser, B. J., McNeill, K. L., Mohan, A., Novak, M., Mohan, L., Affolter, R., McGill, T. A. W., Bracey, Z. B., Noll, J. D., Kowalski, S. M., Novak, M., Lo, A. S., Landel, C., Krumm, A., Penuel, W. R., Van Horne, K., González-Howard, M., & Suárez, E. (2021). Developing research-based instructional materials to support large-scale transformation of science teaching and learning: The approach of the OpenSciEd middle school program. *Journal of Science Teacher Education, 32*(7), 780–804. https://doi.org/10.1080/1046560X.2021.1877457

Elmore, R. F. (1996). Getting to scale with good educational practice. *Harvard Educational Review, 66*(1), 1–26.

Farley-Ripple, E., May, H., Karpyn, A., Tilley, K., & McDonough, K. (2018). Rethinking connections between research and practice in education: A conceptual framework. *Educational Researcher, 47*(4), 235–245.

Feygin, A., Nolan, L., Hickling, A., & Friedman, L. (2020). *Evidence for networked improvement communities: A systematic review of the literature.* American Institutes for Research.

Finnigan, K. S., & Daly, A. J. (2016). Why we need to think systemically in educational policy and reform. *Thinking and acting systemically: Improving school districts under pressure,* 1–9.

Fishman, B. J., & Penuel, W. R. (2018). Design-based implementation research. In F. Fischer, C. E. Hmelo-Silver, S. R. Goldman, & P. Reimann (Eds.), *International handbook of the learning sciences* (pp. 393–400). Routledge.

Fishman, B. J., Penuel, W. R., Allen, A.-R., Cheng, B. H., & Sabelli, N. (2013). Design-based implementation research: An emerging model for transforming the relationship of research and practice. In B. J. Fishman, W. R. Penuel, A.-R. Allen, & B. H. Cheng (Eds.), *Design-based implementation research: Theories, methods, and exemplars* (Vol. 112, Issue 2, pp. 136–156). National Society for the Study of Education.

Fishman, B. J., Penuel, W. R., Hegedus, S., & Roschelle, J. (2011). What happens when the research ends? Factors related to the sustainability of a technology-infused mathematics curriculum. *Journal of Computers in Mathematics and Science Teaching, 30*(4), 329–353.

Gage, N., MacSuga-Gage, A., & Detrich, R. (2020). *Fidelity of implementation in educational research and practice*. The Wing Institute. https://www.winginstitute.org/systems-program-fidelity

Gersten, R., Chard, D., & Baker, S. (2000). Factors enhancing sustained use of research-based instructional practices. *Journal of Learning Disabilities, 33*(5), 445–456.

Hargreaves, A., & Goodson, I. (2006). Educational change over time? The sustainability and nonsustainability of three decades of secondary school change and continuity. *Educational Administration Quarterly, 42*(1), 3–41.

Kamdar, D., Leones, T., Vidiksis, R., & Dominguez, X. (2024). Shining light on preschool science investigations: Exploring shadows and strengthening visual spatial skills. *Science and Children, 61*(3), 20–24.

Kirschner, B., & Polman, J. L. (2013). Adaptation by design: A context-sensitive, dialogic approach to interventions. In B. J. Fishman, W. R. Penuel, A.-R. Allen, & B. H. Cheng (Eds.), *Design based implementation research: Theories, methods, and exemplars. National Society for the Study of Education* (Vol. 112, Issue 2, pp. 215–236). Teachers College.

Klingner, J. K., Vaughn, S., Tejero Hughes, M., & Arguelles, M. E. (1999). Sustaining research-based practices in reading: A 3-year follow-up. *Remedial and Special Education, 20*(5), 263–287.

Lees, A., & Bang, M. (2022). We're not migrating yet: Engaging children's geographies and learning with lands and waters. *Occasional Paper Series*, (48), 33–47. https://doi.org/10.58295/2375-3668.1454

LeMahieu, P. G. (2011). *What we need in education is more integrity (and less fidelity) of implementation*. Carnegie Foundation for the Advancement of Teaching. https://www.carnegiefoundation.org/blog/what-we-need-in-education-is-more-integrity-and-less-fidelity-of-implementation/

Lewis Presser, A. E., Kamdar, D., Vidiksis, R., Goldstein, M., & Dominguez, X. (2017). Growing plants and minds: Using digital tools to support preschool science learning. *Science & Children, 55*, 41–47.

McLaughlin, M. W., & Mitra, D. (2001). Theory-based change and change-based theory: Going deeper, going broader. *Journal of Educational Change, 2*(4), 301–323.

McWayne, C. M., Greenfield, D., Zan, B., Mistry, J., & Ochoa, W. (2021). A comprehensive professional development approach for supporting science, technology, and engineering curriculum in preschool: Connecting contexts for dual language learners. In S. T. Vorkapić & J. LoCasale-Crouch (Eds.), *Supporting children's well-being during the early childhood transition to school* (pp. 222–253). IGI Global.

McWayne, C. M., Zan, B., Ochoa, W., Greenfield, D., & Mistry, J. (2022). Head Start teachers act their way into new ways of thinking: Science and engineering practices in preschool classrooms. Science Education. https://doi.org/10.1002/sce.21714

Means, B., & Penuel, W. R. (2005). Scaling up technology-based educational innovations. In C. Dede, J. P. Honan, & L. C. Peters (Eds.), *Scaling up success: Lessons from technology-based educational improvement* (pp. 176–197). Jossey-Bass.

Morel, R. P., Coburn, C. E., Catterson, A. K., & Higgs, J. (2019). The multiple meanings of scale: Implications for researchers and practitioners. *Educational Researcher, 48*(6), 369–377. https://doi.org/10.3102/0013189X19860531

National Academies of Sciences, Engineering, and Medicine. (2022). *The future of education research at IES: Advancing an equity-oriented science*. The National Academies Press.

O'Donnell, C. L. (2008). Defining, conceptualizing, and measuring fidelity of implementation and its relationship to outcomes in K–12 curriculum intervention research. *Review of Educational Research, 78*(1), 33–84. https://doi.org/10.3102/0034654307313793

Penuel, W. R. (2019). Infrastructuring as a practice of design-based research for supporting and studying equitable implementation and sustainability of innovations. *Journal of the Learning Sciences, 28*(4–5), 659–677. https://doi.org/10.1080/10508406.2018.1552151

Penuel, W. R., & Fishman, B. J. (2012). Large-scale science education intervention research we can use. *Journal of Research in Science Teaching, 49*(3), 281–304.

Penuel, W. R., Fishman, B. J., Cheng, B. H., & Sabelli, N. (2011). Organizing research and development at the intersection of learning, implementation, and design. *Educational Researcher, 40*(7), 331–337.

Peurach, D. J., Russell, J., Cohen-Vogel, L., & Penuel, W. R. (Eds.). (2022). *The foundational handbook on improvement research in education.* Rowman & Littlefield.

Presser, A. L., Dominguez, X., Goldstein, M., Vidiksis, R., & Kamdar, D. (2019). Ramp It UP! *Science and Children, 56*(7), 30–37.

Reiser, B. J., Michaels, S., Moon, J., Bell, T., Dyer, E., Edwards, K. D., McGill, T. A. W., Novak, M., & Park, A. (2017). Scaling up three-dimensional science learning through teacher-led study groups across a state. *Journal of Teacher Education, 68*(3), 280–298. https://doi.org/10.1177/0022487117699598

Rogers, R., Kramer, M. A., Mosley, M., & Literacy for Social Justice Teacher Research Group. (2009). *Designing socially just learning communities: Critical literacy education across the lifespan.* Routledge.

Roschelle, J., Mazziotti, C., & Means, B. (2021). Scaling up design of inquiry environments. In C. Chinn & R. G. Duncan (Eds.), *International handbook on learning and inquiry.* Routledge.

Russell, J. L., & Penuel, W. R. (2022). Introducing improvement research in education. In D. J. Peurach, Russell, J., Cohen-Vogel, L. & Penuel, W. R. (Eds.), *The foundational handbook on improvement research in education* (pp. 1–20). Rowman & Littlefield.

Russell, J., Bryk, A. S., Dolle, J. R., Gomez, L. M., LeMahieu, P., & Grunow, A. (2017). A framework for the initiation of networked improvement communities. *Teachers College Record, 119*, 1–36.

Russell, J. L., Correnti, R., Stein, M. K., Bill, V., Hannan, M., Schwartz, N., Booker, L. N., Pratt, N. R., & Matthis, C. (2020). Learning from adaptation to support instructional improvement at scale: Understanding coach adaptation in the TN Mathematics Coaching Project. *American Educational Research Journal, 57*(1), 148–187. https://doi.org/10.3102/0002831219854050

Scheirer, M. A. (2005). Is sustainability possible? A review and commentary on empirical studies of program sustainability. *American Journal of Evaluation, 26*(3), 320–347.

Stein, M. K., Russell, J. L., Bill, V., Correnti, R., & Speranzo, L. (2022). Coach learning to help teachers learn to enact conceptually rich, student-focused mathematics lessons. *Journal of Mathematics Teacher Education, 25*(3), 321–346. https://doi.org/10.1007/s10857-021-09492-6

Tabak, R. G., Khoong, E. C., Chambers, D. A., & Brownson, R. C. (2012). Bridging research and practice: models for dissemination and implementation research. *American Journal of Preventive Medicine, 43*(3), 337–350.

Thomas, J., Cook, T. D., Klein, A., Starkey, P., & DeFlorio, L. (2018). The sequential scale-up of an evidence-based intervention: A case study. *Evaluation Review, 42*(3), 318–357. https://doi.org/10.1177/0193841X18786818

Thompson, J., Richards, J., Shim, S.-Y., Lohwasser, K., Von Esch, K. S., Chew, C., Sjoberg, B., & Morris, A. (2019). Launching networked PLCs: Footholds into creating and improving knowledge of ambitious and equitable teaching practices in an RPP. *AERA Open, 5*(3), 1–22. https://doi.org/10.1177/2332858419875718

van Dijk, W., Lane, H. B., & Gage, N. A. (2023). How do intervention studies measure the relation between implementation fidelity and students' reading outcomes? A systematic review. *Elementary School Journal, 124*(1), 56–84. https://doi.org/10.1086/725672

What Works Clearinghouse (2023). Pre-K mathematics. Institute of Education Sciences, U.S. Department of Education. https://ies.ed.gov/ncee/wwc/Intervention/425

Zoblotsky, T., Bertz, C. Gallagher, B., & Alberg, M. (2017). *The LASER model: A systemic and sustainable approach for achieving high standards in science education: SSEC i3 validation final report of confirmatory and exploratory analyses.* The University of Memphis, Center for Research in Educational Policy. Summative report prepared for Smithsonian Science Education Center.

5

Navigating the Landscape of STEM Innovation and Implementation

As noted in previous chapters, one of the most distinctive features of the U.S. public education system is its decentralized structure and the resulting complexity and variability across national, regional, and local levels in how policies are made and how resources are invested in public education. In this chapter, we take a closer look at the current landscape of science, technology, engineering, and mathematics (STEM) education from Pre-K through high school with an eye toward how effective educational innovations arise, take root, and spread. Central to understanding this landscape is recognizing that there is an important distinction to be made between the typical configurations of actors, decision makers, and financial resources that are often involved in the development of evidence-based innovations as compared to the configurations that come into play as innovations are implemented, sustained, and spread across settings and populations. The lack of direct connections and the potential for misalignments across these two layers of the STEM education landscape provide context for why it is so challenging to get promising innovations to spread beyond their original implementation. The committee first takes up this implementation landscape—the dynamic configurations of actors and flow of financial resources—as it pertains to the creation and development of innovations and improvements, with particular attention to how federal investments are made. We then turn to the features of this landscape that are relevant to whether and in what ways evidence-based innovations are adopted, scaled, or sustained beyond the development stage, and whether and in what ways, too, the information is disseminated.

THE INNOVATION DEVELOPMENT LANDSCAPE

This section starts by examining the role of federal funding agencies in supporting research and development in STEM education. It first considers the knowledge that is created by these federal investments, and discusses challenges to mobilizing that knowledge in forms that are taken up by decision makers and enactors in educational settings. We then turn to instructional resources and interventions that arise from research grants and discuss some of the demands of aligning them with what schools and districts want and need; this includes examination of the difficulties of creating distribution systems with the capacity to disseminate them widely and support them as they take root in new settings. Finally, this section turns to innovations that arise from sources other than federal funding and considers some of the advantages and disadvantages of resources that come through alternative development pathways.

Federal Investments in the Creation, Development, and Evaluation of Innovations and Improvements in STEM Education

Most funding for research and development aimed at creating and studying innovations and improvements in STEM education and at evaluating their efficacy comes from the federal government, through award competitions run by federal agencies. As discussed in Chapter 2, the largest federal investments are channeled through the National Science Foundation's (NSF's) Directorate for STEM Education (formerly the Education and Human Resources Directorate), which is charged with providing national leadership to improve STEM education at all levels, and through the U.S. Department of Education's (ED's) Institute of Education Sciences (IES), which was created in 2002 as ED's research arm and is intended to provide national leadership in expanding "fundamental knowledge and understanding of education from early childhood through postsecondary study" in all disciplines (Education Sciences Reform Act of 2002), including those related to STEM. Competitive awards made through these agencies fund both use-inspired research (Stokes, 1997), aimed at discovering new knowledge and building theoretical foundations to better understand processes and systems of learning, and applied research, which yields new evidence-based programs, practices, technologies, and models in STEM education.

ED has also introduced funding programs specifically focused on innovation. From 2010 to 2016, ED's Investing in Innovation fund (i3), awarded grants with the goals of developing and testing promising new strategies or obtaining further evidence about expanded implementation of innovative strategies that were already supported by evidence. Grantees were expected to produce rigorous evidence about the strategy they were investigating and generally employed strong causal designs, such as randomized controlled trials, designed to provide reliable estimates of the intervention's or strategy's average impacts. About one-third of the grants were validation or scale-up grants, which evaluated the effectiveness of strategies already supported by prior evidence at a larger scale and with new types of students or in new settings. A small set of these studies were focused on innovations related to STEM. The successor program to i3 is the Education Innovation and Research (EIR) program, administered by ED's Office of Elementary and Secondary Education (OESE). Like the earlier i3 program, EIR funds a wide variety of projects at three levels (early-phase, mid-phase, and expansion). All EIR projects must serve high-need students, and mid-phase and expansion grants are expected to contribute to building a knowledge base about the contexts in which practices are effective and cost-effective.

Investigators who receive competitive awards from these agencies are typically academic researchers in universities and colleges or research professionals based in independent research and development organizations (e.g., WestEd, EDC, TERC, etc.) or institutions such as science centers and museums. State departments of education or local districts may also be awardees or may participate as partners on grants run by others for the duration of the funded project. For example, state and local educational agencies on their own or as part of consortiums can submit proposals to the EIR program mentioned above. Other federal agencies, including the National Aeronautics and Space Administration (NASA) and National Oceanic and Atmospheric Administration (NOAA), also fund some STEM-related education and engagement projects related to their agency missions using a somewhat different model, as discussed below. (See Table 5-1 for an overview of investments in STEM education by various federal agencies.)

One type of product that typically results from federal grant-funded endeavors is knowledge, such as theory and evidence related to the investigation of a set of research questions about learning and education, or evidence arising from controlled efficacy studies. Knowledge outcomes are typically distributed through publications, presentations, and repositories of various sorts. Funded projects may also result in prototypes or fully developed resources, such as curricula and related materials (e.g., science kits), technology-based learning resources, professional learning programs for teachers, educational programs for students, and real or virtual exhibits. In this overview of the innovation development landscape, we consider these different types of research products separately, since the affordances and challenges for spreading and scaling them are different.

Mobilizing Research Knowledge About STEM Education Innovations

For projects that result in new knowledge to have impacts beyond the direct participants in the funded project, the knowledge that is produced must be disseminated in ways that will reach relevant decision makers and

TABLE 5-1 STEM Investments across Federal Agencies

Federal Agency	Estimated 3-year Total Investment in STEM Education and Workforce Development	Estimated 3-year Investment Impacting Pre-K–12 STEM Education	Estimated 3-year Investment Primarily for Pre-K–12 STEM Education
Corporation for National and Community Service	368.7M	368.7M	0M
Department of Homeland Security	32.6M	0M	0M
Department of Commerce	153.5M	44.4M	26.5M
Department of Defense	716.4M	233.5M	19.9M
Department of Energy	1074.9M	70.1M	10.7M
Department of Transportation	335.7M	10.5M	0.2M
Department of Interior	3M	Not Collected	Not Collected
Department of Labor	63.2 M	0M	0M
Department of Education	1,607.1M	731.6M	731.6M
Environmental Protection Agency	19.1M	16.7M	6.7M
Department of Health and Human Services	3,242.9M	557.1M	98.1M
National Aeronautics and Space Administration	566.4M	566.4M	60M

Nuclear Regulatory Commission	74M	0M	0M
National Science Foundation	5,003.9M	2,101.1M	814.4M
Smithsonian Institution	17.1M	17.1M	0M
United States Department of Agriculture	882.1M	3M	3M
Department of Veterans' Affairs	374.5M	0M	0M
Total Federal Investment	**14,525.7M**	**4,720.2M**	**1,770.3M**

NOTE: These are the investments that are reported to National Science and Technology Council's Committee on STEM Education (CoSTEM) and may not fully reflect all institutional programming related to Pre-K–12 STEM education. Column 2 is the total amount awarded. The distinction between columns 3 and 4 lies in the constituency of the primary award recipient. Column 3 includes awards to institutions who may indirectly benefit K–12 students or educators while Column 4 excludes such awardees.

SOURCE: Adapted from White House Office of Science and Technology Policy, https://www.whitehouse.gov/wp-content/uploads/2024/04/2023-CoSTEM-Progress-Report.pdf

practice communities. Individual researchers most often disseminate their findings through peer-reviewed publications and presentations within their own research networks, as is required for academic career advancement, though they may also occasionally reach out to practitioners and policymakers through other channels. Increasingly, research outcomes are also being shared in the form of accessible archives of audio and video data banks (e.g., Databrary.org) and annotated datasets, which can support additional analyses or replication efforts, as well as software code and protocols that can be the foundation for additional research or further development and application by other teams. However, these resources are most often accessed by other researchers, and many individual research teams rely on their own networks and local relationships to craft and implement dissemination plans. Wider project dissemination efforts are sometimes pushed to the end of the grant period, with little time, budget, or incentive to provide extended outreach or to follow up on whether dissemination efforts were successful. At the same time, it is important to note that federally funded research that does not lead directly to implementation in an education setting should not be viewed as a dead end. Weiss and others (e.g., Greene, 1988) have described what they term "enlightenment" or "conceptual use" of research and evaluation findings, a process by which knowledge "percolates into the decision arena in direct and indirect ways" (Weiss, Murphy-Graham, & Birkeland, 2005, p. 14). Many projects have yielded strong scientific evidence related to learning processes, the needs of different groups of learners, and strategies for improving instruction and engagement of students in STEM learning, and this evidence has informed theory and provided a more solid foundation for the design of curriculum, assessments, and instructional practices by other groups. However, the absence of systematic national infrastructure connecting researchers with consumers of the knowledge they produce or with reliable knowledge brokers beyond academic research communities likely means that research knowledge is significantly underutilized (National Academies of Sciences, Engineering, and Medicine [NASEM], 2022).

While many school decision makers and practitioners report that they are interested in learning more about education research and are increasingly required to use scientifically-based evidence to make certain kinds of decisions, studies suggest that how school leaders access and use research is not a straightforward linear process, but one that is influenced by organizational and political factors, available resources, and local dynamics as school leaders seek to justify decisions and persuade interested parties and participants within specific contexts (Asen et al., 2013; Coburn, 2006; Coburn et al., 2009a,b; Finnigan & Daley, 2014; Penuel et al., 2018). The sheer number and variety of specialized peer-reviewed research publications makes it challenging even for full-time academic researchers to keep abreast of new developments and to synthesize research findings across STEM education. Efforts such as Institute of Education Science's (IES's) What Works Clearinghouse (WWC) and practice guides attempt to bridge the gap between education research and practice by consolidating information about successful interventions and the evidence that supports them for educators and decision makers. However, surveys and interviews of district leaders indicate that only a minority of leaders access information from the WWC "often" (13%) or "all the time" (4%; Penuel et al., 2017). Instead, school and district leaders report that they are more likely to access education research through books—especially those that present general frameworks or practical guidance—which are sometimes authored by academic researchers but may also be written by educational consultants (Penuel et al., 2018). These alternative publications are seen as more practitioner-friendly and actionable than peer-reviewed reports of empirical studies.

Why might this be? A recent National Academies consensus study report titled *The Future of Research at IES* (NASEM, 2022) noted several factors that may contribute to the difficulty of mobilizing knowledge that results from federally funded education research. First, there may be a mismatch between the types of problems that school decision makers are attempting to address and the structure of the research questions or interventions being investigated in grant-funded projects. In addition, researchers are often primarily concerned with finding reliable average differences between well-defined groups assigned to different conditions in a research design, and they may use local or regional samples of participants and settings that are circumscribed or non-representative in various ways (e.g., students with learning differences or limited English proficiency may be excluded). Emphasis on research designs that can support causal conclusions may overshadow the study of context variables and adaptation to local contexts (Means & Penuel, 2005). Education leaders, in contrast, are typically concerned with the constraints and complexities of their specific contexts and may be attempting to address the learning needs of a highly varied or particular student population; thus, they may be skeptical about the degree to which findings of individual research studies pertain to or could be realistically implemented in their situation. Although IES seeks to support research that informs not just "what works" on average but also "for whom" and "under what conditions" (Spybrook et al., 2020), such research is more difficult and expensive to conduct and hence less common.

Developing and Disseminating Promising Evidence-Based Resources for STEM Education

Research-based innovations in STEM education typically involve more than just new knowledge gained from studies: they also involve resources in the form of new instructional materials, interventions, training programs, and tools. This kind of research can vary considerably in the degree to which the implementations being studied are carried out in normal educational settings or under more controlled conditions, but, most commonly, research teams running federally funded studies are heavily involved in the implementation, potentially conflicting factors are controlled, and adequate resources and support are provided using grant funding. Preparing to scale an innovation beyond the research phase—especially one that requires significant changes in practice, organization, or resources—is both very difficult and often overlooked or neglected. As discussed in Chapter 4, it is most likely to occur successfully if the designers of research-based tools work collaboratively and iteratively with practitioners to figure out how to best enact the intended innovation in realistic contexts. This may present a steep learning curve for many academic researchers, who may be unfamiliar with the practices, routines, and constraints of schools and classrooms. Research teams that have been successful in scaling up ambitious learning innovations have typically begun planning for scaling early in their work and have invested long periods of time working collaboratively in intended implementation settings and incorporating what they learn there (Roschelle, Mazziotti & Means, 2021). As McLaughlin and Mitra (2001) noted in their study of how theory-based educational change reforms are sustained and extended beyond their initial invention, "Moving from 'vitro' to 'vivo' requires the collaboration of reformers and practitioners and assumes that the reform itself is unfinished until that co-construction takes place" (p. 306).

For promising innovations to spread beyond the contexts in which they were first developed, there also have to be pathways for these types of products to be distributed in usable forms to schools. Physical materials (such as science kits) require a manufacturing and distribution system. Other innovations may rely on professional development for teachers to implement them effectively, which requires project staff to create and implement training programs on an ongoing basis. Although it is attractive to think that resources that were developed with federal funding might be widely disseminated at little or no cost, the reality is considerably more complex. Relatively few potent interventions can truly be given away with no additional support. Even online electronic resources have to be maintained and updated on secure websites, with features such as user registration systems, secure data transfer protocols, operating system updates, and interoperability across different platforms—all of which entail ongoing costs for professional services that persist after the original grant funding has expired. Unlike commercial developers, recipients of federal research grants who create new educational products and resources often lack the expertise to market, distribute, and support products on their own. While innovation developers may wish to see their products disseminated and sustained, accruing the time and resources to do this themselves may be an especially uncomfortable fit with the constraints and incentives of academic jobs and may conflict with the demands of publishing research and pursuing new grant funding. Research labs in academic institutions are ill-suited to selling and distributing products, and academic designers may run into problems or resistance if they try to market what they have developed. They may face scrutiny from their own institution about conflicts of interest or time commitments, or they may be reluctant to publish their research with disclosures of a financial interest.

In recent decades, there has been a move toward open educational resources (OER) shared through various platforms that post materials that have been placed in the public domain or that have been released under licenses that permit various combinations of access, duplication, redistribution, adaptation, and repurposing. Creative Commons (creativecommons.org), for instance, is an international nonprofit organization that provides a variety of licenses that have been widely used to share resources at no cost for educational purposes. Materials shared in this way are typically digital resources that can be easily uploaded and downloaded through web browsers. Because there are few barriers to sharing resources in this way, OER can be an attractive mechanism for facilitating dissemination and spread. However, this model does not solve the problems of generating revenue to support resources more robustly, providing ways to track field-based revisions, or assuring that either original resources or modified versions of them are of high quality.

Another challenge in developing and disseminating evidence is that even innovations that have strong evidence demonstrating their potential to improve student learning and engagement may not attract the interest of school districts if their focus is narrow and doesn't cover a sufficiently wide grade band or a large enough portion of the curriculum. School districts may prefer complete packages provided by commercial publishers that include elements such as teacher and student dashboards that integrate with learning management systems commonly used in schools, ready-made standardized assessments, and professional development for teachers.

Products developed with federal research funding can, of course, be transferred to for-profit publishers. While this might have the benefit of harnessing professional sales and marketing capacities, there is also a risk that innovations may be converted into products that are not faithful to what was originally developed and studied; another risk is that they may be acquired but not distributed. Formerly accessible materials may also disappear behind paywalls. While fields such as medicine and engineering have a history of commercializing products that result from research, the norms and processes are less familiar in education research, and standardized business models are lacking (Kathy Perkins, personal communication, December 7, 2023). Nevertheless, as we will see later in this chapter, some innovation developers have successfully found ways to disseminate, scale, and sustain their products.

Some federal agencies, such as NASA and NOAA, also provide funding for STEM education, but their purview is more specific to their agencies' mission, in contrast to the broad mandates carried out by NSF and the U.S. Department of Education. This allows these agencies to both develop educational programs and resources and also to implement and disseminate them widely in a more integrated fashion. The Smithsonian Institution has also received funding via an IMD grant to successfully disseminate, scale, and sustain products. In these cases, the same program, under a single large umbrella, can develop educational resources and also form partnerships to train and support large networks of practitioners using those resources, with opportunities for collaborative and iterative development over long-time spans. Two examples of such initiatives, NASA's Science Activation program (NASEM, 2020) and the GLOBE Program are described in more detail below. This structure circumvents some of the gaps and misalignments that arise when the development and implementation landscapes for educational innovations are not connected.

Finally, it is important to note that federal investments in STEM education have often extended beyond the formal Pre-K–12 education system. Innovation and impact extension in STEM that takes place during out-of-school time (OST) settings have also been supported in a number of ways over the years. Government investment by many federal agencies including NSF, NASA, NOAA, and ED has supported the development and expansion of projects in science media, informal science institutions, and community serving organizations. Investments by ED and NSF in public television programming with a math and science focus, including early childhood programs, have provided broad access to learners of all ages across the nation. Focused NSF support has also provided the fuel for the expansion of science centers and experiences with new science, such as the nanotechnology-based Nanoscale Informal Science Education Network. NOAA's Environmental Literacy Program provides grants and in-kind support to the informal science education (ISE) world to improve ecosystem stewardship. NOAA has also developed Science On a Sphere, a global display system to visualize planetary data in support of earth science education. NASA, through its Science Activation program (described in more detail below), develops partnerships between the agency and members of the ISE field to support youth participation in their missions of discovery and to build a connection with authentic science through citizen science activities. Collaborations between the formal and informal science systems have also been supported at the federal level, including museum-based standards-aligned curriculum like Smithsonian Science for the Classroom and accompanying professional learning for teachers, kit-based school curriculum like FOSS, and family support for getting ready for school. These collaborative efforts among school educators, informal science institutions, community organizations, and the federal science agencies demonstrate the impact of collective action.

Innovations Arising from Sources Other Than Federal Funding

Innovative STEM programs and resources also arise from sources other than federally funded initiatives. Private corporations, museums and science centers, professional organizations, foundation and corporate philanthropy, groups of teachers, and local community groups have all contributed to enriching and enlivening opportunities for engaging children and youth in STEM and providing supports and resources for STEM education in both the formal Pre-K–12 system and in the OST sector. For example, in recent years, private funders have been active in creating new programs and resources for computing education, both in and out of school, as described in Box 5-1.

In some cases, private funding supports expanded delivery of a particular program through sponsorship and marketing. In other cases, this funding directly supports innovation efforts through investments in research, evaluation, and scale-up activities. Compared to innovations that are developed through competitive federally funded awards, these alternative development pathways can have both advantages and disadvantages. To the extent that their origin is more "bottom up," these innovations may be closer to the intended implementation environment from the outset and may have local or regional champions who gather resources and build collaborations to sustain them. They may also be more specifically tuned to the needs and goals of a particular community. Another significant benefit is that corporate or philanthropic funding can often be secured quickly, in contrast to federal funding, where a solicitation may only accept applications once per year and the timeline from submission to the start of a funded project may take a year or more. However, if the funding does not include a commitment of resources for research and evaluation, the innovation may lack evidence of educational effectiveness beyond simple counts of numbers of events and participants.

BOX 5-1
The Role of the Private Sector

The current movement for computing and learning has been catalyzed and supported by unique public, nonprofit, and private partnerships. Many in-school initiatives for K–12 STEM+C have been funded and implemented by corporations (e.g., AT&T Aspire, Tata TCS goIT, Google Code Next, Cisco Networking Academy, and Microsoft TEALS). Code.org has developed a number of activities to expand access to computing opportunities in school (e.g., providing computer science curriculum, teacher professional development, and the Hour of Code campaign).

The private sector has been a key driver of tools and programs that support STEM experiences and help develop computing interests and competencies. This involvement includes (a) corporate funding and support for computer science and maker-oriented educational programs and institutions, (b) computing learning programs and tools developed by the educational technology industry, (c) technology learning experiences fostered through recreational engagement commercial games and technology platforms, (d) corporate-developed training and curriculum, and (e) corporate support for employee volunteer opportunities.

The private sector has also been a longstanding supporter of out-of-school STEM learning and making programs. Intel was a key sponsor of the Computer Clubhouse Network. Other companies have also sponsored technology centers and makerspaces such as the Best Buy Teen Tech Centers. The maker movement and the Maker Faire were, until recently, championed by the for-profit company Maker Media, which also helped launch nonprofit educational efforts such as Maker Ed.[a] Many of the early maker education efforts were seeded, and continue to be sponsored, by corporations such as Cognizant, Google, Infosys, and Chevron, among many others. Family and community foundations, as well as federal agencies, have also played critical roles, but corporate funds supported the momentum of these initiatives, developed in in-school and OST spaces alike. Smaller local businesses are often also critical to a maker program's fundraising and community building.

While large corporations have supported public-sector and nonprofit computing programs such as Code.org, other companies have developed businesses centered on afterschool and summer programs for STEM learning. Summer camp providers such as ID Tech, Galileo, and Rolling Robots offer programs that can cost more than $1,000 a week to learn robotics, coding, and digital creation. A number of for-profit afterschool centers offer programming and computing experiences for youth, although their membership dues are often prohibitive for large portions of the youth population. A smaller number of startups have sought to establish online STEM learning programs and platforms, such as DIY.org and Apex Learning.

---

[a] See https://www.edsurge.com/news/2019-0

SOURCE: Recopied from NASEM, 2021, p. 10.

THE INNOVATION IMPLEMENTATION LANDSCAPE

In contrast to the innovation development landscape, where federal policy and funding play a predominant role in concert with designers situated primarily outside of the Pre-K–12 public education system, the innovation implementation landscape for STEM education in the United States involves actors, financial resources, and decision-making processes that are located within the public education system, mostly at the state and local levels. There are relatively few direct routes guiding the flow of innovations arising from federally funded projects to schools and districts throughout the country. This situation is somewhat akin to the state of travel in the United States before the interstate road system was established: some schools and districts—such as large city districts, districts that have connections with research universities, or districts in states that develop their own initiatives—sit on well-traveled thoroughfares with ready access to new ideas and resources, while others are only reached by circuitous, lightly traveled routes and have little capacity to investigate or invest in education innovations.

Implementing Innovation: Key Considerations

As discussed in Chapters 2 and 3, the United States has a long history of state and local control in education policy and decision making. Leaders at state, regional, and local levels who identify, vet, and implement innovations in educational settings have distinct sets of concerns that may be quite different from the concerns of innovation designers. As they consider a potential innovation, they may ask whether it addresses an important need or issue; whether it is responsive to the local population and context; what resources are required to implement it and whether those resources can be easily acquired; whether additional staff development will be required; whether it will be welcomed or resisted by staff, students, and the local community; whether it is compatible with or potentially in competition with or disruptive to existing curriculum and routines; what timeline is required for implementation; and how they will know whether it is achieving intended outcomes.

The degree to which a particular innovation is likely to spread and endure depends not just on research data of effectiveness, but also on the extent to which it can provide answers and solutions to these questions of practical implementation. Some innovations are narrowly targeted and can be implemented fairly readily with existing resources under standard conditions in the educational setting. For example, a classroom teacher may decide to incorporate an online tool for math homework assignments and formative assessments that is compatible with curriculum already in use and can be easily integrated with the school's existing learning management system (e.g., ASSISTments).[1] A more ambitious or unconventional innovation, in contrast, might require a lengthy and carefully planned campaign to gather resources, develop a team with appropriate skills, build community support, and address challenges such as dissent or resistance to change.

NEGOTIATING THE TERRAIN BETWEEN THE LANDSCAPES OF INNOVATION DEVELOPMENT AND IMPLEMENTATION

As noted previously, many funded projects are not spread beyond their initial instantiation, and if they are spread, are not sustained. Although they may generate important research evidence of impacts on STEM learning or other desired outcomes in their original context, they lack a functional dissemination model that reaches directly into classrooms or other educational settings. Since 2002, IES has funded types of projects (originally referred to as "goals") that suggest an implicit linear progression from initial development of innovations to focused efficacy studies and then effectiveness or replication studies at larger scales, with the latter goals encouraging studies with new and larger populations under typical rather than ideal circumstances. However, evidence suggests that relatively few innovations progress through these project types in a connected way, and only a minority of grants are associated with future grants (NASEM, 2022). As a result, many research-based innovations may be very promising and have evidence of effectiveness, but they have not completed the process to be fully developed into forms that can be readily implemented in realistic educational settings with diverse populations of learners. In recent years, as discussed in Chapter 4, there has been increasing interest in STEM education in a contrasting nonlinear perspective, in which decision makers and practitioners are directly involved with researchers in designing, adapting, and scaling innovations (Roschelle, Mazziotti & Means, 2021).

Where innovations have gone through a complete development process and are ready to be implemented more widely, the question of how they are promoted or discovered comes into play. One potent route for evidence-based instructional resources is to become part of state adoption cycles. Historically, local school district leaders have had the authority to select and purchase materials, in line with the U.S. tradition of local control, but a growing number of states have developed policies to evaluate and adopt or approve materials at the state level, with the goal of ensuring consistent access to high-quality instructional materials (HQIM) throughout the state (Doan & Kaufman, 2024). These efforts are also in line with the federal

---

[1] See https://new.assistments.org/

Every Student Succeeds Act, which encourages districts and schools to choose interventions that have been rigorously studied and shown to improve student outcomes. Boards in states with adoption policies periodically review materials and evidence of their effectiveness in various subject areas and publish lists of approved materials, which may be either mandated, such that districts must adopt them or apply for a waiver or recommended but not mandated. States with adoption policies may further incentivize the use of selected materials by providing aligned professional development or negotiating master contracts with publishers to make it easier and more affordable for districts to acquire them.[2] State education agencies also receive both federal and private grants, some of which may then be awarded to LEAs to support HQIM and teacher learning. Whether mandated and incentivized or not, adoption lists are a direct way for states to call attention to high-quality materials and save districts the time and money required to carry out their own reviews or figure out procurement strategies. In 2017, the Council of Chief State School Officers formed the High-Quality Instructional Materials and Professional Development (IMPD) Network,[3] which currently includes 13 states and helps states develop policy, communications strategies, and professional learning opportunities aligned with HQIM. Some adoption states also partner with EdReports, which is an independent organization that conducts regular reviews of curriculum materials with national teams of educators (Doan & Kaufman, 2024).

Evidence suggests that state adoption policies increase use of standards-aligned HQIM to some degree. For example, the American Instructional Resources Survey Project, conducted independently by the RAND Corporations, has found that adoption and usage of HQIM was significantly higher for teachers in states in the IMPD network (Doan et al., 2022). State adoption policies can be viewed as an example of what Weiss, Murphy-Graham, and Birkeland (2005) have described as "imposed use" of research and evaluation evidence, where a higher level of government mandates or incentivizes specific actions based on evidence. Local districts may vary in whether they are responding to the evidence itself or to the mandate or incentives, but this is a pathway of influence that appears to be effective and can allow federal, state, and local levels to negotiate varying degrees of control and decision making.

Some adoption policies are limited to particular subjects (especially English language arts and mathematics) or grade levels (e.g., reading materials for early elementary grades), and so state adoption may not be an

---

[2] The federal government has also provided funding support: partially in response to the shocks of pandemic schooling, emergency funding through Elementary and Secondary School Emergency Relief included funding for states to advance the adoption of mathematics and English language arts HQIM.

[3] See https://learning.ccsso.org/high-quality-instructional-materials

option for many STEM innovations. However, professional organizations and other non-profit organizations are another route by which high quality, standards-aligned STEM materials and programs can be highlighted and promoted. Organizations such as the National Science Teachers Association, the National Council of Teachers of Mathematics, and the Council of State Science Supervisors routinely call attention to instructional materials and programs through a variety of channels that reach educators, including their websites, regional and national conferences, journals, reports, and online seminars.

Though state approval is one route to widespread dissemination of innovations, many innovation designers are left to develop their own pathways to spread and sustain the resources they have created. Although we have highlighted many of the challenges of trying to move innovations beyond the environments in which they are initially developed, the committee also documented a number of cases in which designers have been successful in spreading or sustaining their own innovations, or other parties have sought out effective innovations and worked to bring them to more schools and students. A notable finding is that the pathways by which they have done so are almost as varied and numerous as the innovations themselves. In this section, we feature a series of examples, drawn from both programs in the commissioned compendium and from others documented in published research, to illustrate this variety. At the same time, we note that they tend to share some common features, such as ensuring that their interventions and programs address important needs in educational settings, mobilizing and supporting both enactors and facilitators, and partnering to build necessary capacity and infrastructure (Cohen & Mehta, 2017; McLaughlin & Mitra, 2001).

Innovations Starting with Research & Development

We first consider several innovations that started with funding for research and development, accumulated evidence of their effectiveness, and—either simultaneously or successively—have engaged in significant efforts to extend or sustain their innovation. These tend to fall along a continuum of scaffolding for sustainability. Some innovations are able to develop their own distribution model that enables them to stay active over time and to successfully spread the innovation to more users or further develop it in new contexts or with new applications; however, they continue to struggle with achieving a sustainable financial model and are at risk of not remaining viable over a longer time. Some also thrive under the direction and leadership of a founder or key advocate but struggle to create a succession plan for maintaining the innovation when that leader is no longer involved. PhET Interactive Simulations is an instructive example of a program that has been active for more than 20 years and has been impressively successful in spreading worldwide but that finds it challenging to maintain a sustainable business model that can support the full potential of its innovative resources.

PhET Interactive Simulations

PhET has created 169 open-source simulations to support sustained inquiry learning in math and science across multiple topics and grade levels from elementary through higher education. These simulations have been used more than 1.4 billion times around the world, with about half of that usage in the United States and with a notable increase during and following the COVID-19 pandemic. Development has been ongoing since the early 2000's, with support from numerous NSF grants as well as private foundation money. Multiple published research studies indicate that PhET simulations lead to significantly higher learning gains than traditional instruction (Antonio & Castro, 2023; Banda & Nzabahimana, 2021) with substantial effect sizes. However, federal grant funding in the United States has only supported new research and development, with no funding for scaling or sustainability. In recent years, PhET has built a scalable teacher professional development model and a teacher-leader network, but this was done with funding available in Latin America and Africa, not the United States PhET has followed several strategies to make the simulations more available, including building them in such a way that they can be embedded in other education products (e.g., those produced by commercial publishers). Although the PhET website is free, the program's developers have also tried to develop some revenue sources to build a more sustainable financial model, with modest revenues coming from individual donations from teachers, from a low-cost direct to consumer app, and from business-to-business partnerships. These, however, account for less than 15 percent of annual expenses. Despite their notable success in scaling and sustaining PhET simulations, the developers call attention to several intractable issues. Their open education resources—which they believe are too expensive and require too much specialized knowledge to have been produced by the private sector—do not have a compatible business model that generates sustainable revenue. They lack the funding to maintain and update simulations as technology changes (most notably the disruptive transition from Java and Flash to HTML, which has resulted in mothballing dozens of simulations with proven efficacy). Finally, while they have completed research on how to effectively implement inclusive design features in simulations to serve students with special needs and learning differences, they do not have funding to scale these features.

Innovations with a Robust Distribution System

A bit further along this continuum are evidence-based innovations that have developed a robust distribution system that is financially sustainable over a long term. These typically involve having a home in or partnership with a stable organization that can handle sales, marketing, distribution, and support on an ongoing basis. The first case highlights Youth Engineering Solutions (YES) and Engineering is Elementary (EiE), engineering curricula for grades Pre-K through 8, which were originally developed by academic researchers with funding from NSF and are now distributed through the Museum of Science, Boston, with additional support from industry and foundation partners. The second case is the Building Blocks Pre-K Math curriculum, which was developed by Douglas Clements and Julie Sarama with funding from NSF and has been extensively studied during scale up using the TRIAD scale up model, also developed by the same research team.

Youth Engineering Solutions (YES) and Engineering Is Elementary (EiE)

YES and EiE are innovative curricular resources designed to introduce engineering in Pre-K–8 classrooms and out-of-school settings, such as afterschool and camp programs. Initially supported with grant funding, including several NSF grants, the designers of YES/EiE work closely with teachers in design-based development and research cycles to create materials that can be used effectively in typical classroom environments. The YES/EiE approach situates problems in societal contexts and invites students to think critically about the impact of their engineered solutions. It also uses flexible, multimodal activities to encourage all students to generate original solutions to problems, to manipulate physical objects to deepen their conceptual knowledge, and to persist and learn from failure. The programs are accompanied by professional learning resources attuned to teachers' needs, with the understanding that engineering is an unfamiliar discipline for most preschool and elementary teachers.

Because engineering is a new discipline in Pre-K–12 education, it often faces barriers to finding a regular place in school curricula. Clearing instructional time for engineering during the school day, making time for teachers to participate in professional learning opportunities, and developing a system to provide and replenish physical materials have been persistent challenges. To facilitate uptake, the YES/EiE development team has aligned classroom-based materials with state standards and Next Generation Science Standards and also worked with researchers to demonstrate impacts on desirable student outcomes, including engineering and science knowledge, interest, and attitudes. The curricula are also used in out-of-school programs, where there is often more freedom and flexibility to focus on engineering. There have been over 60 published conference papers and journal articles that the team has written about YES/EiE and over 40 others written by scholars outside the team. These includes measures of fidelity of implementation (Lachapelle & Cunningham, 2019), a randomized controlled trial to examine student outcomes (Cunningham et al., 2020), and studies to examine the influence on different populations of learners including English language learners (Cunningham, Kelly, & Meyer, 2021), and low-income students (Robinson et al., 2018).

YES/EiE resources are used nationwide and reach over five million youth a year. The Museum of Science, Boston is the home organization for the resources and has provided some financial support as well as organizational stability over the years. Digital resources, which were originally provided for sale, are now available for free download, and kits and print materials are available for purchase. External grants from corporate, federal, and individual sources fund the development of new resources and the purchase of materials and professional learning for schools and districts. This combination of financial resources has been stable and is expected to be sustainable.

Building Blocks™ Pre-K Math and the TRIAD Scale-up Model

The work of Julie Sarama and Douglas Clements is notable in having devoted attention to (a) the development of theory and evidence about children's learning trajectories in mathematics (Clements & Sarama, 2004), (b) the creation of an extended curriculum for preschool children aligned with progressions of how children learn mathematics, known as the *Building Blocks™* curriculum (Clements et al., 2011), and (c) development of a comprehensive, generalizable model for scaling up evidence-based practices and programs known as Technology Enhanced Research-based Instruction, Assessment and professional Development (TRIAD; Sarama et al., 2008; Sarama & Clements, 2013). Their work on learning trajectories involves theorizing and testing descriptions of the progression of children's thinking and learning within a domain (mathematics, in this case) and then developing a set of instructional tasks that facilitate pathways through the trajectory (Clements & Sarama, 2004). With support from NSF through multiple grants in the last two decades, Sarama and Clements co-evolved the curriculum and the TRIAD scale-up model and conducted multiple research studies, including large randomized controlled trials with thousands of children in hundreds of preschool classrooms across several states.

Sarama and Clements define scale-up "as the instantiation of an educational intervention in varied settings with diverse populations, addressing the needs of multiple sociopolitical stakeholders, so as to achieve (1) satisfactory fidelity of implementation and, as a result, (2) the intervention's goals for over 90% of the children who could benefit from the intervention and ultimately

(3) eventual transfer of the intervention to local ownership, sustainability, persistence of effects, and continuing diffusion" (2013, p. 174). The TRIAD scale-up model includes a set of research-based guidelines for working with teachers and administrators, children, families, and communities to achieve scale-up that successfully fulfills this definition. These guidelines include planning for the long term and preparing for increasing complexity as the intervention scales; continuously communicating and building commitment to a shared vision among administrators, teachers, and families; promoting equity among all participants, including in the allocation of resources; and providing in-depth, ongoing professional learning opportunities and coaching situated in the classroom with a focus on understanding developmental progressions in children's mathematical thinking and their pedagogical application in the curricular activities and assessments in the *Building Blocks*™ curriculum. Their approach anticipates the need for schools and teachers to make adaptations as they increasingly take ownership of the program but supports them in maintaining the integrity of the intervention by helping them learn to distinguish productive adaptations from those that would dilute or undermine it.

The full *Building Blocks*™ *PreK Math*, including manipulative kits, digital activities, and assessment and resource guides for teachers (e.g., printable masters and family letters) is now available for purchase through McGraw Hill. Professional learning resources for teachers are offered in the form of an online course, on-demand video and other resources, and live training sessions.

Standing Program Provides Larger Umbrella

As mentioned above, federal funding, particularly through NASA and NOAA, has provided support for STEM learning using a somewhat different model, in which a standing program provides a larger umbrella with internal infrastructure and longer funding horizons to enable the iterative development of a set of shared resources and to develop robust collaborations to disseminate and implement those resources. The examples below present two cases that exemplify this approach: the Science Activation (SciAct) Program and the GLOBE Program, both of which are based at NASA.

NASA Science Activation Program

The NASA Science Mission Directorate's (SMD) SciAct "connects diverse learners of all ages with science in ways that activate minds and promote a deeper understanding of our world and beyond." Started in 2015, the Science Activation program is a cooperative network of competitively selected teams from across the Nation working with NASA infrastructure activities to share NASA science with learners of all ages" (NASEM, 2020).

The program has its own office and program team embedded within NASA's SMD, and the infrastructure provided by NASA connects these teams to scientific expertise and a large library of NASA resources. SciAct uses a "collective impact" model, with NASA's SciAct team serving as a "backbone" to coordinate organizations and activities that share a common interest in space science and an agenda for promoting accurate and compelling learning experiences.

In 2023, SciAct facilitated almost 76 million learner interactions in the United States and across the globe (National Aeronautics and Space Administration, 2023). The program also supports data collection and publication of peer-reviewed reports. Key to SciAct is the integration of NASA science mission experts and internal education production resources, such as scientific visualization laboratories, NASATV and NASA.gov, with the development and distribution capabilities of the external education experience providers and networks, such as museums, libraries, and media providers. The successful integration effort requires monthly and annual meetings attended by members of all of the teams, annual identification of cross collaboration opportunities, and whole group education opportunities on issues such as diversity, citizen science, and mission science. SciAct features cooperative agreements of up to five years with the potential for renewal, which provides the time necessary to create a thriving community of collaboration. The program bridges the landscape of innovation and implementation through the careful cultivation of a portfolio of diverse projects, partnerships and dissemination opportunities (NASEM, 2020).

GLOBE Program

First announced by the U.S. government on Earth Day in 1994, GLOBE is an international inquiry-based education program focused on environmental science and earth system science. GLOBE, which stands for Global Learning and Observation to Benefit the Environment, aims to engage students in scientific activities, improve science education, and increase environmental awareness and understanding of the Earth as a system. GLOBE operates in 127 countries, with around 41,000 schools and 50,000 educators involved historically. There are about 278,000 GLOBE observers who engage with the program.

GLOBE aims to increase STEM literacy, particularly in earth system science, environmental science, and climate and resilience science, through purposeful active learning, community engagement, and building a community of practice. GLOBE's theory of change is engaging people in taking environmental observations and measurements, analyzing the data, and optionally putting it into GLOBE's open database. The backbone of the GLOBE Program is a set of 40+ measurement protocols. Initially, the program was scientist-driven, with scientists designing protocols for students to collect data. Over time, it has evolved to enable more student-driven investigations using GLOBE tools, with scientists providing context and motivation.

GLOBE operates in coordination with U.S. federal agencies like NASA (which is now the lead agency), NOAA (which was the former lead), NSF, and the Department of State, all of whom have goals aligned with GLOBE's mission around STEM education, environmental literacy, and international collaboration. The core GLOBE infrastructure is primarily funded through federal appropriations to NASA. This supports the GLOBE Implementation Office for training, materials, and community engagement, as well as a data management system. Although securing funding commitments and maintaining interagency agreements has been bureaucratically challenging, the longstanding support for GLOBE's core infrastructure helps explain its longevity and widespread expansion.

Partners obtain additional funding from various sources such as federal agencies, school districts, philanthropies, and international contributions based on bilateral agreements. In U.S. schools, factors such as school administration support, alignment with local standards, and availability of partner support have been persistent challenges, as detailed in program evaluations. Program leaders continue to explore opportunities to secure additional funding commitments from federal agencies beyond in-kind support, as well as other sources, to support their scaling and sustainability efforts.

Independent yearly evaluations of the GLOBE Program were conducted during the first ten years of the program. These evaluations included evidence of GLOBE participants achieving STEM learning goals and skills, and many other aspects of GLOBE implementation and impact, including how implementation varied in different contexts. Since the initial evaluation, many projects based on GLOBE have also included an evaluation component. Going forward, the project would like to enhance program evaluations to further understand factors impacting domestic scale and sustainability, such as teacher turnover and instability in school administration support (Amy Chen, personal communication, April 26, 2024).

Building Durable Systems

The examples discussed so far represent cases in which a distribution system was purposely built to drive a given innovation or a collection of related innovations from development through widespread implementation. While the system allows the targeted resources to evolve and expand in various ways over time, the system is not intended to serve other unrelated innovations or to support STEM education more generally. A different approach is to build "durable systems" with the capacity to identify, implement, and support multiple programs and resources so that unrelated STEM education innovations can successfully reach and serve the intended constituents and communities. These systems will be discussed further in Chapter 8, but here, we provide a brief introduction by way of several examples, which vary considerably in how they came into being, who the main partners are, and how they operate to connect participants, supporters, and resources in the service of STEM education.

Regional Educational Laboratories

The first example is Regional Educational Laboratories (RELs), which are federally funded through ED to disseminate research evidence and build resources to support the application of high-quality research in educational settings. Organized around geographic regions, RELs are one of the few examples of a federally funded pathway that directly connects national research investments with their application and scaling across all levels of the education system.

IES funds a network of ten RELs (see Box 2-4 in Chapter 2) covering American states and territories. RELs partner with educators and policymakers in their regions to support local, regional, or state decisions about educational policies, programs, and practices, with an emphasis on the use of evidence and data to improve student outcomes. Their purview includes but is not limited to STEM education. The authorizing legislation for the REL Program stipulates three main activities:

- *Applied Research and Development:* RELs partner with districts and states to identify high-priority needs and to develop peer-reviewed research products intended to be actionable for teachers and educational leaders in schools. They also develop other products to support scaling up of best practices, such as toolkits, with accompanying professional development programs.
- *Training, Coaching and Technical Support for Use of Research:* RELs provide a variety of professional learning opportunities, including intensive professional development focused on important topics; coaching to apply research evidence to inform critical decisions; and technical support to build capacity in collecting, analyzing, and utilizing data.
- *Dissemination:* RELs are charged with synthesizing and communicating research and evidence so that high-quality, scientifically valid information is readily available and provided to educators and policymakers in ways that support action and application in local contexts.

These activities are intentionally designed to complement other federal investments in research and development in education and to create functional bridges between research and practice, with the goal of translating research for decision makers in schools and building tools and professional capacity to leverage evidence-based improvements in education.

RELs are involved in a number of specific projects related to STEM teaching and learning, but their approach is illustrated by two current mathematics projects. The Teaching Fractions Toolkit Partnership, run by REL Midwest with the Illinois State Board of Education and school districts in Illinois, focuses on strengthening 6th grade students' conceptual understanding of fractions and narrowing gaps in math achievement among student groups. The Toolkit includes intensive professional development and supports for teachers to understand and apply evidence-based practices for teaching fractions and related concepts. It also works with math leaders and school and district administrators to develop wraparound supports to reinforce the broader developmental trajectory of fraction understanding across grades Pre-K–8 in complex school systems.

REL Northeast is partnering with district leadership teams from a group of districts in Connecticut to improve mathematics outcomes for multilingual learners, who typically score low on state assessments. One part of this project is building capacity among district leaders to support English learners and multilingual learners through a workshop series in which participants create district logic models, analyze district data, learn about evidence-based practices, and create action plans. A second component is a research study on the impacts of a related teacher professional development program using an intervention called Visual Access to Mathematics, which helps teachers explore how visual representations can support problem solving and communication for both English learners and other students learning critical middle grades content.

As they work to develop resources to help scale research-based practices and resources, REL projects typically undergo usability and feasibility testing as their components are iteratively developed and then later test them in formal studies to examine their summative impact. RELs also engage in cross-REL activities to further disseminate and scale high-quality programs and products. The REL program has had notable longevity since the first RELs were authorized and established in the mid-1960s as a network of large-scale labs. Although the number of RELs and their priority areas have changed periodically through the program's history, their focus on connecting high-quality research with practice and on creating strong, long-term partnerships and networks to support scaling and impact has been continuous.

State STEM Ecosystems

A second type of durable system designed to support the scaling of multiple STEM innovations is state STEM ecosystems (see Chapter 2 for a brief discussion of STEM learning ecosystems in relation to regional actors). Many states (or regions within states) now have some form of a STEM ecosystem.[4] The committee met with a panel of representatives from four such state-level STEM organizations: Jeff Weld from the Iowa Governor's STEM Advisory Council, Lee Meadows from the Alabama STEM Council, Michael Vargas from the Arizona STEM Acceleration Project, and Jeremy Babendure from the Arizona-based SciTech Institute. Although these groups vary in the specifics of how they are organized, where their funding comes from, and what particular initiatives they support, they share an ecosystems approach to building long-term regional partnerships to call attention to STEM education and to aggregate and channel resources to support it.

Many state STEM ecosystem initiatives have been motivated by local businesses and industries concerned with STEM workforce development, including the development of competencies such as critical thinking, problem solving, communication, and facility with technology, and they have typically been launched with support from the governor's office or the state legislature. In Iowa, for instance, a group of people from industry, higher education, and the K–12 system gathered on their own over several weekends and drafted a STEM education roadmap with a short set of recommendations to policy leaders about how to cultivate a future workforce in the state with strong STEM capabilities. Their plan gained the support of the governor, who created the Iowa STEM Advisory Council by executive order in 2011, and then garnered an initial appropriation of $4.7 million from the legislature in 2012. In Alabama, advocates similarly developed a STEM education strategic plan rooted in workforce development that was presented to the governor, who formed the Alabama STEM Council by executive order in 2020 with financial support from the legislature. State STEM ecosystems leverage these public investments by securing contributions from business and industry partners and grants from foundations and funding agencies. Their ability to create long-lasting partnerships and to raise flexible funds on a consistent basis allows them to grow and maintain efforts over a longer time horizon than efforts that depend on one-time project funding. However, leaders also note that they bear a heavy and continuous burden of fund-raising, and funding streams are not consistently reliable.

---

[4]See https://stemecosystems.org/. Note that this is not an exhaustive list. Other empirically grounded ecosystems exist, such as the Chicago City of Learning initiative (Pinkard, 2019; Quigley et al., 2016) and the Synergies project (Falk et al., 2015, 2016a,b).

Central to the notion of a state STEM ecosystem is the development of regional networks and partnerships that engage state and local organizations in the support of STEM education activities, events, and infrastructure development, both in and out of schools. They also connect teachers and educational leaders with each other, which helps ideas and resources flow to districts throughout the state, including those that are chronically underresourced and understaffed in STEM-related areas. For example, Arizona's SciTech Institute uses a dual strategy of creating regional hubs, which connect local resources and foster collaboration, and also supporting statewide working groups, which can share expertise and develop collaborative projects focused on high-priority needs and challenges across the state.

State STEM ecosystems have supported a great variety of programs and initiatives, including professional learning opportunities and externships for teachers; small competitive grants to teachers and districts to develop specific projects; out-of-school events and programs for youth; STEM ambassador programs for students; and STEM festivals for the general public. As just one example, the Arizona STEM Acceleration Project has supported more than 450 teachers from every corner of the state as STEM Fellows, who receive a stipend of $4,500 plus $2,000 to purchase STEM supplies. Fellows complete at least 30 hours of STEM professional development and also submit four lesson plans, which are reviewed and then added to a repository that is available to other teachers statewide. State ecosystems have also targeted specific critical needs in their respective states. For example, in order to address the state's critical shortage of STEM teachers, the Alabama STEM Council has created partnerships and obtained annual funding from the legislature to launch new UTeach STEM teacher preparation programs at six universities in Alabama, with the goal of preparing 250 new STEM teachers every year.

A noteworthy feature common to many state STEM ecosystems is that they have embraced the need to develop sophisticated communication strategies about the importance of STEM and the value of providing engaging and effective STEM learning opportunities to children and youth across the state. They produce blogs, podcasts, and radio and television ads that showcase students actively pursuing their STEM-related aspirations to raise awareness among the general public and to drive support for STEM education.

State STEM ecosystems vary in their approaches to measuring and documenting their outcomes. Most regularly compile statistics on participation in their programs and also conduct analyses of return on public investments. They may also look for gains in students' interest in STEM and persistence in STEM education and career pathways, general gains in academic performance on state-wide math and science tests, and public support for STEM education.

STEM NOLA

A third example, STEM NOLA, illustrates a markedly different approach to building a durable system to support STEM education. In contrast to many efforts that attempt to import STEM learning opportunities from more resourced to less resourced communities, STEM NOLA has grown a thriving STEM ecosystem from the ground up, using local leadership, partnerships, and resources to create a dynamic suite of programs in neighborhoods in New Orleans that have traditionally struggled with weak schools and lack of opportunity. In an unusual turn of events, the quality and popularity of these programs now draw participants from more affluent communities and have prompted families and educators to work with STEM NOLA to upgrade STEM education in the public schools.

Launched in New Orleans in 2013 under the leadership of Calvin Mackie, STEM NOLA is a community-based STEM learning ecosystem that designs and delivers a variety of hands-on learning activities, events, and programs with an emphasis on engaging and serving youth in underserved neighborhoods. Its history stands in marked contrast to initiatives that originated with grant funding to STEM education researchers and professional developers. Dr. Mackie, who had previously been a tenured professor of mechanical engineering at Tulane University, and his wife Tracy, who was a trained pharmacist, saw that STEM education in local schools was inadequate and uninspiring, with the result that students were being turned off rather than engaged by STEM, risking a tremendous loss of talent. Initially working out of their garage, the Mackies built a robust learning ecosystem from the ground up, engaging local STEM professionals and college students as volunteers and interns to provide a full menu of hands-on learning opportunities in local neighborhoods during out-of-school time. STEM NOLA focuses on children and youth, with the goals of laying an early foundation of STEM exposure and inspiration, building trust-based intergenerational relationships with local STEM mentors and role models, and providing connections to help young people make sense of and advance through education and career pathways in STEM. Their flagship program has been STEM Saturdays, where familiar local facilities are transformed into temporary laboratories with a series of hands-on activity stations staffed by at least one college student and STEM professional volunteer and a maximum of four students. Activities, which are divided into four grade bands, are related to the theme or topic of the day and selected to be engaging and culturally and environmentally relevant. Each activity culminates with students building or making something, such as functional catapults, rocket cars, circuits, batteries, levees, and motorboats. STEM NOLA has also branched into other formats, including summer camps, larger-scale STEM Fests, and, more recently, providing kits, curriculum, and teacher professional learning opportunities for school-based STEM.

The program's community engagement model has generated a remarkable response: since its inception, STEM NOLA has engaged over 130,000 Pre-K–12 students and over 25,000 families, 87 percent of whom qualify for free and reduced lunch programs, as well as more than 3,500 STEM professionals and trained student volunteers. It has attracted more than $20 million of financial and partnership support from numerous businesses and industries, universities, foundations, the state of Louisiana, and the Department of Defense, and has paid more than $4 million to college student interns. STEM NOLA has expanded into other cities in Louisiana and across the Gulf Coast and beyond using a versatile scaling model. One-time pop-up events can be managed by a central team and delivered either in-person or virtually to any location with a local organization supporting recruitment. If support from a funding sponsor or industry partner is available, full-time STEM NOLA staff members can work with local partners to help accelerate the development of a new learning ecosystem with local ownership.

To date, STEM NOLA has primarily documented its impact in terms of numbers of participants and events and their geographic distribution and spread. They have also conducted pre/post surveys of students, which show notable gains in their level of interest in STEM. These measures are in line with their stated goals of increasing exposure, participation, and engagement, especially in underserved communities. STEM NOLA has not created formal curriculum frameworks for materials they develop and distribute, though they do aim for topical alignment with state STEM standards. Nor have they measured other outcomes and impacts, such as student learning or depth and sustainability of program implementation and ecosystem development in new locations. While they would welcome participation by researchers, they note that they do not have internal capacity to conduct research beyond participation metrics.

The Importance of Systemic Capacity

Stepping back from individual initiatives to take a broader view, a theme that emerged repeatedly from the committee's analysis of innovations that have achieved some success in growing and evolving along one or more of the dimensions of scaling, as identified in Chapter 4 is that networks of functional partnerships among actors in multiple roles at multiple levels often enabled and facilitated the progress of those innovation. The more ambitious an innovation is, the more likely it is to require not just immediate strategic partnerships but also durable systemic infrastructure in order to take root and be sustained in new settings. The committee believes that building interconnected systemic capacities across the education landscape would provide more robust and hospitable environments for effective innovations to scale and spread in equitable ways and be productively adapted to meet the needs different groups of learners.

Systemic infrastructure weaves together elements such as the interplay between designers, facilitators, and enactors; the aggregation of human, social, and material resources; the need for collective learning opportunities for actors in different roles; and the dynamics of leadership, agency, and ownership over time. Building systemic infrastructure involves connecting people and organizations who occupy different roles and who have responsibility and agency for different spheres of influence in ways that promote alignment and integration, so that goals and activities are complementary and mutually reinforcing rather than divergent and in tension (Hopkins & Woulfin, 2015). Building such collective capacity takes considerable time and consistent effort. Actors and participants at boundaries and intersections—whether across the development and implementation landscapes, at different levels of the formal education system, or at any of the many junctures where non-system actors engage with educational settings—need to develop mutual understandings of each other's positions and concerns and of how to align what each party can bring in the service of STEM teaching and learning for all students. What's more, these systemic structures need to be dynamically sustainable. Many initiatives in education tend to devolve over time unless commitment and communication are maintained and continually renewed, in order to survive turnover of personnel, changes in priorities and accountability structures, and new demands on budgets and other resources. These issues are considered further in Chapter 8.

SUMMARY

The configurations of actors, decision makers, and resources that are active when evidence-based STEM education innovations are being developed are typically very different from the configurations that populate the implementation landscape in the public education system. This is particularly true for projects that have been funded with grants from federal agencies to researchers and designers who generally work outside local schools and districts or state education agencies. Many promising research-based innovations never scale because they are not set up to navigate the transition from their original research and development environment to implementation in real-world settings. The innovations may not integrate easily with existing curricula or practices, they may not be readily adaptable to the needs of diverse student populations, or they may be ineffective in the absence of professional learning opportunities for teachers and school leaders to learn how to implement them independently. Innovations may also fail to spread because the original designers lack the knowledge and resources to engage in professional marketing or to provide reliable distribution systems. These barriers to successful transitions from initial development to widespread implementation are primarily structural rather than intentional, arising from divergent incentives, knowledge bases, resources, and needs across the development and implementation landscapes. In general, most designers would like to see their innovations take root and spread and school leaders would like to access high-quality research-based innovations if they are responsive to school needs and can be tailored to local circumstances.

Where programs and resources have been able to spread and be sustained over time, they have done so in many different ways and with varying degrees of success. This variety is due, in part, to the sparseness of standard pathways across national, regional, state, and local levels for bringing innovations to scale, with the result that many individual innovations create their own unique systems and networks. Interventions and programs that have scaled successfully also tend to share some general features, such as ensuring that they address important needs in educational settings, mobilizing and supporting both enactors and facilitators, and partnering to build necessary capacity and infrastructure. They also tend to start the process of planning for scaling early in their lifespan and to find ways to sustain their efforts over multiple years. There are also some models of durable systems that have created networks of relationships, partnerships, and resources with general capacity to spread and support multiple STEM programs and resources. These include RELs, funded by ED, state policies to support the adoption of HQIM, and state and community-led STEM ecosystems. Actors and supporters outside the formal education system, such as professional organizations, informal science organizations, families and community members, and industry partners, can be influential in advocating and leveraging additional resources for new and improved STEM opportunities and shaping them to be responsive to the needs of local participants and settings.

REFERENCES

Antonio, R. P., & Castro, R. R. (2023). Effectiveness of virtual simulations in improving secondary students' achievement in physics: A meta-analysis. *International Journal of Instruction, 16*(2), 533–556.

Asen, R., Gurke, D., Conners, P., Solomon, R., & Gumm, E. (2013). Research evidence and school board deliberations: Lessons from three Wisconsin school districts. *Educational Policy, 27*(1), 33–63. https://doi.org/10.1177/0895904811429291

Banda, H. J., & Nzabahimana, J. (2021). Effect of integrating physics education technology simulations on students' conceptual understanding in physics: A review of literature. *Physical Review Physics Education Research*, *17*(2), 023108.

Clements, D. H., & Sarama, J. (2004). Learning trajectories in mathematics education. *Mathematical Thinking and Learning*, *6*, 81–89.

Clements, D. H., Sarama, J., Spitler, M. E., Lange, A. A., & Wolfe, C. B. (2011). Mathematics learned by young children in an intervention based on learning trajectories: A large-scale cluster randomized trial. *Journal for Research in Mathematics Education*, *42*(2), 127–166. https://eric.ed.gov/?id=EJ918252

Coburn, C. E. (2006). Framing the problem of reading instruction: Using frame analysis to uncover the microprocesses of policy implementation. *American Educational Research Journal*, *43*(3), 343–349.

Coburn, C. E., Honig, M. I., & Stein, M. K. (2009a). What's the evidence on districts' use of evidence? In J. D. Bransford, D. J. Stipek, N. J., Vye, L. M. Gomez, & D. Lam (Eds.), *The role of research in educational improvement* (pp. 67–86). Harvard Education Press.

Coburn, C. E., Toure, J., & Yamashita, M. (2009b). Evidence, interpretation, and persuasion: Instructional decision making at the district central office. *Teachers College Record*, *111*(4), 1115–1161.

Cohen, D. K., & Mehta, J. D. (2017). Why reform sometimes succeeds: Understanding the conditions that produce reforms that last. *AERJ*, *54*(4), 644–690.

Cunningham, C. M., Kelly, G. J., & Meyer, N. (2021). Affordances of engineering with English learners. *Science Education*, *105*(2), 255–280. https://doi.org/10.1002/sce.21606

Cunningham, C. M., Lachapelle, C. P., Brennan, R. T., Kelly, G. J., Tunis, C. S. A., & Gentry, C. A. (2020). The impact of engineering curriculum design principles on elementary students' engineering and science learning. *Journal of Research in Science Teaching*, *57*(3), 423–453.

Doan, S., & Kaufman, J. (2024). What role do states play in selecting K-12 textbooks? *State Education Standard*, *24*(1), n1.

Doan, S., Kaufman, J. H., Woo, A., Tuma, A. P., Diliberti, M. K., & Lee, S. (2022). *How states are creating conditions for use of high-quality instructional materials in K-12 classrooms: Findings from the 2021 American Instructional Resources Survey*. RAND Corporation. https://www.rand.org/pubs/research_reports/RRA134-13.html

Falk, J. H., Dierking, L., Staus, N., Penuel, W. R., Wyld, J., & Bailey, D. (2016a). Understanding and connecting youth STEM interest and participation across the community: The Synergies Project. *International Journal of Science Education, Part B*, *16*(4), 369–384.

Falk, J. H., Dierking, L. D., Staus, N., Wyld, J., Bailey, D., & Penuel, W. R. (2016b). The Synergies research-practice partnership project: A 2020 Vision case study. *Cultural Studies of Science Education*, *11*(1), 195–212.

Falk, J. H., Staus, N., Dierking, L. D., Wyld, J., Bailey, D., & Penuel, W. R. (2015). The Synergies project: Preliminary results and insights from two years of longitudinal survey research. *Museology Quarterly*, *29*(1), 15–21.

Finnigan, K. S., & Daly, A. J. (Eds.). (2014). *Using research evidence in education: From the schoolhouse door to Capitol Hill*. Springer.

Greene, J. C. (1988). Communication of results and utilization in participatory program evaluation. *Evaluation and Program Planning*, *11*, 341–351.

Hopkins, M., & Woulfin, S. L. (2015). School system (re) design: Developing educational infrastructures to support school leadership and teaching practice. *Journal of Educational Change*, *16*, 371–377.

Lachapelle, C. P., & Cunningham, C. M. (2019, June). *Measuring fidelity of implementation in a large-scale research study (RTP)*. Paper presented at 2019 ASEE Annual Conference & Exposition, Tampa, Florida.

McLaughlin, M. W., & Mitra, D. (2001). Theory-based change and change-based theory: Going deeper, going broader. *Journal of Educational Change, 2,* 301–323.

Means, B., & Penuel, W. R. (2005). Scaling up technology-based educational innovations. In Dede, C., Honan, J. P., & Peters, L. C. (Eds.) *Scaling up success: Lessons learned from technology-based educational improvement.* Jossey-Bass.

National Academies of Sciences, Engineering, and Medicine (NASEM). (2020). *NASA's Science Activation Program: Achievements and opportunities.* The National Academies Press.

———. (2021). *Cultivating interest and competencies in computing: Authentic experiences and design factors.* The National Academies Press.

———. (2022). *The future of education research at IES: Advancing an equity-oriented science.* The National Academies Press.

National Aeronautics and Space Administration. (2023). *2023 NASA Science Activation impact report.* https://science.nasa.gov/wp-content/uploads/2024/05/2023-sciact-impact-report-tagged.pdf

Penuel, W. R., Briggs, D. C., Davidson, K. L., Herlihy, C., Sherer, D., Hill, H. C., Farrell, C., & Allen, A. R. (2017). *How school and district leaders access, perceive, and use research.* AERA Open.

Penuel, W. R., Farrell, C. C., Allen, A., Toyama, Y., & Coburn, C. E. (2018). What research district leaders find useful. *Educational Policy, 32*(4), 540–568. https://doi.org/10.1177/0895904816673580/

Pinkard, N. (2019). Freedom of movement: Defining, researching, and designing the components of a healthy learning ecosystem. *Human Development, 62*(1/2), 40–65. https://doi.org/10.1159/000496075

Quigley, D., Dibie, O., Sultan, M. A., Van Horne, K., Penuel, W. R., Sumner, T., Acholonu, U., & Pinkard, N. (2016). Equity of learning opportunities in the Chicago City of Learning program. In T. Barnes, M. Chi, & M. Feng (Eds.), *Proceedings of the 9th International Conference on Educational Data Mining* (pp. 618–619). International Educational Data Mining Society.

Robinson, A., Adelson, J. L., Kidd, K. A., & Cunningham, C. M. (2018). A talent for tinkering: Developing talents in children from low-income households through engineering curriculum. *Gifted Child Quarterly, 62*(1), 130–144.

Roschelle, J., Mazziotti, C., & Means, B. (2021). Scaling up design of inquiry environments. In C. Chinn & R. G. Duncan (Eds.), *International Handbook on Learning and Inquiry.* Routledge.

Sarama, J., & Clements, D. H. (2013). Lessons learned in the implementation of the TRIAD scale-up model: Teaching early mathematics with trajectories and technologies. In T. G. Halle, A. J. Metz & I. Martinez Beck (Eds.), *Applying implementation science in early childhood programs and systems* (pp. 173–191). Brookes.

Sarama, J., Clements, D. H., Starkey, P., Klein, A., & Wakeley, A. (2008). Scaling up the implementation of a pre-kindergarten mathematics curriculum: Teaching for understanding with trajectories and technologies. *Journal of Research on Educational Effectiveness, 1,* 89–119.

Spybrook, J., Zhang, Q., Kelcey, B., & Dong, N. (2020). Learning from Cluster Randomized Trials in education: An assessment of the capacity of studies to determine what works, for whom, and under what conditions. *Educational Evaluation and Policy Analysis, 42*(3), 354–374. https://doi.org/10.3102/0162373720929018

Stokes, D. E. (1997). *Pasteur's quadrant: Basic science and technological innovation.* Brookings Institution.

Weiss, C. H., Murphy-Graham, E., & Kirkland, S. (2005). An alternative route to policy influence: How evaluations affect D.A.R.E. *American Journal of Evaluation, 26*(1), 12–30.

6

Technology in STEM Education and the Emerging Frontier

Over the past decades, computer technologies have had profound impacts on education, especially as access to computers and the internet have increased in Pre-K–12 education settings. The creation and sale of educational technologies and related software (often referred to as "Ed Tech") is a huge global industry. Already a multibillion dollar market, projections for the global K–12 Ed Tech sector predict that it will reach multiple hundreds of billions of dollars by the end of this decade, with much of the growth in North America.[1] The goals and applications of Ed Tech products are quite varied, and include personalizing instruction, supporting learners with special needs, enabling collaborative learning, providing continuity between in- and out-of-school settings, assisting teachers in managing instruction and assessment, and preparing students to be digitally literate and capable as future workers and citizens. As technology tools are now being increasingly used in Pre-K–12 schools, it is important to understand how novel technologies can affect learning and teaching in science, technology, engineering, and mathematics (STEM) education, as they may commonly be embedded across a range of types of innovations.

It is beyond the scope of this report to conduct a comprehensive review of technology in education (see Duran, 2022 for an overview). The focus in the first part of this chapter is on an overview of some of the types of technology-based resources created specifically for STEM education that have been developed iteratively and studied sufficiently in recent decades

---

[1] See https://market.us/report/k-12-education-technology-edtech-market/#overview

to provide an evidence base on their potential impacts and the factors that affect how likely they are to spread more widely and to be taken up and adapted effectively in new contexts. The chapter also considers the emerging frontier of rapidly developing AI technologies in education, which have some distinctive and unprecedented advantages as well as risks. The chapter goes on to examine the potential of new technologies for expanding opportunities to learn and participate in STEM in powerful ways, while also considering persistent challenges of ensuring that these opportunities are fully and equitably accessible to students and schools regardless of geographic location, socioeconomic status, or student demographics. Finally, the chapter considers issues related to the rapid pace at which new technology-based resources may stream into Pre-K–12 education—a pace that is increasingly outstripping the standard capacities of research and policy making processes to vet their quality in a timely way and ensure their alignment with educational goals and student needs.

TECHNOLOGIES DESIGNED TO SUPPORT STEM LEARNING AND TEACHING

The committee begins with a brief discussion of research-based technologies that have demonstrated positive effects on students' learning and teaching practices in STEM through empirical research. It is important to note that the review is not exhaustive but describes some of the most widely used and researched technologies (see Table 6-1).

Simulations and Virtual Experiments

Virtual experiments using simulations have been widely used to help students learn, and research has found several strengths of virtual experiments for supporting students' learning such as enabling unique testing conditions that are impossible in real-world laboratories, highlighting conceptually salient features of experiments while constraining students' manipulation of relevant variables, allowing for the presentation of dynamically changing graphs and tables to enable students to test multiple "what-if" scenarios, seeing relationships between variables, and interpreting data more accurately (Chini et al., 2012; de Jong, Linn, & Zacharia, 2013; Puntambekar et al., 2021; Sullivan et al., 2017). However, educators also need to understand that simulations rely on models of real-world scenarios and, by necessity and definition, models strip away contextual elements to focus on specific phenomena. Further, students can quickly run trials during virtual labs, potentially leading them to engage in more trial and error or "play" types of behaviors, without thinking about underlying reasons for their experimental choices (Bumbacher et al., 2018; Renken &

TABLE 6-1 Technologies to Support Learning and Teaching

Type of Technology	What It Supports	Who It Supports	Benefits	Challenges
Simulations/ Virtual Experiments	• Support learning of macro & micro processes • Can visualize microscopic phenomena not visible to humans • Help understand time scales • Helps visualize large events • Support learning of science practices such as planning & carrying out investigations, analyzing data & generating explanations	Students	• Provide access to experimentation that may otherwise be impossible or too expensive • Integrate visualizations & multiple representations to support learning • Can constrain scenarios to help students focus on variables of interest • Provide opportunities for testing ideas quickly & conducting multiple trials	• Virtual experiments are models & scaled down versions of real phenomena • Students may not gain a full understanding of measurement & experimental error • Students may engage in play-like, less reflective use of the technology
Visualizations, Representations	• Help visualize macro & macro processes explore time scales and invisible phenomena • Visualize data & patterns to support science practices	Students	• Can support understanding of complex science phenomena at multiple scales • Data visualizations across time can support science practices • Promote representational competence	• Students might focus on surface, rather than deep features • Translating & making connections between representations can be difficult for novice learners
Models and Modeling	• Support learning of scientific content & processes at multiple scales • Help students understand multiple interacting levels in complex systems • Support practices such as using evidence to evaluate & revise science ideas	Students	• Help students engage in argument with evidence • Develop computational & systems thinking • Help make predictions about emergent phenomena	• Open-ended & complex, nonlinear practice that can be difficult for students

(*continued*)

TABLE 6-1 Continued

Type of Technology	What It Supports	Who It Supports	Benefits	Challenges
Immersive Environments	• Allow merging of digital content with physical environment • Allow students to experience 3D phenomena • Augmented reality, virtual reality environments can illustrate the spatial & temporal contiguity of scientific events	Students	• Allow learners to physically interact with complex science ideas allowing for richer experiences, and haptic feedback • AR systems are easy to use for younger students because they can use their body movements	• Use of AR & VR equipment classrooms may be costly and impractical • Space constraints & finding personnel to supervise activities can be challenging
Intelligent Tutoring Systems, Conversational and Dialogue Agents	• Support learning through virtual agents	Students	• Make thinking processes visible • Help students develop metacognitive processes & reflection skills	• Students might need additional scaffolds & support from teachers
Automated Assessments	• Assessment of science writing & revision • Assessment of students' inquiry skills • Provide summary of students' progress to teachers	Students and Teachers	• Reduce burden on teachers to provide formative, feedback on students' work • Provide immediate feedback on students' work to both students and teachers	• Not all automated feedback is comprehensible to students • Students may not know how to use the feedback
Dashboards for Classroom Orchestration	• Help teachers understand current states of students' learning & progress at the individual, group, & whole-class level	Teachers	• Support teachers in orchestrating complex, inquiry-based learning environments • Provide teachers with visualizations & information about students' activity, learner states, & performance to support pedagogical decision making	• Attending to multiple data streams in dashboards may be burdensome for teachers • Determining the right balance between amount & level of information provided is challenging

SOURCE: Puntambekar, 2024.

Nunez, 2013). Simulations can be used strategically to support learning of abstract content, or in instances where setting up physical labs might be expensive, dangerous, or time consuming—all of which are important considerations when selecting and potentially scaling innovations.

Visualizations and Multiples Representations

Visualizations can be part of simulations where students can manipulate variables, or they can be used as stand-alone entities to provide graphical, multiple representations of complex or invisible phenomena to foster learning. Visualizations range from static depictions to dynamic visualizations and can also range from concrete representations to abstract (Braithwaite & Goldstone, 2013), to mathematical and symbolic. Mathematical representations play an important role in helping students visualize data (Wu & Shah, 2004) across time scales. Research suggests that visual representations can support students' deeper content understanding (e.g., de Jong, 2006) and "representational competence," or the ability to understand and translate between representations (Shafrir, 1999). Nonetheless, research has also acknowledged that deeper learning with multiple representations depends on how students *translate* between representations, i.e., how students understand the connections across representations (e.g., Ainsworth 2006, 2014; Kozma & Russell, 2005) based on the core principles of the domain. Scaffolding translation by building support into the representations and by incorporating appropriate instructional strategies by the teacher are both effective in ameliorating difficulties that students face in understanding multiple representations.

Models and Modeling

While simulations are models created by others and made available as tools for teaching, modeling practices involve students in constructing, evaluating, and revising models. Research suggests that immersing students in model building means that they are engaging with content in authentic ways as they create, evaluate, and revise their ideas; in these ways, model building is an integral aspect of STEM (Gilbert & Justi, 2016). Studies have focused on various types of scaffolding that can be built in modeling environments to provide task- and strategy-specific adaptive feedback (Basu, Biswas, & Kinnebrew, 2017). Instructional scaffolds designed to support students' more open-ended, self-directed science inquiries using models can promote a greater understanding of science and the processes underlying the phenomena under study. Further, research has indicated that prompts to scaffold students' self-reflection and monitoring as they learn with models promote a more comprehensive grasp of the scientific concepts under investigation (Linn et al., 2018).

Immersive Environments

Immersive environments can include such things as augmented reality (AR) or mixed reality (MR) and virtual reality (VR) technologies. This is an emerging class of technologies that combine physical objects, actions, and environments with digital representations, either through augmenting the physical world with digital attributes or by augmenting a digital environment with aspects of the physical world. VR uses technologies that simulate an artificial environment; users experience this environment through senses such as sight, sound, and touch, and may be able to interact with it or receive feedback from it (Cromley, Chen, & Lawrence, 2023). AR technologies superimpose virtual objects onto the existing environment; users may be able to interact with them but are still able to see the real world around them (Scavarelli, Arya, & Teather, 2021). While meta-analyses have found that VR and AR interventions have positive effects on factual and conceptual learning as well as transfer tasks compared to instruction without the technology, it may vary by the pedagogical strategies used, subject, and classroom settings (Cromley, Chen, & Lawrence, 2023; Garzón et al., 2020; Xu et al., 2022). For example, Cromley and colleague's 2023 meta-analysis of studies of STEM learning in middle and high school found the strongest effects for VR combined with active learning, such as a specific constructive task or answering transfer questions that required students to transform information presented in the VR, rather than engaging in passive viewing. Garzón and Acevedo's 2019 meta-analysis of the impact of AR technologies on student learning classified three types of pedagogical strategies used in comparisons groups—multimedia, traditional lectures, and traditional pedagogical tools—and analyzed them as a moderator, finding that AR yielded significantly larger impacts on student learning than each of these. They also report particularly large effects on learning content related to engineering.

Immersion in the learning experiences seems to be a major affordance of VR/AR learning technologies; however, evaluating the ethical, practical, and safety implications of incorporating immersive VR in classrooms is essential before large-scale deployment. Practical considerations such as the constraints of time and curricula, not to mention the high hardware costs of immersive VR (e.g., head-mounted devices) must be taken into account. Not having adequate space or people to supervise students in immersive virtual environments has been found to be a major constraint, in addition to regular classroom constraints such as time and integration into full curricula (Southgate et al., 2019).

Intelligent Tutoring Systems and Agents

Automated intelligent technology systems have been used to support students learning for several decades. Intelligent Tutoring Systems (Koedinger & Corbett, 2006; VanLehn et al., 2016), conversation agents (e.g., Graesser, 2016; Ward et al., 2013), and dialogue agents (Katz et al., 2021) have been used to support STEM learning with benefits for learners in terms of mastery of the content knowledge addressed by the interventions. Teachable agents embedded in technology applications are based on research showing that learning by social interactions (Palincsar & Brown, 1984) and by teaching others have positive effects on learning (Biswas et al., 2005; Roscoe & Chi, 2007), as well as the benefits of active learning (Bransford, Brown, & Cocking, 2000). One of the notable aspects of teachable agents is that they can also make the thinking process visible to students (Chase et al., 2009), which can significantly impact learning and metacognition (Schwartz et al., 2009).

Automated Assessments

One of the key areas of intelligent technologies in education is that of automated scoring of students' written work (Celik et al., 2022), including assessments of students' inquiry skills (Gobert et al., 2018). This is an important area where Natural Language Processing (NLP) techniques can help by providing immediate feedback to students (Gerard & Linn, 2022; Zhai et al., 2020), while at the same time supporting teachers who often have little time to provide detailed feedback on students' written work. In a meta-analysis of 24 studies comparing automated adaptive guidance versus guidance provided in typical instruction, automated adaptive guidance was found to be significantly more effective. However, teachers can play an important role by using automated assessments and guidance provided by automated systems to inform their instruction (Puntambekar, 2024). New and emerging generations of such systems are discussed further in this chapter in the section on Artificial Intelligence.

Dashboards for Classroom Orchestration

Intelligent adaptive dashboards can help with classroom orchestration (Holstein, McLaren, & Aleven, 2019) by providing visualizations of critical real-time data on complex states (Dickler, Gobert, & Pedro, 2021), assisting with adaptive decision making, and identifying areas requiring attention. Dynamic algorithms can be applied to assess progress based on features sensed within the environment and correspondingly inform dashboard visualizations. Research suggests that visualizations of group progress and individual student's work helps teachers to identify groups and/or individuals requiring the teacher's attention and support (Martinez-Maldonado et al., 2015). Although real-time dashboards on dedicated teacher devices have proven effective, they can also increase the burden on teachers by requiring them to manage multiple data streams simultaneously (Martinez-Maldonado et al., 2015). However, co-designing and prototyping dashboards with input from teachers has helped in designing dashboards that balance orchestration loads and the important information that teachers need for effective management orchestration (Olsen, Rummel, & Aleven, 2021).

EMERGING FRONTIERS: ARTIFICIAL INTELLIGENCE IN EDUCATION

Given the current moment, it is important to consider the role of innovation within Pre-K–12 STEM education with respect to some of the contemporary shifts caused by recent advances in artificial intelligence (AI). In the time since this report was commissioned, society has seen an explosion in the prominence and ubiquity of AI, largely fueled by large language models (LLMs). In some respects, the large organizations that develop and maintain widely used LLMs are dominating the innovation landscape, and exemplify scaling, but with minimal indications around how these technologies might be used most effectively. It is worth noting that applications of AI to STEM education have been in development for more than half a century, including some of the applications discussed in the previous section. What distinguishes many of the current technologies from early developments of AI in education is the wider set of activities that current AI in education technologies can afford teachers, learners, administrators, parents, and organizations; the opportunity to significantly shift who participates in STEM; what that participation looks like; where these experiences take place; and how learning and engagement are recorded and analyzed.

Looking across the AI in education landscape, and specifically examining ways that AI can shift who participates in learning, there are several examples where AI has enabled new forms of access. For instance, technologies that support speech recognition (Southwell et al., 2024), eye tracking (Ke et al., 2024), and gesture-based input (Abrahamson, Ryokai, & Dimmel, 2024) have created additional opportunities for people with disabilities to engage with otherwise inaccessible STEM content and experiences (Worsley et al., 2021). This expansion in accessibility can result from offering multimodal input and by enabling multimodal outputs that make fewer assumptions about user ability. While far from perfect, many of these input and output modalities are available through contemporary VR headsets and through the use of computer vision. These interfaces can also allow younger students to access and engage with increasingly complex concepts and ideas, once again, pointing to a shift in who is invited to participate in STEM learning experiences (Worsely et al., 2021).

Examples of gesture-based input, or embodied learning experiences, also point to innovations in what learning itself looks like. Instead of the traditional practices of reading textbooks, learners may be transported into a virtual world where they conduct scientific experiments alongside peers and adults from around the world (Lester al., 2014).[2] Such programs exemplify how educational technology can help realize computer-supported collaborative learning. Even in the absence of other humans participating in a virtual space, recent technological innovations can support learners through intelligent virtual agents that embody human-like characteristics and can support guided inquiry across an infinite number of learning contexts (Johnson & Lester, 2016). These intelligent virtual agents, or intelligent tutors, take many forms and can offer the types of personalization that society has grown to expect from commercial recommendations systems.

In the traditional in-person classroom context, AI technologies are being used to transform the classroom experience. Technologies that hinge on AI capabilities can be found in the robots and AI-partners that support classroom inclusion, discussion, and engagement (D'Mello et al., 2024). Broadly speaking, researchers and educators are able to leverage AI to shift the classroom experience into something that is more collaborative and fluid than the types of experiences that dominated the 20th century classroom.

Technology is also transforming where learning takes place. The COVID-19 pandemic and the shift to remote learning is one example of how technological innovations enabled classroom-based learning to become increasingly accessible from home. Additionally, researchers are leveraging mobile technologies, for example, to support learning within community-based settings and while navigating different geographical spaces. Many of the initiatives within this line of work take advantage of GPS technologies, and the exciting ways that learners can leverage technology to interact with and capture rich information about the world around them (Marin et al., 2020; Taylor, 2017). As previously highlighted, AI technologies are also being used to support learning within and through virtual reality. Virtual experiences, which range from the use

---

[2]Note, that this might not be fully aligned with contemporary standards and ideas about science practices. More generally, emerging technologies may usher in paradigm shifts and new modes of activity that may challenge current views of learning and best practices in instruction. Research will be necessary to evaluate whether they are successful, and if so, for whom and under what conditions.

of specialized headsets to content experienced through a computer screen, might enable learners to navigate a distant geographical location, tour a nearby museum, or visit a mythical world of their own creation. The idea of students creating their own virtual content is one of the unique aspects of contemporary AI. The level of technical proficiency needed to create digital content has drastically decreased over the past ten years. Students and teachers now have access to powerful AI tools in easy-to-use, low-cost, web-based platforms that require little prior experience with traditional programming languages (Vadaparty et al., 2024; Weintrop, 2019).

Finally, researchers and schools are using AI to rethink important aspects about how to study, support, and measure student learning. This ranges from analytics approaches (Blikstein & Worsley, 2016) to detecting how students might feel about a given learning experience (Loderer, Pekrun, & Lester, 2020) to building computational models of student pathways through different educational settings (Pardos, Chau, & Zhao, 2019; Shao, Guo, & Pardos, 2021). It also includes ways for expanding what the field considers as indicators of student learning. For instance, many researchers have access to automated transcripts of learner-spoken utterances that can be used to better understand how well students are connecting with course content and adopting disciplinary content. To take this one step further, educators might then use that information to inform how they design upcoming lessons. These are simply a small collection of the vast integration points between AI and educational technology. And that landscape continues to grow as additional tools become increasingly accessible to learners, educators, and communities around the country.

CLOSING DIGITAL DIVIDES AND CREATING EQUITABLE STEM LEARNING OPPORTUNITIES FOR ALL STUDENTS

Although the development and implementation of Ed Tech resources in STEM has great promise and may empower more students in many cases, it can also be biased in various ways or distributed unevenly in ways that perpetuate inequities in education (National Academies of Sciences, Engineering, and Medicine [NASEM], 2022; U.S. Department of Education, Office of Educational Technology, 2024). The recent 2024 National Educational Technology Plan (NETP) highlighted three digital divides that impact the equitable support of learning with Ed Tech:

1. *Digital use divide*: refers to the divide between students who have access to innovative digital tools that help them actively analyze, build, produce, and create such as those described in the previous section, versus students who are asked to use technology only for passive assignments;

2. *Digital design divide*: refers to inequitable opportunities for educators to build their professional capacity to design learning experiences for students that use Ed Tech resources; and
3. *Digital access divide*: refers to inequitable access to connectivity, devices, and digital content.

Each of these digital divides is important, and they need to be considered together. The abrupt need for remote learning during the COVID-19 pandemic, and the emergency funding that became available as a result, spurred many schools to dramatically increase their students' access to devices and improved connectivity (NASEM, 2020). Because so many tech-enabled educational resources are web-based, robust internet access in all schools and access to a sufficient number of devices that are available on demand in classrooms and kept updated and functioning have become foundational necessities for modern education. As of the end of 2023, about three-quarters of public school districts across the country were meeting the goal of bandwidth of at least 1 Mbps per student, which the Federal Communications Commission (FCC) has deemed sufficient to support digital learning, as reported in the ConnectK12 *2023 Report on School Connectivity*. Although this has been a heartening increase over previous years, many millions of students are in public schools that still lack adequate bandwidth. Students' access to internet outside of school also remains a challenge. Due to a lack of continuing funding from Congress, the FCC's Affordable Connectivity Program, which had helped lower income households afford broadband, was discontinued as of June 2024.[3] Patterns of access in both schools and homes have mirrored the well-known problems of uneven and inequitable distribution of resources, often correlated with social and economic segregation and school funding policies. Rural areas, and rural tribal areas in particular (Mack et al., 2022), have been especially vulnerable to the higher costs per megabit of broadband and the sparseness of internet fiber systems.

As noted previously, some technology-enhanced learning resources have requirements that go well beyond merely having broadband access. Technologies that require specialized hardware, such as VR headsets, may be prohibitively expensive to provide in sufficient numbers to entire classrooms and hard to manage even in wealthier schools with smaller class sizes and good staff support. Many technologies also impose a heavy burden of set-up and maintenance, battery charging, and maintaining compatibility with school or district operating systems and firewalls. However, new technologies often become more affordable and easier to use as they are on the market for a while. As individual schools and districts make local decisions

---
[3] See https://www.fcc.gov/acp

about trade-offs between costs of implementation and return on investment, it is likely that socioeconomics will be a significant driver in which schools acquire new technologies, when they acquire them, and how they distribute or ration them.

While making progress on reducing the *digital access divide* is necessary, it is not sufficient on its own. Research indicates that improved access by itself has little impact on student outcomes and may even have negative impacts (Escueta et al., 2020). Consistent positive results are seen when access to devices and good connectivity are coupled with high-quality digital content and pedagogical activities, as highlighted in the NETP's framing of the *digital use divide*. However, as discussed in the next section, many Ed Tech products have not been thoroughly researched and lack evidence one way or the other as to their educational effectiveness. During the COVID-19 pandemic, many schools took up new digital resources on an emergency basis, without the benefit of careful selection and planning processes or systems for managing and evaluating change. Often, the technological solutions were attempts to find quick substitutes for traditional teaching practices, such as having students view online content or take online tests, and many administrators and teachers still have not had sufficient time or support to systematically build their capacity to understand, evaluate, and coordinate more active and innovative uses of educational technologies. Many factors, such as pedagogy, underlying curricula, participatory structures, and teachers, play an essential role in helping students understand how and why these tools have been designed in certain ways and how they can be used to promote reflection, solve problems, and accomplish goals. Ensuring that all educators have equitable access to time and professional learning resources to build this capacity is central to bridging the *digital design divide*.

Recognizing and closing the existing digital divides described in the 2024 NETP is essential to overcoming traditional patterns of inequity in who has access to and who benefits from the distribution of educational resources. However, it is also important to consider ways in which emerging technologies may be powerful tools for promoting and sustaining new kinds of opportunities for all learners, with inclusiveness built into their foundations. One challenge for addressing equity in education is that it often entails disrupting entrenched patterns that tend to reify inequities or that routinely exclude or marginalize certain students, such as students with learning differences (NASEM, 2022, 2024). Incorporating new technologies into teaching and learning tends to be disruptive by its nature, but this disruption can be viewed as offering opportunities to remake learning experiences in new ways that promote participation, a sense of belonging, and meaningful learning for all students. The recent National Academies consensus report on *Equity in K–12 STEM Education* emphasizes the importance of goals such as promoting students' agency, supporting sense-making during learning, and leveraging linguistic and cultural assets and ways of knowing (NASEM, 2024). As highlighted in the previous section of this chapter, there is striking potential for innovative technologies to be shaped and applied in ways that expand and diversify types and modalities of participation in STEM learning, while also cultivating interest and broadening opportunities for all students to form a strong identity as someone who can learn and use STEM. Technologies can also provide opportunities to connect classrooms—in potentially vivid and engaging ways—to other people and resources in students' local communities as well as around the world. This may help cultivate a sense of STEM as a dynamic shared enterprise with many different participants. If they are properly designed and deployed, new technologies offer the means to advance these goals. The NETP provides examples of principles and practices, such as the research-based Universal Design for Learning (UDL) framework, that can guide the design and use of Ed Tech to improve and optimize teaching and learning by reducing barriers and addressing individual and sociocultural learning needs.

Finally, Ed Tech offers the potential for new solutions to the persistent problem of the role of assessment in improving and reforming education to promote equity. As noted in Chapter 3, the current large-scale assessment practices ushered in with No Child Left Behind (NCLB) have exposed persistent performance gaps across groups of students but have also led to frustration that many existing high stakes assessments do not illuminate what is or is not happening during learning to explain those gaps and to understand what might be done to change them. Current and emerging technologies provide access to new types of data and analytic methods to better reveal and understand student learning processes and classroom activity, including fine-grained data about what individuals and interacting groups are doing and what they are accomplishing throughout learning. These go well beyond summative assessments and standardized test scores and have the potential to provide new windows into learning for students and families as well as teachers and administrators. As innovative assessment technologies are developed and implemented, it is imperative to ensure that their purposes and uses are clearly and transparently articulated and appropriately aligned to specific goals (NRC, 2001), while also attending to concerns about algorithmic or analytic biases and students' and teachers' autonomy and privacy.

MANAGING THE RAPID PACE OF EMERGING TECHNOLOGIES IN EDUCATION

An increasing proportion of innovations in STEM education involve the creation and application of various kinds of digital technologies, and, while some of the benefits and challenges to implementation and scaling are similar to resources that are not technology-based, new applications of technology in education also have some unique features and considerations. In this section, we look at factors that are specific to educational improvements that are rooted in new applications of digital technologies.

While innovation is robust in the Ed Tech industry, it also poses some unique challenges. Ed Tech is an unusually fastmoving enterprise with many players, often working in market-driven contexts and capitalizing on the availability of new technologies in the general consumer market (Dube & Wen, 2022). The speed at which new technologies and products are marketed and purchased (or otherwise acquired) far outpaces the ability of researchers and decision makers to keep up with evaluating them (Escueta et al., 2019). Traditional research cycles used to obtain high-quality evidence of effectiveness or impact are much longer than the time it takes for new Ed Tech products to appear and become obsolete. Products that are heavily marketed or that incorporate popular features (e.g., gaming features) may achieve widespread adoption without any assurance that they are educationally effective. This rapid pace of development and change has prompted a need to re-think the relationship between research processes and implementation of Ed Tech resources. A recent National Academies report on the *Future of Education Research at IES* (NASEM, 2022) addressed this issue and highlighted the need for new research to guide the design of new tools so that they are grounded in theoretical mechanisms of learning and serve the needs of learners, to build understanding of relationships between new technologies and the learning environments in which they are employed, and to cultivate the capacity of educators to evaluate and integrate new Ed Tech resources.

A recent comprehensive review (Escueta et al., 2020) found that relatively few Ed Tech products have robust data that can support causal conclusions, such as evidence obtained from a randomized controlled trial or a regression discontinuity design. For products in the general category of computer-assisted learning, null results are common. A few mathematics products have demonstrated the strongest results, including the online math homework support system ASSISTments (Roschelle et al., 2016) and interactive SimCalc software for algebra and preparation for calculus (Hegedus, Dalton, & Tapper, 2015; Roschelle et al., 2010). Key positive features for products with good evidence of results are adaptivity to students at different levels, rapid feedback and guidance to students, and formative assessment data for teachers. It is worth noting that this level of evidence represents a high bar, and very few of the Ed Tech resources marketed to schools have been studied in this way.

In part because it is so challenging for education research to keep up with the pace of change in AI in particular, it is essential to formulate principles and policies to govern and support the use of these powerful new technologies in ways that will address priorities in teaching and learning and advance equity, while modulating potential risks or unintended consequences. Compared to prior technologies, emerging AI is now accelerating a shift from capturing data efficiently to detecting patterns in very large and fine-grained sets of data and automating decisions about teaching and learning processes. As discussed above, it enables new forms of engagement and interaction among teachers, learners, and automated systems, and does so in ways that can address variability among learners and increase adaptivity. It can also provide teachers with data and tools to make their work easier and better. At the same time, it poses significant risks, including issues of data privacy and security, lack of alignment with educational goals and priorities, and algorithmic discrimination in the development and application of tools. As AI algorithms and models may increasingly be used for automating decisions about learning processes as well as about students' status and access to resources (e.g., tracking into special programs, school admissions, or support services), methods for evaluating and ensuring the fairness of algorithmic decision making is consequential but such methods are currently unsettled (Holstein & Doroudi, 2021). The potential for bias can arise for reasons both internal and external to how these algorithms operate. Whose data are represented in the historical data used to train them, what evaluation metrics are used, and whether technical development is informed by broader contexts of usage and how different students may experience those contexts are critical considerations. As one example of how AI algorithms and models can propagate bias, if certain groups of learners or learning contexts are overrepresented in training datasets, then generalization to new and different groups and settings may be poor and could even end up widening divides among groups. Machine learning algorithms generally try to optimize overall prediction accuracy and may thus bias or overweight data from majority groups in the data. As a result, predictions and classifications may be less accurate for various subgroups of users if they are not well represented in the training set (Ocumpaugh et al., 2014).

In stark contrast to many other innovations the committee reviewed, some powerful AI resources are widely accessible as consumer products and have the potential to spread very rapidly among individuals and groups (including students), without going through formal processes to vet them and integrate them in educational settings in an intentional and thoughtful manner. A recent report from the U.S. Department of Education's Office of Educational Technology analyzed the current state of AI in education and formulated a set of recommendations as guidance (U.S. Department of Education, Office of Educational Technology, 2023). These recommendations are summarized in Box 6-1.

BOX 6-1
Recommendations on AI and the Future of Teaching and Learning

A recent report by the U.S. Department of Education's Office of Education Technology analyzed the current state of AI in education. Based upon that analysis, the group made the following recommendations:

- **Emphasize Humans-in-the-Loop.** Teachers and other people must be "in the loop" whenever AI is applied in order to notice patterns and automate educational processes.
- **Align AI Models to a Shared Vision for Education.** Educational decision makers, researchers, and evaluators are needed to determine the quality of an educational technology based not only on outcomes, but also on the degree to which the models at the heart of the AI tools and systems align to a shared vision for teaching and learning.
- **Design AI Using Modern Learning Principles.** Achieving effective systems requires more than processing "big data." Applications of AI must be based on established, modern learning principles, and the wisdom of educational practitioners, and leverage the expertise in the educational assessment community around detecting bias and improving fairness.
- **Prioritize Strengthening Trust.** Technology can aid in achieving educational objectives when there is trust. Trust develops as people meet and relate to each other; there needs to be a focus on building trust and establishing criteria for trustworthiness of emerging educational technologies.
- **Inform and Involve Educators.** Educational leaders need to prioritize informing and involving educational constituents so that they are prepared to investigate how and when AI fits specific teaching and learning needs, and what risks may rise.
- **Focus Research & Development on Addressing Context and Enhancing Trust and Safety.** Researchers and funders need to prioritize investigations of how AI can address the long tail of learning variability and seek advances in how AI can incorporate contextual consideration when detecting patterns and recommend options to students and teachers. Immediate research is needed on how to enhance trust and safety in AI-enabled systems for education.
- **Develop Education-specific Guidelines and Guardrails.** Data privacy regulation already covers educational technology; further, data security is already a priority of school educational technology.

SOURCE: Based on U.S. Department of Education, Office of Educational Technology, 2023.

SUMMARY

It is clear that multiple forms of technology have shown evidence for supporting STEM learning and teaching. Although digital technologies can be powerful learning tools, simply giving students access to technology does not necessarily promote learning. Tools and technologies rarely fully communicate meaning or information about how they can be best used, especially to support learning and cultural practices. Many other factors such as pedagogy, underlying curricula, participatory structures, and teachers play an essential role in helping students understand how and why these tools have been designed in certain ways and how they can be used to promote reflection, solve problems, and accomplish goals. Therefore, it is important to interrogate promising, evidence-based innovations for the features that support (and constrain) their scalability and sustainability. In considering how technology-based resources are acquired by schools and are adapted to new settings and learners, equity concerns are particularly prominent, given that they simultaneously have strong potential to both increase existing digital divides, as well as open powerful new avenues for including and supporting students who have often been under-served or left out of STEM learning.

Emergent AI-based technologies hold unique promise for addressing difficult problems in new ways, but they also bring some potential risks, and scaling them and applying them effectively in education involves some special considerations. The educational technology industry tends to be fast-moving and market-driven, with many developers based in for-profit companies rather than research organizations or education-focused organizations. As a result, concerns may be less about how quickly or robustly a given innovation can be scaled and more about whether there is reliable evidence of its efficacy, whether it is aligned with educational goals and policies, and whether students' needs are being served safely and equitably.

REFERENCES

Abrahamson, D., Ryokai, K., & Dimmel, J. (2024). Learning mathematics with digital resources: Reclaiming the cognitive role of physical movement. In B. Pepin, G. Gueudet, and J. Choppin. (Eds.) *Handbook of digital resources in mathematics education. Springer International Handbooks of Education.* Springer.

Ainsworth, S. (2006). DeFT: A conceptual framework for considering learning with multiple representations. *Learning and Instruction, 16*(3), 183–198.

———. (2014). The multiple representation principle in multimedia learning. In R. E. Mayer (Ed.), *The Cambridge handbook of multimedia learning* (2nd ed., pp. 464–486). Cambridge University Press.

Basu, S., Biswas, G., & Kinnebrew, J. S. (2017). Learner modeling for adaptive scaffolding in a computational thinking-based science learning environment. *User Modeling and User-Adapted Interaction, 27*, 5–53.

Biswas, G., Leelawong, K., Schwartz, D., Vye, N., & The Teachable Agents Group at Vanderbilt. (2005). Learning by teaching: A new agent paradigm for educational software. *Applied Artificial Intelligence, 19*(3–4), 363–392.

Blikstein, P., & Worsley, M. (2016). Multimodal learning analytics and education data mining: Using computational technologies to measure complex learning tasks. *Journal of Learning Analytics, 3*(2), 220–238.

Braithwaite, D. W., & Goldstone, R. L. (2013). Integrating formal and grounded representations in combinatorics learning. *Journal of Educational Psychology, 105*(3), 666–682.

Bransford, J. D., Brown, A. L., & Cocking, R. R. (2000). *How people learn.* The National Academy Press.

Bumbacher, E., Salehi, S., Wieman, C., & Blikstein, P. (2018). Tools for science inquiry learning: Tool affordances, experimentation strategies, and conceptual understanding. *Journal of Science Education and Technology, 27*(3), 215–235.

Celik, I., Dindar, M., Muukkonen, H., & Järvelä, S. (2022). The promises and challenges of artificial intelligence for teachers: A systematic review of research. *TechTrends, 66*(4), 616–630.

Chase, C. C., Chin, D. B., Oppezzo, M. A., & Schwartz, D. L. (2009). Teachable agents and the protégé effect: Increasing the effort towards learning. *Journal of Science Education and Technology, 18*(4), 334–352.

Chini, J. J., Madsen, A., Gire, E., Rebello, N. S., & Puntambekar, S. (2012). Exploration of factors that affect the comparative effectiveness of physical and virtual manipulatives in an undergraduate laboratory. *Physical Review Special Topics-Physics Education Research, 8*(1), 010–113.

ConnectK12. (2023). *Report on school connectivity: Connect K–12.* ConnectK12.org, https://s3.amazonaws.com/connected-nation/898e8ecb-8046-4850-af4b-b89b12c1a4a1/Connect_K12_Connectivity_Report_2023_FINAL.pdf

Cromley, J. G., Chen, R., & Lawrence, L. (2023). Meta-analysis of STEM learning using virtual reality: Benefits across the board. *Journal of Science Education and Technology, 32*(3), 355–364.

D'Mello, S. K., Biddy, Q., Breideband, T., Bush, J., Chang, M., Cortez, A., Flanigan, J., Foltz, P. W., Gorman, J. C., Hirshfield, L., Ko, M. L. M., Krishnaswamy, N., Lieber, R., Martin, J., Palmer, M., Penuel, W. R., Phillip, T., Puntambekar, S., Pustejovsky, J., Reitman, J. G., Sumner, T., Tissenbaum, M., Walker, L., & Whitehill, J. (2024). From learning optimization to learner flourishing: Reimagining AI in education at the Institute for Student-AI Teaming (iSAT). *AI Magazine, 45*(1), 61–68.

de Jong, T. (2006) Computer simulations: Technological advances in inquiry learning. *Science, 312,* 532–533.

de Jong, T., Linn, M. C., & Zacharia, Z. C. (2013). Physical and virtual laboratories in science and engineering education. *Science, 340*(6130), 305–308.

Dickler, R., Gobert, J., & Pedro, M. S. (2021). Using innovative methods to explore the potential of an alerting dashboard for science inquiry. *Journal of Learning Analytics, 8*(2), 105–122.

Dube, A. K., & Wen, R. (2022). Identification and evaluation of technology trends in K-12 education from 2011 to 2021. *Education and Information Technologies, 27,* 1929–1958. https://doi.org/10.1007/s10639-021-10689-8

Duran, M. (2022). *Learning technologies: Research, trends, and issues in the U.S. education system.* Springer International Publishing.

Escueta, M., Nickow, A. J., Oreopoulos, P., & Quan, V. (2020). Upgrading education with technology. *Journal of Economic Literature, 58*(4), 897–996.

Garzón, J., & Acevedo, J. (2019). Meta-analysis of the impact of Augmented Reality on students' learning gains. *Educational Research Review, 27,* 244–260.

Garzón, J., Baldiris, S., Gutiérrez, J., & Pavón, J. (2020). How do pedagogical approaches affect the impact of augmented reality on education? A meta-analysis and research synthesis. *Educational Research Review, 31,* 100334.

Gerard, L. F., & Linn, M. C. (2022). Computer-based guidance to support student revision of their science explanations. *Computers & Education, 176,* 304–351.

Gilbert, J. K., & Justi, R. S. (2016). *Modelling-based teaching in science education.* Springer.

Gobert, J., Moussavi, R., Li, H., Sao Pedro, M., & Dickler, R. (2018). Real-time scaffolding of students' online data interpretation during inquiry with Inq-ITS using educational data mining. In A. K. M. Azad, M. Auer, A. Edwards, and T. de Jong (Eds.), *Cyber-physical laboratories in engineering and science education.* Springer.

Graesser, A. C. (2016). Conversations with AutoTutor help students learn. *International Journal of Artificial Intelligence in Education, 26,* 124–132. https://doi.org/10.1007/s40593-015-0086-4

Hegedus, S. J., Dalton, S., & Tapper, J. R. (2015). The impact of technology-enhanced curriculum on learning advanced algebra in US high school classrooms. *Educational Technology Research and Development, 63*(2), 203–228.

Holstein, K., & Doroudi, S. (2021). Equity and artificial intelligence in education: Will "AIEd" *amplify* or *alleviate* inequities in education? *arXiv.* https://doi.org/10.48550/arXiv.2104.12920

Holstein, K., McLaren, B. M., & Aleven, V. (2019). Co-designing a real-time classroom orchestration tool to support teacher–AI complementarity. *Journal of Learning Analytics, 6*(2), 27–52.

Johnson, W. L., & Lester, J. C. (2016). Face-to-face interaction with pedagogical agents, twenty years later. *International Journal of Artificial Intelligence in Education, 26,* 25–36. https://doi.org/10.1007/s40593-015-0065-9

Katz, S., Albacete, P., Chounta, I. A., Jordan, P., McLaren, B. M., & Zapata-Rivera, D. (2021). Linking dialogue with student modelling to create an adaptive tutoring system for conceptual physics. *International Journal of Artificial Intelligence in Education, 31*(3), 397–445.

Ke, F., Liu, R., Sokolikj, Z. Dahlstrom-Hakki, I., & Israel, M. (2024). Using eye-tracking in education: Review of empirical research and technology. *Educational Technology Research and Development,* 1–36.

Koedinger, K. R., & Corbett, A. (2006). Cognitive tutors: Technology bringing learning sciences to the classroom. In R. K. Sawyer (Ed.), *The Cambridge handbook of the learning sciences* (pp. 61–77). Cambridge University Press.

Kozma, R., & Russell, J. (2005). Students becoming chemists: Developing representational competence. In J. Gilbert (Ed.), *Visualization in science education.* Kluwer.

Lester, J. C., Spires, H. A., Nietfeld, J. L., Minogue, J., Mott, B. W., & Lobene, E. V. (2014). Designing game-based learning environments for elementary science education: A narrative-centered learning perspective. *Information Sciences, 264,* 4–18. https://doi.org/10.1016/j.ins.2013.09.005

Linn, M. C., McElhaney, K. W., Gerard, L., & Matuk, C. (2018). Inquiry learning and opportunities for technology. In F. Fischer, C. E. Hmelo-Silver, S. R. Goldman, & P. Reimann (Eds.), *International handbook of the learning sciences* (pp. 221–233). Routledge.

Loderer, K., Pekrun, R., & Lester, J. C. (2020). Beyond cold technology: A systematic review and meta-analysis on emotions in technology-based learning environments. *Learning and Instruction, 70,* 101162. https://doi.org/10.1016/j.learninstruc.2018.08.002

Mack, E. A., Helderop, E., Keene, T., Loveridge, S., Mann, J., Grubesic, T. H., Kowalkowski, B., & Gollnow, M. (2022). A longitudinal analysis of broadband provision in tribal areas. *Telecommunications Policy, 46*(5), https://doi.org/10.1016/j.telpol.2022.102333

Marin, A., Taylor, K. H., Shapiro, B. R., & Hall, R. (2020). Why learning on the move: Intersecting research pathways for mobility, learning and teaching. *Cognition and Instruction, 38*(3), 265–280. https://doi.org/10.1080/07370008.2020.1769100

Martinez-Maldonado, R., Clayphan, A., Yacef, K., & Kay, J. (2015). MTFeedback: Providing notifications to enhance teacher awareness of small group work in the classroom. *IEEE Transactions on Learning Technologies*, 8(2), 187–200.

National Academies of Sciences, Engineering, and Medicine (NASEM). (2020). *Reopening K–12 schools during the COVID-19 pandemic: Prioritizing health, equity, and communities*. The National Academies Press. https://doi.org/10.17226/25858

———. (2022). *The future of education research at IES: Advancing an equity-oriented science*. The National Academies Press. https://doi.org/10.17226/26428

———. (2024). *Equity in K–12 STEM education: Framing decisions for the future*. The National Academies Press. https://doi.org/10.17226/26859

National Research Council. (2001). *Knowing what students know: The science and design of educational assessment*. National Academies Press.

Ocumpaugh, J., Baker, R., Gowda, S., Heffernan, N., & Heffernan, C. (2014). Population validity for educational data mining models: A case study in affect detection. *British Journal of Educational Technology*, 45(3), 487–501.

Olsen, J. K., Rummel, N., & Aleven, V. (2021). Designing for the co-orchestration of social transitions between individual, small-group and whole-class learning in the classroom. *International Journal of Artificial Intelligence in Education*, 31, 24–56.

Palinscar, A. S., & Brown, A. L. (1984). Reciprocal teaching of comprehension-fostering and comprehension-monitoring activities. *Cognition and Instruction*, 1(2), 117–175.

Pardos, Z. A., Chau, H., & Zhao, H. (2019, June). Data-assistive course-to-course articulation using machine translation. In *Proceedings of the Sixth (2019) ACM Conference on Learning@ Scale* (pp. 1–10).

Puntambekar, S. (2024). [Technology for science learning and teaching]. Paper commissioned by the Committee on Pre-K–12 STEM Education Innovations. https://nap.nationalacademies.org/resource/27950/Technology%20for%20Science%20Learning%20and%20Teaching_Puntambekar.pdf

Puntambekar, S., Gnesdilow, D., Dornfeld Tissenbaum, C. D., Narayanan, H. N., & Rebello, S. (2021). Supporting middle school students' science talk: A comparison of physical and virtual labs. *Journal of Research in Science Teaching*, 58(3), 392–419.

Puntambekar, S., Gnesdilow, D., Passonneau, R. J., & Kim, C (2024). AI-human partnership to help students write science explanations. *Learning as a cornerstone of healing, resilience, and community: Proceedings of the 18th International Conference of the Learning Sciences -ICLS 2024*. International Society of the Learning Sciences.

Renken, M. D., & Nunez, N. (2013). Computer simulations and clear observations do not guarantee conceptual understanding. *Learning and Instruction*, 23, 10–23.

Roschelle, J., Feng, M., Murphy, R. F., & Mason, C. A. (2016). Online mathematics homework increases student achievement. *AERA Open*, 2(4), 2332858416673968.

Roschelle, J., Shechtman, N., Tatar, D., Hegedus, S., Hopkins, B., Empson, S., Knudsen, J., & Gallagher, L. P. (2010). Integration of technology, curriculum, and professional development for advancing middle school mathematics: Three large-scale studies. *American Educational Research Journal*, 47(4), 833–878.

Roscoe, R. D., & Chi, M. T. (2007). Understanding tutor learning: Knowledge-building and knowledge-telling in peer tutors' explanations and questions. *Review of Educational Research*, 77(4), 534–574.

Scavarelli, A., Arya, A., & Teather, R. J. (2021). Virtual reality and augmented reality in social learning spaces: A literature review. *Virtual Reality*, 25(1), 257–277.

Schwartz, C. V., Reiser, B. J., Davis, E. A., Kenyon, L., Achér, A., Fortus, D., Shwartz, Y., Hug, B., & Krajcik, J. (2009). Developing a learning progression for scientific modeling: Making scientific modeling accessible and meaningful for learners. *Journal of Research in Science Teaching*, 46(6), 632–654.

Shafrir, U. (1999). Representational competence. In I. E. Sigel (Ed.), *Development of mental representation: Theories and applications* (pp. 371–389). Lawrence Erlbaum Associates Publishers.

Shao, E., Guo, S., & Pardos, Z. A. (2021). Degree planning with Plan-Bert: Multi-semester recommendation using future courses of interest. *Proceedings of the AAAI Conference on Artificial Intelligence, 35*(17), 14920–14929. https://doi.org/10.1609/aaai.v35i17.17751

Southgate, E., Smith, S. P., Cividino, C., Saxby, S., Kilham, J., Eather, G., Scevak, J., Summerville, D., Buchanan, R., & Bergin, C. (2019). Embedding immersive virtual reality in classrooms: Ethical, organisational and educational lessons in bridging research and practice. *International Journal of Child-Computer Interaction, 19*, 19–29.

Southwell, R., Ward, W., Trinh, V. A., Clevenger, C., Clevenger, C., Watts, E., Reitman J., D'Mello, S., & Whitehill, J. (2024, April). Automatic speech recognition tuned for child speech in the classroom. In *ICASSP 2024–2024 IEEE International Conference on Acoustics, Speech and Signal Processing (ICASSP)* (pp. 12291–12295). IEEE. https://doi.org/10.1109/ICASSP48485.2024.10447428.

Sullivan, S., Gnesdilow, D., Puntambekar, S., & Kim, J. S. (2017). Middle school students' learning of mechanics concepts through engagement in different sequences of physical and virtual experiments. *International Journal of Science Education, 39*(12), 1573–1600.

Taylor, J., Roth, K., Wilson, C., Stuhlsatz, M., & Tipton, E. (2017). The effect of an analysis-of-practice, videocase-based, teacher professional development program on elementary students' science achievement. *Journal of Research on Educational Effectiveness, 10*(2), 241–271.

U.S. Department of Education, Office of Educational Technology. (2023). Artificial intelligence and the future of teaching and learning: Insights and recommendations. https://www.ed.gov/sites/ed/files/documents/ai-report/ai-report.pdf

———. (2024). A call to action for closing the digital access, design, and use divides: 024 National Educational Technology Plan. https://www.govinfo.gov/content/pkg/GOVPUB-ED-PURL-gpo229250/pdf/GOVPUB-ED-PURL-gpo229250.pdf

Vadaparty, A., Zingaro, D., Smith IV, D. H., Padala, M., Alvarado, C., Gorson Benario, J., & Porter, L. (2024). CS1-LLM: Integrating LLMs into CS1 instruction. In *Proceedings of the 2024 on Innovation and Technology in Computer Science Education* (Vol. 1, pp. 297–303).

VanLehn, K., Wetzel, J., Grover, S., & van de Sande, B. (2016). Learning how to construct models of dynamic systems: The effectiveness of the Dragoon intelligent tutoring system. *IEEE Transactions on Learning Technologies*.

Ward, W., Cole, R., Bolaños, D., Buchenroth-Martin, C., Svirsky, E., & Weston, T. (2013). My science tutor: A conversational multimedia virtual tutor. *Journal of Educational Psychology, 105*(4), 1115–1125.

Weintrop, D. (2019). Block-based programming in computer science education. *Communications of the ACM, 62*(8), 22–25.

Worsley, M., Mendoza Tudares, K., Mwiti, T., Zhen, M., & Jiang, M. (2021). Multicraft: A multimodal interface for supporting and studying learning in Minecraft. In X. Fang (Eds.) *HCI in Games: Serious and Immersive Games. HCII 2021. Lecture Notes in Computer Science, 12790*. Springer.

Wu, H., & Shah, P. (2004). Exploring visuospatial thinking in chemistry learning. *Science Education, 88*(3), 465–492.

Xu, W. W., Su, C. Y., Hu, Y., & Chen, C. H. (2022). Exploring the effectiveness and moderators of augmented reality on science learning: A meta-analysis. *Journal of Science Education and Technology, 31*(5), 621–637.

Zhai, X., Haudek, K. C., Shi, L., Nehm, R. H., & Urban-Lurain, M. (2020). From substitution to redefinition: A framework of machine learning-based science assessment. *Journal of Research in Science Teaching, 57*(9), 1430–1459.

7

Promising Pre-K–12 STEM Education Innovations

As highlighted throughout the report, Pre-K–12 science, technology, engineering, and mathematics (STEM) education initiatives can have a complex constellation of goals and related outcomes for beneficiaries (e.g., students, teachers). For example, they might be designed to advance the STEM workforce, to develop skills and competency in STEM disciplines, to foster a sense of belonging and identity as a STEM professional, and/or as a way to cultivate just, sustainable, and thriving human communities (National Academies of Sciences, Engineering, and Medicine [NASEM], 2024a). Innovations might be designed to meet multiple goals, some of which are explicitly stated, others that are more implicit. As an innovation is implemented, enactors (educators and administrators) may emphasize specific outcomes or introduce additional goals. Some of the goals may be measured, and others may not be. Regardless, throughout the curricula, programs, and experiences, the intended outcomes are intertwined. Recent research in STEM education has focused on understanding and measuring these broadened goals and outcomes of educational approaches, programs, curricula, and interventions (National Academy of Engineering [NAE] & National Research Council [NRC], 2014; NASEM, 2020, 2021a,b, 2022, 2023, 2024a; NRC, 2011, 2013).

A goal for some Pre-K–12 STEM education innovations is to scale beyond the contexts in which it was designed. Chapters 4 and 5 described some of the approaches to scaling and sustaining that innovations might take and the ways in which innovations can propagate. Throughout these discussions, the committee navigates the tensions between the landscape of innovation and implementation as well as the tensions between features of the innovation itself that are necessary to support the scaling and sustainability, and broader system-level supports. These issues are necessarily intertwined and highly dependent.

Pre-K–12 STEM education innovations are highly variable in their implementation and reach, which presents challenges for understanding the landscape of access and opportunity. A number of recent reports have attempted to catalogue the patterns of opportunity and access to Pre-K–12 STEM education innovations (see NASEM, 2022, 2023, 2024a,b). Given the variability, the committee was unable to provide a detailed analysis of this opportunity landscape; however, as can be observed through the case summaries in the compendium that was completed by the Education Development Center (EDC; Appendix C), there are a number of innovations designed to increase opportunity and develop a sense of belonging and identity with STEM.

The goal for this chapter is to provide what is known about the features at the innovation level that support the scaling of promising, evidence-based Pre-K–12 STEM education innovations. This is accomplished by drawing on the findings recorded in the compendium that was completed by the EDC. First, the committee describes the development of the compendium. The committee then explores the conditions that support scaling promising, evidence-based, Pre-K–12 STEM education innovations. The chapter concludes with a brief introduction of the factors that were identified as hindrances to scaling innovations, issues that are taken up more fully in the subsequent chapter.

IDENTIFYING PROMISING PRE-K–12 STEM INNOVATIONS[1]

The committee was tasked with producing a compendium of promising, evidence-based Pre-K–12 STEM education innovations. As noted in Chapter 1, the committee recognized the importance of this task and the enormity of the undertaking. Therefore, the committee commissioned the production of the compendium, which was developed by EDC. What follows is a brief outline of the methodology and a brief overview of promising innovations identified through this process.

---

[1] It should be noted that the compendium was produced while the committee was engaged in its analysis of the literature and reaching consensus on its evidence-based conceptualization of scaling. Therefore, the production of the compendium did not include questions that would allow for a more nuanced analysis and understanding of scaling using the dimensions of scale as described by the committee.

Methodology

EDC conducted a seven-step process with the goal of identifying promising Pre-K–12 STEM education innovations that have gone through a scaling-up process. This process included these steps:

1. Conduct a literature search to identify an initial set of factors that facilitate or hinder scaling of innovations that are broadly supported by the existing research literature.
2. Set parameters for inclusion in the compendium, which mainly follow from the charge to the committee.
3. Develop program nomination form to be used in an open call for online submissions. The form was guided by the factors identified in the literature review to ensure that the online submissions would provide information that would be likely to be relevant to the committee's considerations of factors that facilitate or hinder scalability of innovations.
4. Work with a list of sources and field experts to generate the names of likely promising programs to make targeted invitations.
5. Invite identified programs to submit and also conduct an outreach campaign to advertise the call for submissions more broadly.
6. Review and analyze nominations.
7. Summarize programs, including their approach to scaling and sustainability and evidence of success.

The full methodology for the development of the compendium can be found in Appendix B, and the full compendium is provided in Appendix C.

Literature Search

Before identifying innovations, EDC first conducted a literature search to identify factors that appear to support innovations in their scaling efforts and those that may hinder them in service of understanding how innovations scale. EDC systematically searched Google Scholar and EBSCO using various combinations of the following keywords: STEM, science, mathematics, engineering, education, innovation, scaling, and scale-up. Results were filtered to identify literature published in the last ten years. In EDC's review, it was determined that there is a growing body of research that has attempted to uncover the factors that enable or constrain the scaling of innovations (Dearing et al., 2015; Krainer et al., 2019; Looi & Teh, 2015; Lowrie, Leonard, & Fitzgerald, 2018; Maass et al., 2019; Sabelli & Harris, 2015; Young et al., 2016). From the literature, the following promising factors were identified:

- A "tight but loose" framework
- Alignment of goals, policies, and practices

- Capacity building and organizational support
- Study the innovation in a variety of settings
- Ease of adoption
- Partnerships and networks

These promising factors were intentionally built into the questions asked by EDC in its solicitation and in the rubric so that EDC could provide the committee with an understanding of how the innovations accounted for these factors during scaling and sustainability efforts.

Set Parameters for Inclusion

For an innovation to be considered, it needed to meet the following characteristics:

- Occur within the Pre-K–12 grade band
- Focus on one or more of the traditional STEM disciplines (i.e., science, technology, engineering, and mathematics), which could include computer and data science
- Be connected to formal classroom teaching and learning (e.g., curricula, professional learning)
- Have evidence of scaling (although this was not a strict requirement)
- Have conducted a formal evaluation process to measure their impact and outcomes (i.e., external evaluation or other peer review process)

Develop Nomination Form

A Google form was created for potential programs to self-nominate. The form requested general information (e.g., program name and point of contact); program information (e.g., Pre-K–12 grade band, subject domain[s], intended audience[s]); evidence of scale; and evidence of impact. Evidence of scale and evidence of impact were collected mostly as open-ended responses to allow programs maximum flexibility to explain how they view these parameters and apply them in their individual contexts.

Identify Programs

EDC developed a working list of sources and field experts to assist in identifying programs to directly contact regarding the self-nomination process. Based on this, EDC identified programs through the following:

- Professional connections internal and external to EDC
- Recommendations from Board on Science Education and the committee

- Recommendations from relevant organizations (e.g., National Science Foundation [NSF], Education Innovation and Research)
- Federal program databases for programs meeting the criteria that received an award in the past seven years (e.g., NSF and Department of Education [ED] award search databases, the Institute of Education Sciences What Works Clearinghouse database)
- Additional projects discovered throughout the process (e.g., through literature review)

In order to identify specific programs to reach out to, EDC first solicited suggestions from their personal contacts as well as through conversations with program officers from the ED, NSF, National Aeronautics and Space Administration, and National Oceanic and Atmospheric Administration. This resulted in 41 programs identified.

EDC then utilized publicly available databases to review federally funded projects from the past 15 years. This included programs funded by Education Innovation and Research scale-up grants from ED, as well as Innovative Technology Experiences for Students and Teachers (ITEST) and Discovery Research Pre-K–12 (DRK–12) grants from NSF. EDC included a search for the terms "scale" or "scale-up" in order to limit the results to those referencing scale. The list of programs was then reviewed to include only those programs that had scaled, were focused on a field of STEM, and were connected to formal classrooms. EDC also reviewed the What Works Clearinghouse to identify programs that met criteria. This resulted in the identification of an additional 81 programs.

Finally, EDC's review of the literature identified an additional 14 programs that had not already been identified through other means. In total, EDC sent invitations to 136 programs inviting them to self-nominate (see Table B-1 in Appendix B).

In addition to reaching out to specific programs, EDC also sent information about this opportunity to organizations asking them to share the opportunity with programs that may be eligible for inclusion in the compendium. In total, EDC contacted individuals representing 64 organizations (see Table B-2 in Appendix B).

Invite Programs to Self-Nominate

Program contacts received an outreach email encouraging them to nominate their programs and share the opportunity with their networks. EDC also utilized social media for outreach with posts shared by EDC, Community for Advancing Discovery Research in Education, and STEM Learning and Research Center. Moreover, EDC sought word-of-mouth recommendations from knowledgeable colleagues and others in the field whenever possible.

Review Nominations

All programs were asked to provide a brief summary of evidence of impact to include evidence that (a) STEM learning goals were achieved (e.g., content-specific knowledge), (b) STEM skills were developed (e.g., critical thinking, problem solving, communication), (c) affective goals were achieved (e.g., generated interest in STEM), and/or (d) the innovation helped participants make connections to STEM careers. The various innovations were evaluated against a rubric to determine the strength of evidence for scale, impact, and additional factors related to the scalability of an innovation as noted above (see Appendix B for the Rubric). EDC examined innovations looking for: (a) evidence of fidelity during scaling,[2] (b) evidence of scaling to new audiences or contexts, (c) evidence that participant outcomes were achieved or skills developed, and (d) understanding of effectiveness for different contexts/learners. The innovations were also reviewed to determine to what extent there was evidence for the factors identified by the literature search that have contributed to successful scaling efforts.

Overview of Promising Innovations

A total of 65 nominations were received. Four submissions were excluded because they did not include an external evaluation or peer review, another four were excluded because they were not connected to formal classroom settings, and one was excluded because it did not focus on STEM. The remaining 56 programs were reviewed and an overview of their breakdown is summarized below (see Appendix C for individual descriptions of all of the programs).

Grade Bands and Subject Domains

At least half of the innovations were intended for elementary, middle, and/or high school with two-thirds focused on middle school. Fewer innovations focused on Pre-K (30%). More than half of the innovations (66%) indicated that they focused on two or more grade bands. Most innovations (70%) included a focus on science content, whereas about half (48%) included a focus on engineering or mathematics. More than half of the identified nominations (63%) indicated more than one domain, and 13 innovations (23%) selected all four of the main STEM disciplines.

---

[2] As previously noted, this work was done in parallel as the committee was reaching consensus on the more nuanced characterization of scaling; the committee recognizes that focusing on "fidelity of implementation" represents a limited view on scaling an innovation.

TABLE 7-1 Nominated Innovations by Domain and Grade Band

% Nominations	Science	Technology	Engineering	Mathematics	Computer Science	Data Science
Pre-K (n=17)	65%	41%	53%	82%	29%	29%
Elementary (n=29)	62%	41%	62%	59%	38%	34%
Middle (n=38)	79%	37%	58%	45%	34%	26%
High (n=32)	78%	38%	44%	41%	34%	31%

*Innovations could select more than one response option.
SOURCE: EDC, 2024.

Looking at the distribution of domains across grade bands, as seen in Table 7-1, most Pre-K programs included a mathematics component (82%). Science was a component of the majority of middle and high school programs (79% and 78%, respectively). Elementary school programs had a more even distribution across the domains, but were most likely to include science, engineering, or mathematics.

Implementation Contexts

Innovations can arise from and be implemented in a variety of contexts (see Chapter 5 for more discussion). Although innovations needed to have a connection to Pre-K–12 settings, innovations were also frequently implemented in informal learning and afterschool settings. Twenty-eight (50%) of the innovations indicated that they take place in or are connected to formal Pre-K–12 settings only. Moreover, about half of the innovations (52%) have been in operation for more than 10 years, 23 percent have been operating for 2–5 years, and 20 percent for 6–10 years.

In terms of the intended audiences for the identified innovations, all but one program indicated that teachers/educators were the intended audience in addition to most (86%) also selecting students. At least half of the innovations also identified low-income communities, individuals from ethnic or racial groups traditionally underrepresented in STEM, and under-resourced geographic areas as intended audiences (see Table 7-2). Given these intended audiences, many of the innovations (87%) incorporated supports for building teacher capacity (e.g., professional learning, differentiated teaching/learning, cultural/contextual responsiveness) to implement the innovation successfully with the anticipated participants.

INNOVATION-LEVEL FACTORS THAT SUPPORT SCALING

As described in the earlier methodology section, EDC conducted a review of the literature to identify conditions that hinder or support the

TABLE 7-2 Nominated Innovations by Audience

Audiences	n*	%
Teachers/educators	55	98%
Students/youth	48	86%
Low-income communities	34	61%
Individuals from ethnic or racial groups traditionally underrepresented in STEM	31	55%
Under-resourced geographic areas	29	52%
Multilingual learners	27	48%
Girls	23	41%
Parents/caregivers/families	14	25%
Other **	5	9%

*Programs could select more than one choice.
**Other responses: All; School/District Administrators; designed to work for all students taking a science class; Tribal communities and high schools with a minimum of 60% enrollment of Native American, Alaska Native, Native Hawaiian and/or Pacific Islander students; teacher leaders, professional learning providers, administrators, state-level leaders.
SOURCE: EDC, 2024.

scaling of innovations (Dearing et al., 2015; Krainer et al., 2019; Looi & Teh, 2015; Lowrie, Leonard, & Fitzgerald, 2018; Maass et al., 2019; Sabelli & Harris, 2015; Young et al., 2016). As listed above, key factors identified as supportive conditions for scaling were:

- A "tight but loose" framework
- Alignment of goals, policies, and practices
- Capacity building and organizational support
- Study the innovation in a variety of settings
- Ease of adoption
- Partnerships and networks

These are the factors that are inherent (or need to be considered) in the design and implementation of an innovation and are related to the approaches articulated in Chapter 4. Many of these factors are also related to systems-level factors that can enable or constrain the scaling and sustaining of innovations—these system-level ideas will be taken up in Chapter 8. What follows is a discussion of each factor, using case studies from the compendium to support the ways in which the various factors supported the scaling (and sustainability) of the innovation. In describing each case study, the committee discusses the factors that contributed to the innovation's success and how challenges were managed.

A "Tight but Loose" Framework

For innovations to successfully scale, it is important that they include a proven core with ample room for adaptation to different contexts and learners (Looi & Teh, 2015). Wylie and colleagues (2008) note that a "tight but loose" framework focuses on the tension between two opposing factors in school reform: the need for an innovation to stay consistent with its governing principles, while also offering ample opportunity to adapt to the countless STEM learning environments in which it makes sense to take up said innovation. The framework "combines an obsessive adherence to central design principles (the tight part) with accommodations to the needs, resources, constraints, and particularities that occur in any school or district (the loose part), but only where these do not conflict with the theory of action of the intervention" (p. 2). This is akin to the mutual adaptation discussion in Chapter 4.

The flexibility offered by this framework can also support educator autonomy, which can aid in motivation and buy-in. It is important that the core of the innovation be clearly stated and shown to be sufficient to meet desired outcomes (Dearing et al., 2015). As an example of an innovation using the "tight but loose" approach, the framework utilized by SCRIPT supports schools and districts in creating a plan for high-quality computer science implementation in a way that considers their individual contexts and goals (see Box 7-1). The SCRIPT framework not only allows but trains educators to appropriately adapt the innovation to support local relevance, leading to adoption across a variety of settings.

Additionally, adaptations by practitioners can have the added benefit of serving as a source of additional resources that could be used to expand upon the materials offered by the innovation (Sabelli & Harris, 2015). For example, the compendium describes FUSE,[3] which is a program that is guided by core design principles while offering individual educators the freedom to design the program according to the needs of the school/organization and their community, including logistics like classroom schedules. Research-based recommendations are shared with all partners as they develop their plans to guide adaptation to fit their local needs. FUSE was first piloted in the Chicago area but has been expanded to additional urban, suburban, and rural partners.

Alignment of Goals, Policies, and Practices

For innovations to have the potential to scale, it is important for the innovation to be aligned with the priorities set by policy, organizations, and

---

[3] FUSE is not an acronym. The name originated from youth who had participated in the program, which had been called 'YouSTEM' (see https://www.fusestudio.net/about).

> **BOX 7-1**
> **Strategic CSforALL Resource & Implementation Planning Tool (SCRIPT)**
>
> SCRIPT utilizes a framework to guide strategic planning for school and district leadership teams to implement computer science education. The SCRIPT team works with school and district leadership teams to create a plan for K–12 implementation in a way that considers their individual contexts and goals—so although the SCRIPT framework itself is stable, it is flexible so that the plan can be adapted to fit the context, a factor critical for the scalability of this innovation. As part of the planning, SCRIPT helps leadership teams consider capacity building, including teacher professional learning, technology implementation, and community resources. SCRIPT has worked with over 950 school districts in the United States, increasing its reach by over 25 times since its inception, and has multiple states with facilitators trained and certified and currently offering workshops; the utilization of trained facilitators across the country primed to support adaptation based on local contexts and goals has aided in the scalability of the innovation.
>
> Research has shown that SCRIPT has had impact on buy-in, decision making, goal setting, and actions at the district level (Cobo et al., 2024), with more recent research focusing on longitudinal impact on student course taking and equity.
>
> SOURCE: EDC, 2024.

individual practitioners (Looi & Teh, 2015; Lowrie, Leonard, & Fitzgerald, 2018). As noted earlier, innovations can be developed with multiple goals and purposes—from broadening participation and access, to developing skills and content knowledge, to advancing a sense of belonging and identity as a person who participates in STEM (among others). Each of these goals might be attended to in various ways in the construction and implementation of an innovation, and some of these may be easier to advance when they are aligned with other goals as well as existing policies and practices (this will be taken up more in Chapter 8).

Alignment with goals, policies, and practices helps to facilitate alignment across levels of the system and the different partners (Maass et al., 2019); alignment in this way can lead to lasting organizational and policy related changes (Sabelli & Harris, 2015). For example, showing how the program is aligned with standards can help with buy-in by showing how implementing the program can be incorporated with existing practices and help achieve goals for learners (Sabelli & Harris, 2015). The IRCEDE STEM for Our Youngest Learners (see Box 7-2) is an innovation that is aligned with both the Early Learning Outcomes Framework[4] and the Next Generation Science Standards (NGSS Lead States, 2013). By providing aligned materials and

---

[4] See https://iowaccrr.org/training/IELS/

> **BOX 7-2**
> **IRCEDE STEM for Our Youngest Learners**
>
> STEM for our Youngest Learners is a framework for a student-centered, inquiry-based approach to STEM that engages young children in sensemaking as they design solutions to self-defined engineering problems. The framework of STEM for Our Youngest Learners is aligned with both the Early Learning Outcomes Framework and the Next Generation Science Standards. The program is not a stand-alone curriculum or a package of lessons but is an approach to pedagogy that is taught in hands-on teacher play sessions for adults using the same open-ended materials they will offer children in their settings. The goal is for teachers to develop the skills and confidence to enhance their existing science curriculum and sequential lesson plans, adapting to their local contexts and learners while considering other factors such as grade, time schedules, culture, and mandated curricula.
>
> The framework was originated with Pre-K–2 teachers at an inclusive laboratory school serving primarily low-income urban Black families. Additional funding allowed for expansion to the predominantly rural northeast part of the state. The Iowa Governor's STEM Advisory Council has funded the program annually since 2017 to provide professional learning and classroom materials to over 1,000 of Iowa's early childhood educators and informal learning programs, in under-resourced rural as well as urban sites, across the state. Additional funding has also allowed for ongoing improvement of materials, and dissemination occurs through a partnership with Pre-K–2 teachers at North Tama County Community Schools, a rural public school.
>
> An NSF DRK-12 grant enabled a pilot test and field test in multiple sites in different states. The evaluation revealed that most of the participating teachers created an environment that supports science teaching and learning and that children made gains in physical science content knowledge. Additionally, teachers reported that they had gained important knowledge, skills, and abilities in terms of science content, supporting science inquiry, and facilitating inquiry-based learning.
>
> SOURCE: EDC, 2024.

professional learning, teachers gain important knowledge, skills, and abilities that support student learning across a variety of contexts and student populations. As teachers gain more confidence with STEM, they are able to adapt the program to their local contexts and learners, considering such factors such as grade, time schedules, cultures, and mandated curricula.

To ensure that all learners have access to STEM-related opportunities, there has been increasing focus on equity-related goals. Some studies have revealed that explicit connections to equity-oriented components within innovations yield better outcomes for learners who have been traditionally underrepresented in STEM (Cunningham et al., 2020; NAE & NRC, 2014; NASEM, 2021a,b). Box 7-3 presents the example of the Beauty and Joy of Computing (BJC) course—a high school Advanced Placement Computer

BOX 7-3
Beauty and Joy of Computing (BJC)

BJC is a College Board-endorsed Advanced Placement (AP) Computer Science Principles (CSP) course designed to provide students with a rigorous and engaging introduction to CS and to support the participation of students from groups historically underrepresented in computer science. The BJC course uses the blocks-based visual programming language Snap! to increase accessibility and engagement for students. It employs a project-centered approach, with projects in a variety of contexts (e.g., games, art/design, mathematics); supports culturally responsive instruction; and incorporates critical social implications of computing in the content of the course.

Findings from a BJC field-test indicate that teachers using the BJC curriculum and participating in summer professional learning made statistically significant pre/post gains in content knowledge, self-efficacy, self-rated preparation/effectiveness, self-rated programming ability, and knowledge/fluency (Price et al., 2016). External evaluation reports revealed that students in the BJC course in 2016–2017 (n = 311) showed significant pre/post gains on a content assessment, with small to medium effect sizes. Findings for student engagement and attitudes included significant gains for confidence and identity sub-scales, but no significant gains for interest and belongingness. Girls and Black and Latinx students achieved similar gains on the content assessment and on engagement and attitude measures as male and non-Black and Latinx students.

Student enrollment data in NYC indicate gains in the percentages of female, Black, and Hispanic students participating in BJC classes, and taking and passing the AP CSP exam. On the 2017 AP CSP exam, 2,854 NYC students took the exam, and 2,076 passed—a 73 percent pass rate compared with 74 percent nationwide, with higher percentages of female, Black, and Hispanic students in NYC taking the AP CSP exam than nationwide (Mark & Klein, 2019). National AP CSP exam data from the College Board in 2021 indicated female BJC students passed at a rate of 6.4 percentage points higher than the national average, Black BJC students passed at 1.2 points higher, and Hispanic BJC students at 4.6 points higher than the national average.

With support from NSF (grant #1441075), the initial cohort of teachers that piloted the high school BJC curriculum in 2015 included 28 NYC high school teachers. Between 2015 and 2022, BJC curriculum training was provided to over 200 NYC teachers from 136 schools. Those teachers, in turn, served over 25,000 NYC high school students. BJC AP CSP has been offered in the NYC Public Schools (NYCPS) continuously since the 2015–2016 school year with teacher professional learning opportunities offered through the NYCPS Computer Science for All (CS4All) initiative led by NYCPS teachers. Hundreds of additional BJC teachers have been trained nationally through annual summer professional development offerings at North Carolina State University. With additional support from EIR program at ED, an additional 38 teachers from 36 schools across the country are using BJC as part of a school CS equity program designed to broaden participation in CS coursework through recruitment, enrollment, and retention of high-need students in AP CSP courses. While the program is currently focused on working and expanding within a specific population (NYC schools), additional funding is currently supporting expansion across the country with a focus on equity.

SOURCE: EDC, 2024.

Science Principles course that has scaled to over 200 New York City (NYC) teachers and 600 non-NYC teachers. It is endorsed by the College Board, aligning to goals which can help administrators and teachers feel confident that this curriculum will help them meet their objectives. The objectives of BJC include providing students with a rigorous and engaging introduction to computer science and supporting participation of students from groups historically underrepresented in computer science. Findings from studies evaluating BJC have shown not only improved academic performance but also significant gains in confidence and identity for girls and Black and Latinx students.

Capacity Building and Organizational Support

In addition to ensuring that there is a core, adaptable framework and alignment with goals, policies, and practices, there is also a need for capacity building and organizational support. This can come from a variety of different forms, such as providing support for practitioners through professional learning (Maass et al., 2019; Young et al., 2016). Professional learning can support teachers as they navigate the changing landscape with growing expectations for what they need to know and do in their day-to-day practice of teaching (as described in Chapter 1; NASEM, 2020). Teachers are increasingly charged with ensuring that classrooms serve as equitable learning communities, fostering trusting and caring relationships among students and with teachers, and serving as a bridge between the school and families and communities. These increased expectations for learning, combined with the demand to create a responsive learning environment that supports the needs of all students, call for innovative approaches to instruction that may differ substantially from teachers' own experiences as students or their preservice education (NASEM, 2020). At the same time, in the case of many STEM education innovations designed for students, teachers are considered key players in implementation. Thus, they are often supported through professional learning in an effort to facilitate effective implementation of these STEM education innovations. For example, STeLLA, a program included in the compendium, is a year-long science professional learning program for K–12 teachers, integrating video-based analysis of practice and a focus on student thinking (see Box 7-4). It provides approximately 90 hours of professional learning, including a summer institute and school year study groups. Research has provided evidence of impacts on teacher content knowledge, teacher pedagogical content knowledge, and teacher classroom practice that resulted in improved student achievement.

Beyond ensuring opportunities for professional learning, there is also a need for support from the organization via an investment in resources and continued support/buy-in (Krainer et al., 2019; Maass et al., 2019). In some cases, this might mean focusing on a bigger shift in the organization or

> **BOX 7-4**
> **Science Teachers Learning from Lesson Analysis (STeLLA)**
>
> STeLLA, by BSCS Science Learning, began with 32 upper elementary school teachers in California in 2003. This innovation is a year-long science professional learning program for K–12 teachers, integrating video-based analysis of practice and a focus on student thinking. The goal is to improve students' science achievement by improving teachers' science content knowledge and their abilities to (a) explain science concepts to students, (b) clearly identify to students the science concepts used in student learning activities, and (c) engage students in thinking about science. Teachers learn to use these strategies by analyzing classroom videos and units, and sharing their thinking in facilitated sessions with other teachers. Throughout the school year, teachers apply what they are learning in their own classrooms. In 2009, STeLLA expanded to Colorado, initially serving 144 elementary teachers and then again in 2015 to reach middle and high school teachers in the same state. In 2019, the program expanded to Kentucky and Tennessee.
>
> STeLLA's approach to scaling was to steadily grow the project over time through additional funding and partnerships. This allowed them to test out their model in different contexts (e.g., different states and with different grade levels). They also utilize expert mentors to provide in-person, online, or hybrid teacher professional learning experiences.
>
> Randomized controlled trial and quasi-experimental studies of the core program provide evidence of impacts on student achievement (effect size 0.68), teacher content knowledge, teacher pedagogical content knowledge, and teacher classroom practice (e.g., Roth et al., 2011, 2019; Taylor et al., 2017; Wilson et al., 2018). Additional studies have included online adaptations and application in preservice education and across settings (elementary, middle, and high school), as well as small- and large-scale implementation.
>
> SOURCE: EDC, 2024.

policies to establish a system where the essential principles of an innovation can be adopted and sustained (Looi & Teh, 2015; Sabelli & Harris, 2015). An example is Making Sense of Science, a train-the-trainer approach that can support local leaders in facilitating high-quality teacher professional learning that, coupled with support from administrators, can develop systems of support for STEM learning (see Box 7-5). In this way, an organization's capacity for adopting any new program could be strengthened. These ideas are expanded upon in Chapter 8.

Study the Innovation in a Variety of Settings

As introduced in Chapters 4 and 5, research has suggested that practitioners can be key to providing developers with a better sense of what works

> **BOX 7-5**
> **Making Sense of SCIENCE (MSS)**
>
> Making Science of SCIENCE (MSS) provides leadership development, professional learning, and needs-based technical assistance to teachers, coaches, leaders, and administrators. The program has been brought to scale through two key mechanisms: (a) a train-the-trainer model to support local leaders in facilitating high-quality teacher professional learning, and (b) work with administrators and local leaders to develop systems of support for STEM learning. These approaches work hand-in-hand to build local capacity in ways that account for differing contexts and authentically meet the needs of partnering schools, districts, and states. As two examples of state-wide scaling, MSS partnered with the Math and Science Bureau of the New Mexico Public Education Department and the Texas Regional Collaboratives to lead Facilitation Academies for regional leaders on a variety of topics. These trained regional leaders then provided MSS professional learning across the state, reaching 400–1,000 teachers each year for multiple consecutive years.
>
> As reported by Heller and colleagues (2012), the MSS train-the-trainer approach has been shown to produce facilitators who successfully lead impactful teacher professional learning. A national randomized controlled trial (RCT) showed that teacher preparation in just 24 hours of MSS professional learning resulted in statistically significant gains in teacher and student content knowledge. Teacher content knowledge was maintained during the following school year and the new cohort of students also experienced gains in content knowledge. Following the national RCT, a follow-up study analyzed videos of 30 classrooms to better understand shifts in teacher instruction resulting from participation in the professional learning The MSS professional learning had a large, statistically significant effect on the overall quality of classroom instruction. Teacher participation in the professional learning resulted in statistically significant improvements in student cognitive engagement, student engagement in scientific sensemaking practices, and teacher elicitation of and attention to student thinking.
>
> SOURCE: EDC, 2024.

for whom and in what contexts (Looi & Teh, 2015; McLaughlin & Mitra, 2001; Sabelli & Harris, 2015; Sarama & Clements, 2013). Additionally, testing the program in a variety of different settings (e.g., via design-based research) with different learners and including the input of educators whenever possible can provide valuable insights to identify challenges and adaptations (Lowrie, Leonard, & Fitzgerald, 2018). NURTURES (see Box 7-6) is an innovation that began with implementation in urban districts before expanding to rural districts and then military-connected districts in seven states. Throughout the program, research has been conducted to understand how to implement the innovation in different settings and with different audiences.

> **BOX 7-6**
> **NURTURES**
>
> NURTURES provides professional learning for Pre-K–3 teachers and family engagement for families of young children (take-home Family Science packs and family engagement activities hosted in the community after school or on weekends). NURTURES began with implementation in urban districts in Toledo, Ohio. Building on the success of the initial phase of the program, they received additional NSF funding to implement the program in rural districts in Ohio and Michigan. A particularly important facet of this follow-up project was to research how each component (teacher professional learning versus family engagement) impacts student learning. Further funding from the Department of Defense allowed the program to expand to military-connected districts in seven states. Throughout the life of the program, the NURTURES team has conducted research to understand how to implement the program in different settings and with a wider audience. Continuous federal funding has supported this.
>
> An initial evaluation documented the first five years of the program. Findings verified fidelity of implementation, and corrections or modifications to implementation were made due to early detection of variance from implementation plans. Findings indicated that NURTURES is a successful intervention for improving science teaching and student outcomes in early childhood classrooms as well as for increasing family science participation and the quality of that participation.
>
> A longitudinal case study revealed improved pedagogical practices among teachers, increased science content knowledge and confidence to teach science, and increased use of technology in the classroom. A randomized controlled trial study found that K–2 students whose teachers had participated in NURTURES demonstrated higher achievement than peers whose teachers had not been in the program. Longitudinal studies also demonstrate the long-term impact of the program on student learning with gains in science, early literacy, and mathematics being sustained to grade 5.
>
> Current research, funded through the Department of Defense, focuses on the delivery of program elements, examining methods of program delivery, multisite facilitation, impacts on student learning, and the feasibility of offering NURTURES at scale.
>
> SOURCE: EDC, 2024.

Ease of Adoption

If the goal is to get many practitioners from a variety of contexts to try out a program, considering the feasibility ("trialability"), usability ("simplicity"), and cost can help increase the chances that the program will be implemented. Dearing and colleagues (2015) described case studies from three community college advanced technological education programs as they were supported in scaling innovations. Several lessons were learned through these case studies. First, it was determined that scaling required critical thinking, trial and error, and reflection during implementation. That is, factors aiding in scale included the ease with which adopters can experiment with an innovation (i.e., trialability), how easy the innovation is to understand and use (i.e., simplicity), compatibility with diverse settings, and how much implementation of the innovation costs in terms of both time and money. As discussed in Chapter 4, an inherent tension exists between the ease of adoption and the depth of change that is needed to scale and sustain an innovation, and it is important to recognize that just because an innovation might by easy to adopt does not mean that it will result in the depth of change that is needed to be sustained.

Moreover, scaling benefits from encouraging adopters to adapt the innovation (within limits) and utilize these adaptations to improve the innovation. For example, Project Learning Tree (PLT) is an innovation that is supported by a network of state-level coordinators to engage with educators and communities at the local level. Because PLT programs are directed and implemented locally, educators received state-specific supplements to PLT's educational materials that address the local environment, which aids in the ease of adoption of the materials. As another example, AlgebraByExample (Box 7-7) is a set of supplementary assignments that were explicitly designed to narrow the achievement gap for minority students.

BOX 7-7
AlgebraByExample

Easily incorporated into any existing Algebra 1 curricula, AlgebraByExample is a set of freely downloadable supplementary Algebra 1 assignments that require students to analyze correctly- and incorrectly-worked examples that target common misconceptions and errors. These assignments can be used for practice, probes, personal reflection, and jumping off points for discussion. Developed via design-based research through the Strategic Education Research Partnership (SERP) and educators from the Minority Student Achievement Network (MSAN) within a year-long random-assignment study in over 300 classrooms with over 6,000 students, this set of assignments was developed with the intent of narrowing the achievement gap for minority students in the MSAN without isolating minority students in intervention settings (see Booth et al., 2015).

On average, students using AlgebraByExample demonstrated statistically significant gains in procedural and conceptual understanding, as well on released items from standardized tests, but the lowest performing students showed the most significant gains. More research needs to be done to see the impact on minority students.

Although not much information was provided about their scaling efforts, the fact that it is freely accessible and designed to supplement classroom teaching may contribute to scaling due to the ease of accessing and integrating the materials.

SOURCE: Booth et al., 2015; EDC, 2024.

However, in striving to develop an innovation that can be scaled across a variety of contexts, it is key to not fall into the "trap of perfection" (Dearing et al., 2015). As described in Chapter 4, there are a number of dimensions for scaling. Maintaining depth (what the program is supposed to do) while also allowing for simplicity and flexibility is desirable for scalability. Therefore, there can be a tradeoff between ease of adoption and impact. That which is easily adopted in terms of curricular innovation may be less likely to push on practice in the way today's STEM standards require. The committee returns to this issue in Chapter 8.

Partnerships and Networks

Partnerships can be valuable for scaling in a variety of ways (Lowrie, Leonard, & Fitzgerald, 2018; Maass et al., 2019; Young et al., 2016). For example, the common online data analysis platform (CODAP) is free educational software for data analysis with wide uptake and acknowledgement among the statistics education community and beyond. This web-based data science tool is designed both as a platform for curriculum developers and as an application for students in grades 6–12. CODAP has utilized partnerships with other projects to incorporate and spread their work and is currently in broad use by approximately 60,000 users monthly. More than 130 learning science researchers have incorporated CODAP into their research and development efforts, resulting in dozens of curricula and lessons nationwide. Through the varied partnerships across multiple communities, CODAP has had the potential to scale across multiple contexts.

Moreover, partnerships can be leveraged to help in scaling culturally specific programming across the country. For example, Seeding Innovation, described in the compendium, is an innovation in which American Indian Science and Engineering Society (AISES) and the Kapor Center have partnered to provide a sequence of culturally revitalizing computer science curricula to partner schools across the country. The partner organization works collaboratively with school sites to create an engaging computer science curriculum, while also working with teachers and, when possible, community members to integrate cultural traditions, language, stories, art and more.[5]

Although external partners can be valuable sources of resources, funding, and support for those developing innovations, partnering with districts, schools, and teachers can provide in-depth insights into specific contexts to guide development and improvements. Building networks in this way can allow for the innovation to be carried out in a larger number of settings across a larger geographic area. For example, Box 7-8 highlights the

---

[5]For more information, see Kapor Foundation & AISES (2023) report, *State of diversity: The native tech ecosystem*, https://www.kaporcenter.org/wp-content/uploads/2023/10/StateofDiversity.TheNativeTechEcosystem.pdf

> **BOX 7-8**
> **Exploratorium California K–12 Science Leader Network**
>
> The Exploratorium has developed a professional network of over 1,100 science education leaders across California who bring high-quality science professional learning and advocacy to over 100,000 teachers statewide. Leaders in the network access a constellation of professional learning opportunities that begins with a multi-day core institute and includes series of stand-alone virtual and in-person workshops, communities of practice, and access to high-quality teaching leadership resources.
>   The Exploratorium K–12 Science Leader Network spans the state of California and now includes over 950 leaders, 85 percent of whom work with Title I schools. Because this network is aimed at teacher professional learning, their leadership network impact spreads to 95,000 classroom teachers and millions of students. By 2025, they would like to further expand their network to 1,500 leaders serving 150,000 classroom teachers. They provide professional learning programs based on grade band: One to train K–12 Science Leaders, one for K–5 educators, and one for secondary educators.
>   Based on an external evaluation by Inverness Research Inc., the Exploratorium's K–12 Science Leader Network and professional learning programs consistently show positive impact on improved leadership capacities and achieving equity in the science classroom.
>
> SOURCE: EDC, 2024.

Exploratorium California K–12 Science Leader Network, which grew from serving a single county office to spanning the state of California.

CHALLENGES TO SCALING PROMISING INNOVATIONS

The complexity of educational environments results in embedded challenges that can negatively affect successful scaling and sustainability efforts. Challenges identified from the literature review in combination with the compendium submissions include:

- Changing policies and priorities
- Staff turnover
- Keeping materials updated
- Monitoring implementation and outcomes at scale

If an innovation is designed to align with specific policies or to meet specific goals, there can be a large threat to scaling and sustainability when policies or priorities change and are not in line with the direction of the innovation. Scaling and sustainability are aided by buy-in from and capacity building with individuals and organizations who are the enactors. If individuals championing the innovation at an organization or those trained to implement it leave, it can hinder continuity and efforts to scale the innovation. During scaling efforts, it can be difficult to also update materials as these would require additional development and testing. This can lead to materials that are out-of-date with the latest advances in STEM fields. Working with partners, especially teachers, who adapt and update materials can help mitigate this. Lastly, once a program has scaled broadly, it is challenging to monitor and evaluate. When an innovation is being implemented and adapted in many different contexts, it is difficult to draw conclusions across sites and learners. Additionally, the cost of evaluating something at this scale in a deep way can be prohibitive.

Although these issues were identified as having impacts on the individual innovations, they represent more systemic issues. Chapter 8 provides a more in-depth discussion of these challenges and offers suggestions for how the system can respond.

SUMMARY

Pre-K–12 STEM education innovations can be implemented in a variety of contexts to achieve a variety of different goals. As highlighted throughout the compendium commissioned for this report, although there can be notable challenges to scaling and sustaining innovations, there are several factors that support the conditions for scaling, to include a "tight but loose" framework; alignment of goals, policies, and practices; capacity building and organizational support; adaptability to a variety of settings; ease of adoption; and partnerships and networks. It is important to note that these are not the only factors that are needed for scaling, nor are they a requirement for successful scaling efforts. Looking across the various innovations, it is clear that there is not a "one-size-fits- all" approach to scaling, but rather, design of scaling innovations depends on the goals of the innovation, the resources available, and the contexts and learners they are trying to reach. Moreover, the process of evaluating and understanding implementation and outcomes can be challenging at scale, especially harder-to-study aspects such as fidelity of implementation, integrity of implementation (as described in Chapter 4), and implementation in a variety of contexts. Although many innovations in the compendium were able to collect this information and use it to scale the innovation, evidence cannot cover all settings and all participants. Finally, as discussed in Chapter 5, continuous funding, especially larger grants from federal sources, are important to funding these efforts, which can lead to a robust innovation that has scaled across a range of contexts.

Overall, in an effort to best understand the supportive conditions that allow for the scaling and sustaining of innovations, there is a need for consideration as to how and in what ways evidence of scale and implementation is gathered, what types of evidence and understanding are important for the development and scale of innovations, and how funders can support these efforts. Chapter 8 will unpack these ideas more.

REFERENCES

Booth, J. L., Cooper, L. A., Donovan, M. S., Huyghe, A., Koedinger, K. R., & Paré-Blagoev, E. J. (2015). Design-based research within the constraints of practice: AlgebraByExample. *Journal of Education for Students Placed at Risk (JESPAR)*, 20(1–2), 79–100. https://doi.org/10.1080/10824669.2014.986674

Cunningham, C. M., Lachapelle, C. P., Brennan, R. T., Kelly, G. J., Tunis, C. S. A., & Gentry, C. A. (2020). The impact of engineering curriculum design principles on elementary students' engineering and science learning. *Journal of Research in Science Teaching*, 57(3), 423–453.

Dearing, J. W., Dede, C., Boisvert, D., Carrese, J., Clement, L., Craft, E., Gardner, P., Hyder, J., Johnson, E., McNeel, D., Phiri, J., & Pleil, M. (2015). How educational innovators apply diffusion and scale-up concepts. *Scaling Educational Innovations*, 81–104. https://doi.org/10.1007/978-981-287-537-2_5

Education Development Center. (2024). [Compendium of PreK–12 STEM education programs: Impact and scale]. Paper commissioned by the Committee on Pre-K–12 STEM Education Innovations. https://nap.nationalacademies.org/resource/27950/Compendium%20of%20PreK-12%20STEM%20Education%20Programs_EDC.pdf

Heller, J. I., Daehler, K. R., Wong, N., Shinohara, M., & Miratrix, L. W. (2012). Differential effects of three professional development models on teacher knowledge and student achievement in elementary science. *Journal of Research in Science Teaching*, 49(3), 333–362.

Kapor Foundation & AISES. (2023). *State of diversity: The native tech ecosystem*. https://www.kaporcenter.org/wp-content/uploads/2023/10/StateofDiversity.TheNativeTechEcosystem.pdf

Krainer, K., Zehetmeier, S., Hanfstingl, B., Rauch, F., & Tscheinig, T. (2019). Insights into scaling up a nationwide learning and teaching initiative on various levels. *Educational Studies in Mathematics*, 102, 395–415. https://doi.org/10.1007/s10649-018-9826-3

Looi, C. K., & Teh, L. W. (2015). Towards critical discussions of scaling up educational innovations. In C. K. Looi & L. Teh (Eds.), *Scaling educational innovations* (pp. 1–10). Springer. https://doi.org/10.1007/978-981-287-537-2

Lowrie, T., Leonard, S., & Fitzgerald, R. (2018). STEM practices: A translational framework for large-scale STEM education design. *Educational Design Research*, 2(1). https://doi.org/10.15460/eder.2.1.1243

Maass, K., Cobb, P., Krainer, K., & Potari, D. (2019). Different ways to implement innovative teaching approaches at scale. *Educational Studies in Mathematics*, 102, 303–318.

Mark, J., & Klein, K. (2019, February). Beauty and joy of computing: 2016–17 findings from an AP CS Principles course. In *Proceedings of the 50th ACM Technical Symposium on Computer Science Education* (pp. 627–633).

McLaughlin, M. W., & Mitra, D. (2001). Theory-based change and change-based theory: Going deeper, going broader. *Journal of Educational Change*, 2, 301–323.

National Academies of Sciences, Engineering, and Medicine (NASEM). (2020). *Changing expectations for the K–12 teacher workforce: Policies, preservice education, professional development, and the workplace*. The National Academies Press.

———. (2021a). *Call to action for science education: Building opportunity for the future*. The National Academies Press. https://doi.org/10.17226/26152

———. (2021b). *Cultivating interest and competencies in computing: Authentic experiences and design factors*. The National Academies Press. https://doi.org/10.17226/25912

———. (2022). *Science and engineering in preschool through elementary grades: The brilliance of children and the strengths of educators*. The National Academies Press. https://doi.org/10.17226/26215

———. (2023). *Closing the opportunity gap for young children*. The National Academies Press. https://doi.org/10.17226/26743

———. (2024a). *Equity in K–12 STEM education: Framing decisions for the future*. The National Academies Press. https://doi.org/10.17226/26859

———. (2024b). *A new vision for high-quality preschool curriculum*. The National Academies Press. https://doi.org/10.17226/27429

National Academy of Engineering, & National Research Council. (2014). *STEM integration in K–12 education: Status, prospects, and an agenda for research*. The National Academies Press. https://doi.org/10.17226/18612

National Research Council (NRC). (2011). *Successful K-12 STEM education: Identifying effective approaches in science, technology, engineering, and mathematics*. The National Academies Press. https://doi.org/10.17226/13158

———. (2013). *Monitoring progress toward successful K-12 STEM education: A nation advancing?* The National Academies Press. https://doi.org/10.17226/13509

NGSS Leads States. (2013). *Next generation science standards: For states, by states*. The National Academies Press.

Price, T. W., Cateté, V., Albert, J., Barnes, T., & Garcia, D. D. (2016, February). Lessons learned from "BJC" CS Principles professional development. In *Proceedings of the 47th ACM Technical Symposium on Computing Science Education* (pp. 467–472). https://bjc.berkeley.edu/documents/2014%20SIGCSE%20-%20Lessons%20Learned%20from%20BJC%20CS%20Principles%20Professional%20Development.pdf

Roth, K. J., Garnier, H. E., Chen, C., Lemmens, M., Schwille, K., & Wickler, N. I. (2011). Videobased lesson analysis: Effective science PD for teacher and student learning. *Journal of Research in Science Teaching*, 48(2), 117–148.

Roth, K. J., Wilson, C. D., Taylor, J. A., Stuhlsatz, M. A., & Hvidsten, C. (2019). Comparing the effects of analysis-of-practice and content-based professional development on teacher and student outcomes in science. *American Educational Research Journal*, 56(4), 1217–1253.

Sabelli, N. H., & Harris, C. J. (2015). The role of innovation in scaling up educational innovations. In C. K. Looi & L. Teh (Eds.), *Scaling educational innovations*. Springer. https://doi.org/10.1007/978-981-287-537-2_2

Taylor, J., Roth, K., Wilson, C., Stuhlsatz, M., & Tipton, E. (2017). The effect of an analysis-of-practice, videocase-based, teacher professional development program on elementary students' science achievement. *Journal of Research on Educational Effectiveness*, 10(2), 241–271.

Wilson, C. D., Stuhlsatz, M., Hvidsten, C., & Gardner, A. (2018). Analysis of practice and teacher PCK: Inferences from professional development research. *Pedagogical content knowledge in STEM: Research to Practice*, 3–16.

Wylie, E. C., Goe, L., Leusner, D. M., Lyon, C. J., Tocic, C., Wylie, E. C., Cleland, D., Gannon, M., Ellsworth, J., Heritage, M., Maher, J., Mardy, D., Popham, W. J., Snodgrass, D., Taylor, G., Thompson, M., & Wiliam, D. (2008). Tight but loose: Scaling up teacher professional development in diverse contexts. *ETS Research Report Series*, 2008(1), i–141. https://doi.org/10.1002/j.2333-8504.2008.tb02115.x

Young, V. M., House, A., Sherer, D., Singleton, C., & Wang, H. (2016). Scaling up STEM academies statewide: Implementation, network supports, and early outcomes. *Teachers College Record*, 118(13), 1–26. https://doi.org/10.1177/016146811611801310

8

Enabling and Constraining Factors and the Need for System Change

As illustrated throughout this report, there are a number of ways in which an innovation can scale. The committee refers to the potential of an innovation to be "scaled" as its "scalability." Chapter 4 introduced scale as multidimensional and described the varied approaches that could be used to scale and sustain an innovation. Chapter 5 went on to characterize the landscapes of innovation and implementation and the ways in which the configurations of actors, system-level decision makers, and financial resources can facilitate the implementation, scalability, and sustainability of innovations across settings and populations. In particular, the chapter describes the ways in which innovations are funded and how innovations can share new knowledge and resources and the implications these additional factors have for the scalability of innovations. Especially in the case of science, technology, engineering, and mathematics (STEM) innovations that aim to alter core beliefs or principles regarding STEM teaching and learning, consideration of key aspects of the system in which innovations are introduced and intended to thrive is critical.

Chapter 7 identified several factors—at the level of the innovation—that, when baked into the design, can support or hinder the scaling of a particular innovation. Those factors included: a "tight but loose" framework; alignment of goals, policies, and practices; capacity building and organizational support; ease of adoption; studying the program in a variety of settings with practitioners included during the process; and partnerships and networks. These are not the only factors that are needed nor are they a requirement for successful scaling efforts. The chapter concluded with a brief discussion of some of the challenges to scaling such as changing policies and priorities, staff turnover, keeping materials updated, and monitoring implementation and outcomes at scale. Although the issues identified were at the level of the innovation, the implementation, scaling, and sustaining of innovations can be enabled or constrained by system-level factors.

This chapter extends the previous discussion by addressing these systemic issues. It begins with a discussion of many of these enabling and constraining factors and the insights for scaling and sustaining innovations that have been highlighted throughout the report. In particular, the section points to (a) the nature of the innovation, (b) resources that catalyze change, (c) professional learning and support for enactors and enablers, (d) leadership, (e) system capacity to support innovation, and (f) coherence. Building upon this discussion, the committee then considers the affordances of a durable system that allow for innovations to scale and sustain. That is, what opportunities can a durable system provide that allow for deep systemic change through the implementation of innovations and how can this change the "business as usual" model. The chapter concludes with a call for systems change.

ENABLING AND CONSTRAINING FACTORS

Policy structures, design features, resources, infrastructure, and leadership influence the STEM innovation implementation activities of various actors (Hopkins et al., 2013). Certain levers hold the potential to increase the agency of district and school leaders to more deeply implement STEM innovations. Here we discuss how levers enable—and sustain—actors' work related to implementing STEM innovations. Policies and resources can reshape conditions to not only support individual actors, but promote deeper, systemic change. An array of catalysts enables learning so that STEM innovations become implemented in more equitable and sustainable ways across various contexts.

The Nature of the Innovation

The nature of the innovation matters for scalability. As described in Chapter 4, innovations that entail minor adjustments to enactors' current practices are easier to implement and scale. In contrast, innovations that entail substantial change in enactors' current beliefs about teaching and learning or students' capabilities, knowledge, and/or current practices are much harder to implement, sustain, and scale. As elaborated throughout this report, the literature is replete with examples of how substantial changes to teaching and learning require ongoing professional learning as well as attention to and revision of the educational system in which the innovation is integrated (e.g., Cobb et al., 2018; Coburn, 2003; Cohen & Mehta, 2017; Elmore, 1996; McLaughlin & Mitra, 2001; Sarama & Clements, 2013).

Moreover, innovations that provide room for principled adaptation within specific contexts, with specific enactor and beneficiaries in mind, tend to be more scalable, as compared to innovations whose implementation is tightly prescribed, ad discussed in Chapter 4 (National Academies of Sciences, Engineering, and Medicine [NASEM], 2022a). Ample research on implementation points to the importance of local system leaders, educators, and family/community members adapting an innovation to reflect the needs, resources, and challenges of a particular community (Marshall & Khalifa, 2018; Zeichner, 2010).

Need for Resources

A number of resources are needed to support educational improvement in STEM and ensure equitable access and opportunities. Resources can be viewed as the components enabling—or fueling—activities and changes to systems and actors in the education field. Resources include such things as funding, research-based curricula, and tools, as well as time (Grubb, 2008, 2009; Kolbe, Steele, & White, 2020; Pareja Roblin, Schunn, & McKenney, 2018; Woulfin & Spitzer, 2023). These resources matter for the direction and extent of educational improvement efforts (Grubb, 2008; Grubb & Allen, 2011).

First, it remains important to fully fund STEM innovation efforts so that actors at different levels of the education system can respond to their implementation in substantive ways, given the inequitable funding structures across states, regions, and districts (see Chapters 2 and 3). This includes properly funding infrastructural elements aligned with an innovation, such as instructional materials, professional learning, and ongoing support for school and district leaders. Moreover, to promote more substantive forms of implementation, there is also a need to ensure adequate funding for improving working conditions to promote educator retention (NASEM, 2020). It appears educator stability functions as a resource with the potential to support STEM innovation efforts (McLaughlin & Mitra, 2001).

Second, providing teachers access to research-based curricula and the integration of technology into practice are steps toward changing teaching and learning, which is why it is important that decisions are based on educational research rather than policymakers' initiatives (Niederhauser et al., 2018), as adoption of materials mediates access. External review systems (like EdReports) have been put in place to evaluate curricula; however, it is possible that this could create rigidity in curriculum expectations that could impact the scalability of new STEM innovations (see Chapter 5).[1] Aligning technology use with pedagogical goals encourages educators to critically evaluate the relevance and effectiveness of technologies in their teaching

---

[1] However, it is not clear what the impact is of external reviews on the scaling and sustaining of Pre-K–12 STEM education innovations.

objectives. It can be a lot to ask of teachers who are now responsible for the orchestration of tools, participatory structures and routines, and supporting small groups and the whole class at appropriate times. Implementing feedback and evaluation mechanisms to gather input from teachers about their experiences with different technologies helps identify areas for improvement and informs future technology adoption decisions. Partnerships and plans based in research on how technology, teachers, peers, and technology tools can work synergistically are ways to help with successful teaching and learning using novel technologies (Puntambekar et al., 2021).

Third, time functions as a supportive condition for instructional change, permitting various actors to fully respond to the principles and practices of a STEM innovation (Kolb, Steele, & White, 2020; Sarama & Clements, 2013). Time for learning about and enacting STEM innovations is both structured and managed by educational leaders (Kraft & Novicoff, 2022; Woulfin & Spitzer, 2023). That is, district and school leaders make localized decisions on the allocation of time for STEM. Such decisions include guidelines for minutes per day for elementary math instruction, blocks of time for classes to work with a STEM specialist instructor, and number of professional learning sessions addressing science. Notably, the calendar and schedules of the school day, week, and year enable—or derail—STEM innovation efforts (Tyler et al., 2020). This can also include teachers' time for working alongside families and researchers in the design and implementation of STEM education innovations. In sum, it is important to be patient about, and provide additional time for, change associated with the implementation and research of STEM innovation efforts.

Professional Learning and Support for Enactors and Enablers

Another critical factor in the scalability of an innovation regards the provision of high-quality professional learning and support for enactors. In cases where the innovation requires minimal changes to enactors' current beliefs, knowledge, and/or practice, the professional learning needs are likely less, as compared to innovations that entail deep change (NASEM, 2020). For example, an initial workshop or session may suffice for new enactors, paired with occasional opportunities to share and troubleshoot challenges. On the other hand, when the innovation requires substantial changes to enactors' beliefs, knowledge, and/or practice, the literature indicates the need for high-quality, sustained professional learning supports (NASEM, 2020), which can be especially true for increasing teachers' knowledge and skills related to technology (Ertmer et al., 2012; Niederhauser et al., 2018). This might include providing professional learning opportunities that support enactors in deepening their expertise and experience with culturally relevant and sustaining practices (NASEM, 2020). Moreover, professional learning opportunities are needed for both researchers and developers to ensure that considerations are made from the outset regarding the implementation contexts and the implications for adaptation and scaling.

Specific to innovations designed to alter instruction, it is important that the professional learning focuses on making sense of the specific materials, as well as underlying principles and assumptions (e.g., about teaching and learning, about students' capabilities, about the discipline; NASEM, 2020). Further, opportunities for the enactors to participate in the professional learning with their colleagues, and to discuss how they might adapt the materials and/or approach them in ways that are specific to their contexts, students, and communities, is crucial (NASEM, 2020) and helps to ensure that enactors are adapting experiences in meaningful ways for all learners.

Although professional learning opportunities can function as a lever for substantive change, it is rarely optimized inside current systems. It may neglect evidence-based principles of high-quality professional learning, including the importance of content-specific, engaging, collective, and extended duration learning opportunities (Garet et al., 2001; Woulfin, Stevenson, & Lord, 2023). Moreover, there are flaws in the ecosystem for professional learning. Specifically, district and school leaders face challenges for organizing release time, compensation, and space for high-quality, aligned professional learning on STEM innovations for educators, as well as pursuing such opportunities for themselves. And educators, regardless of their role in the school system, encounter challenges for implementing the principles and practices addressed during professional learning in their particular school and/or classroom contexts (MacLeod, 2020).

While the provision of professional learning across educator roles is often essential for scaling innovations, it is important to simultaneously consider the design, implementation, and scale of professional learning itself. In other words, just as it is important to encourage principled adaptation of an innovation for a given context and community, it is often necessary to also consider how a professional learning design may need to be adapted for a new context or community, with specific resources and strengths, as well as challenges. A key challenge that often emerges is developing professional learning facilitators who have the necessary expertise and resources to design and adapt professional learning specific to particular contexts and communities. Indeed, building and sustaining a cadre of professional learning facilitators is a critical aspect of building systemic capacity to support innovation (see below). Relatedly, many designers of innovations—including academic researchers—would benefit from collaborative opportunities to deepen their knowledge of educational systems and settings. Designers who have a deeper understanding of schools and classrooms are better able to prepare for the transition of an innovation from its initial implementation to robust use across new settings and to provide appropriate guidance and responsive support.

Organizational learning also matters for the course and depth of STEM innovation implementation. In particular, the ways that districts, as organizations, adapt in response to evidence on STEM outcomes as well as barriers for change, can be treated as organizational learning. Moreover, when districts apply a continuous improvement approach, rather than a compliance orientation, this enables educators to engage more meaningfully with STEM innovations and work in creative ways to advance implementation efforts, bridging the gap between research and practice (Schneider, 2014). For example, district leaders might pilot new mathematics high-quality instructional materials in a small set of schools, collect evidence on how educators and students respond, and then design more effective systems to enable district-wide curriculum implementation in subsequent years. This incremental approach provides time and space for individual and organizational learning, aiding in ensuring the innovation contributes to substantive—and sustainable—change.

Organizational and adult professional learning opportunities are levers with the potential to boost actors' agency for implementing STEM innovations. Capacity-building instruments play key roles ensuring enactors and enablers—teachers, coaches, and district and school administrators—to understand the rationale for an innovation, key components of the innovation, and how to align their work to the innovation (Coburn, 2001; McDonnell & Elmore, 1987; Woulfin & Gabriel, 2022). In turn, teachers and leaders integrate ideas into their planning and practices for not only implementing the innovation but to create conditions and guidance for others who are involved in implementation.

Leadership

Leadership also functions as a lever catalyzing the implementation of STEM innovations. Leaders positioned at different levels and in various organizations can take steps to select priorities and align initiatives that, in turn, increase the likelihood that teachers (as well as other leaders) take active steps matching the principles and practices of a particular STEM innovation. They play roles in framing innovations (Coburn, 2006; Woulfin, Donaldson, & Gonzales, 2016). The strategic communication about problems as well as solutions associated with STEM teaching and learning can motivate others to shift their beliefs and practices related to STEM (Coburn, 2006; McLaughlin & Mitra, 2017; Sarama & Clements, 2013; Woulfin, 2015). This communication matters for delineating how and why teachers and leaders adopt aspects of a STEM innovation. For example, a district administrator's framing of how teachers use new math high-quality instructional materials can promote changes aligned with the new curriculum. And, if an intermediary organization leader sets up *Framework*-aligned science standards in resonant ways, district and school leaders could be more likely to allocate funding and time necessary for promoting and enacting science instruction.

Leadership activities also serve to promote the agency of other actors involved in implementing STEM innovations (Elmore, 2016). In a sense, leaders who are aware of how learning happens at all levels in STEM education can catalyze the agency of others in the STEM arena. In particular, perceptive leaders in different roles at different levels can create conditions enabling teachers and other system and school leaders to interpret, learn from, and then respond to messages about STEM innovations in substantive ways (Elfers & Stritikus, 2014; Woulfin & Gabriel, 2020).

System Capacity to Support Innovation

Enactors implement innovations in complex contexts, which often entails the management of multiple and competing demands. Providing high-quality professional learning supports for those charged with enacting the innovation is necessary but not sufficient for supporting sustainable implementation at some scale, especially, again, if the innovation entails substantial change to the enactors' current beliefs, knowledge, and/or practice (e.g., Bryk et al., 2015; Cobb et al., 2018; Coburn, 2003; Elmore, 1996, 2016; NASEM, 2020). Instead, if innovations are to take hold, research provides ample evidence that aspects of the educational system must be supportive of—not hindrances to—educators' implementation of the innovation (Coburn, 2003; Elmore, 1996; Fullan, 2016; Johnson, 2019). One aspect is the coherence between the focus of the innovation, and other instructional reform initiatives and materials that educators are expected to simultaneously implement (Desimone et al., 2002; Garet et al., 2001) Teachers, in particular, are often expected to learn about and implement new forms of practice, or new materials, without consideration of how these fit with existing practices and materials, and what might be best to set aside or forgo (Schneider, 2014).

The sustainability of an innovation is easily threatened by turnover in the enactors. Thus, whether the innovation entails a minor or substantial change to "business as usual," it is critical to build in structured opportunities to "onboard" new enactors (McLaughlin & Mitra, 2001). One strategy is to identify and grow a cadre of experienced educators who are provided with resources (e.g., time, compensation) to create ongoing opportunities for new members to learn about the innovation and participate in research activities, as observed in the Tennessee Math Coaching Project (see Box 4-2) and other professional learning community examples discussed in Chapter 4. For example, Yoon and colleagues (2020a) have discussed the importance of designing for "social capital" in teacher professional learning. They describe social capital as "building teacher networks, sharing knowledge and resources, and providing access to expertise" (p. 253). The shift from human capital—that is developing knowledge and skills at the individual level—to social capital emphasizes being connected and a part of a social community in which teachers have access to expertise from peers, and a community in which teachers are "scaffolded to develop social ties, build trust by sharing experiences and resources, participate in collective sensemaking on practice and access peer and expert support through multiple channels" (Yoon et al., 2020b, p. 689). District leaders, principals, and coaches can similarly benefit from participating in peer networks across schools.

Fundamental to this type of work is understanding that schools implement reforms and innovations through localized social processes: members of a school are part of a social system that can gain access to each other's expertise and may respond to social pressures to implement innovations, even if they run counter to their own perceptions of value of the innovation (Frank, Zhao, & Borman, 2004). Schools and teachers within them may develop a shared understanding of their instructional vision (Munter & Wilhelm, 2020), and positive change in instructional practice can be achieved through interactions with close colleagues (Sun et al., 2014), given their expertise (Wilhelm et al., 2016).

A related issue concerns the workplace culture, including the extent to which educators are trusted and encouraged to make sense of, experiment with, and adapt new materials and practices (e.g., Bryk et al., 2010; Johnson, 2019; NASEM, 2020). School leaders play a critical role in establishing and maintaining a school culture that is supportive of innovations in teaching and learning (e.g., Bryk et al., 2015; Grissom, Egalite, & Lindsay, 2021; Kazemi, Resnick, & Gibbons, 2022). Just as school leadership matters, so does district leadership (e.g., Cobb et al., 2018; Honig, 2012). One issue regards the nature of district leaders' accountability relations with school leaders, and whether district expectations are coherent with the focus of the innovation. For example, if principal supervisors primarily press principals to increase student achievement on a limited assessment of learning, absent attention to teaching quality or students' wellbeing, those principals are, in turn, likely to press teachers to focus narrowly on student achievement. On the other hand, if principal supervisors not only expect but encourage school leaders to organize opportunities for teachers to develop more ambitious ways of engaging students in STEM, principals are likely to act accordingly (Honig, 2012; Jackson et al., 2018; Kazemi et al., 2024). These sets of accountability relations (between district leaders and school leaders; and school leaders and teachers) shape the workplace culture and the extent to which the enactors and enablers view experimenting with innovations in service of expansive views of teaching and learning as both expected and desirable.

Since the "implementation of a complex process in the context of a complex system necessitates a rich set of data to facilitate meaningful action," districts have begun to utilize various models of data collection to support planning and measuring implementation of one or more innovations in context beyond simply tracking end-of-implementation student outcomes (Olson et al., 2020, p. 56). One such model, the Concerns Based Adoption Model (CBAM), seeks to measure quality of, degree of, and reactions to the implementation of a given innovation both personally for individual enactors as well as for the educational system as a whole. Utilizing robust data collection models designed to capture the changes systems make to support implementation of innovations can give insight into the enabling conditions for successful implementation across contexts, which can ultimately be used to shape future policy in supporting strong STEM learning.

Coherence

The coherence of STEM innovations with other educational improvement efforts influences the degree of organizational and individual change. By aligning with—or building upon—other improvement strategies and reducing the too-muchness of educational reform, coherence can catalyze the implementation of STEM innovations (Bryk et al., 2015; Honig & Hatch, 2004). Here, leaders play key roles in intentionally aligning and then strategically connecting STEM innovations with other improvement efforts. For instance, state administrators can connect mathematics high-quality instructional materials with school improvement models. And principals and coaches can meld *Framework*-aligned science standards learning with professional learning community routines so that teachers have opportunities to collaborate on—and learn together about—this approach to science instruction. As such, system leaders need opportunities to learn about methods for assessing and revising system-level policies and practices that may be impeding implementation of innovations, which might include developing orientations and enacting principles aimed at fostering experimentation and learning "along the way" as innovations are implemented (Bryk et al., 2015).

Relatedly, there are potential benefits for refining accountability policies, including high stakes testing, to enable the deeper implementation of STEM innovations. By decreasing the pressures of accountability reforms, leaders and teachers could devote greater attention toward STEM innovations. Inside schools, this might involve teachers replacing mathematics and English language arts test preparation activities with *Framework*-aligned instruction that interweaves science, math, and literacy (NASEM, 2022b). Notably, as compared to most STEM innovations, mathematics is more proximal to accountability policies. Based upon this, educators encounter pressure to teach and assess mathematics in particular ways—with consequences for schools and students.

AFFORDANCES OF RESILIENT SYSTEMS

As articulated in earlier chapters, factors that affect scaling of innovations include the need to have a strong, core program with ample room for adaptations for different contexts and learners. In order for innovations to have the potential for scale and sustainability, the innovation and implementation landscapes must be bridged. And for that to happen, there needs to be a system in place that can make it happen. Resilient systems exhibit alignment of goals, policies, and practices.

Some individual innovations have accomplished scaling by growing their own system. That is, these innovations that have achieved some degree of scaling and/or sustainability have invariably done so through creating and leveraging partnerships (see Chapter 5). There have even been some historical attempts through federally funded programs to build resilient systems with durable, sustained capacity and infrastructure to support multiple innovations or a single innovation to scale over time (see Chapter 3).

Research suggests that the design of a resilient, stable system is one that is organized around a "backbone" entity that gathers together the various and varied individuals and organizations that might coalesce around STEM education values, ideas, and/or actions (National Research Council [NRC], 2015). In practice, the backbone may be a government created entity, a grass roots community group, an institution of higher education, a school district, a business, a museum, a foundation, a professional organization, or even an entity created for the sole purpose of providing structural support. Resilient, stable systems also take into account the geography, funding sources, policy, and/or common/cultural identity. Place-based leaders are able to make evidence-informed decisions about local needs and the potential solutions to address those needs given a constellation of factors that matter, such as policy, values, resources, human capital, and facilities aligned with a vision. In other words, there is structure and leadership to enable and encourage the work of tending to the system and making decisions about the implementation needs of an innovation that balances broad understanding of STEM education with deep understanding of localized context.

Figure 8-1 represents the system of actors who engage with an innovation or enable it to take shape. Unlike the system of actors as described in Chapter 1, which positions the learner as the center, or the system of actors as described in Chapter 2, which principally focuses on the formal K–12 education system, Figure 8-1 puts the innovation at the center. From the innovation are the expanding spheres of influence from the learner within the classroom context to the community and formal K–12 education system

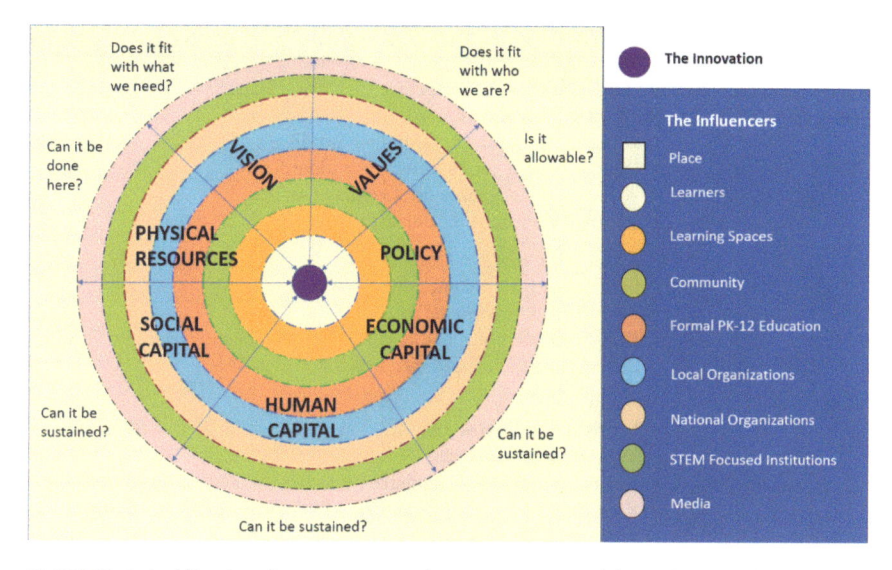

FIGURE 8-1 Aligning factors across the system to enable scaling and sustaining innovations.

to local agencies and STEM focused institutions to national organizations and media all embedded within place. Place serves to acknowledge the histories, cultural practices, ideologies, values, politics, and ethics that are part of both the local context within which an innovation is implemented as well as how it has influenced the broader educational system. Across the expanding spheres, the actors can serve as enablers or enactors, with their positionality changing throughout the life course of an innovation.

Cutting across each of these levels of influence are the enabling and constraining factors highlighted throughout this report. These factors include vision, values, policy, economic capital, human capital, social capital, and physical resources. Starting with the top center wedges (Vision and Values), the overall issue is one of "fit"—enablers and enactors can ask "Does the innovation fit with who we are and where we are going in STEM?" If the answers are, "Yes," then the next issue would be "Can we implement the innovation?" This is where the Policy and Physical Resource wedges come into play as both facilitators and barriers. Again, if the answers to the questions are, "Yes," then it is feasible to consider the scaling and sustaining of the innovation.

For any actor within the system for a given innovation, they can begin to ask themselves questions to help guide implementation of an innovation with considerations related to scaling and sustaining (see Table 8-1). Across all factors and questions, it is important to consider who gets to make the decisions, what influence those decision makers have, and over what time period (see Chapter 2).

TABLE 8-1 Considerations Related to Scaling and Sustaining Innovations

Factors	Questions to Consider
Vision	Does it fit with what we need? • Is this innovation something we need? • Does it solve a problem we have identified? • Will it help us reach a goal we have set? • Where does it rank in our list of priorities?
Values	Does it fit with who we are? • Is this innovation something we want? • Does it fit with who we are? • Does it fit with our STEM culture and other intersecting cultural, demographic and/or identity factors?
Policy	Is it allowable? • Is this innovation something that we can choose to do or is it something we must do? • Are there policies or standards that limit our capacity to do this? • Who can change the policies that limit or promote the innovation, and how difficult is this process?
Economic Capital	Can it be sustained? • Is this something we can afford to do? • What does it cost to implement? To scale? To sustain?
Human Capital	Can it be sustained? • Do we have the leadership support and expertise needed to implement and sustain this innovation? • Do we have the system capacity to build capacity?
Social Capital	Can it be sustained? • How close to our current practice is it? • How aligned is it to other system innovations, including assessments? • What new problems are created? • What accepted practices or people will be replaced? • What will be the reaction of those not involved in the decision-making process? • Can we work around the objections to this innovation?
Physical Resources	Can it be done here? • Do we have the place, space, time, operational structure, learning support systems, equipment, curriculum, professional development, technology, etc. needed to implement and sustain this innovation?

Whereas facilitating the scaling and sustainability of innovations requires a stable, resilient system, systems are vulnerable to disruptions in leadership and funding. These disruptions can bring about an abrupt end to their capacity to act. Strong partnerships among school districts and historically stable organizations such as government agencies, institutions of higher education, trade associations, and business/industry can help safeguard against such disruptions (Krainer et al., 2019; Maas et al., 2019;

Young et al., 2016) and work to move toward a more durable system that can continuously improve itself through cycles of reflection, innovation, implementation, and improvement (Lowrie, Leonard, & Fitzgerald, 2018; Sabelli & Harris, 2015). For this aspirational goal, there is a need for robust systems change.

NEED FOR SYSTEM CHANGE

Scaling is not just about scaling a particular innovation, but rather seen as part of a larger effort to improve the education system as a whole and make lasting changes to organizations and policies that allow for a system that better supports continuous improvement in part through the implementation and sustaining of innovations. Innovation, while necessary to address immediate problems of practice, is insufficient in addressing systemic challenges in STEM education. What is needed is a deeper understanding of scaling across various levels of the system. Stronger systemic infrastructure would enable designers to work with enablers and enactors to set up a system where the essential principles of an innovation can be sustained. This could help to shift the focus from simply putting an innovation into practice to the work of addressing a problem of practice by utilizing an appropriate innovation. Moreover, organizations and systems could then take the lead (Sabelli & Harris, 2015) to ensure that there are policies, practices, and resources available for systems to identify problems of practice so that the system can identify, create, and implement innovations to address those problems, learning along the way.

Schools, districts, and states can have trouble successfully scaling innovations when there is a lack of attention to each classroom's varied context across all levels, including the political context, teacher support from leadership, quality instructional materials, teacher professional learning support, and student learning norms, among other micro- and macro-contextual factors. Each actor is not simply implementing "best practices" but learning to become a different kind of educator (Elmore, 2016). What's more, these leveled contexts need to be considered as interdependent. Maass and colleagues (2019) note that improvement must also take place across interested parties, especially outside of the classroom, and can be addressed through aligning the aims of various partners.

In a decentralized national public education system of nearly 13,000 school districts, large-scale "systems change" can at first seem to be a vague concept with little in the way of a starting point or central locus of power from which change emanates, even within the confines of making the scaling of innovations more practical and possible. This vagueness is in part because, as detailed in Chapter 2, the responsibility to provide public education lies with the states and, across states, most relegate power over school governance to local school boards. One thing that can help to concretize or organize change is data. Central to resilient learning systems are both access to useful data about student learning, instructional practice, and their enabling conditions, as well as the means to utilize these data effectively for organizational change (Peurach et al., 2022).

This report suggests that "systems change" might mean empowering state and local education agencies to build responsive systems that can implement, adapt, and innovate based on local context and the needs of current students to incorporate innovations over time with families and communities as key partners and sources of expertise in the work. Currently, there is a need to ensure that federal agencies are positioned to provide incentives to states and districts to develop policies, practices, and resources that allow for innovation and continuous improvement through the use of locally-collected data that is specific to particular contexts. Developing robust research and development infrastructure within state and local education agencies will require (a) a restructuring of the recipients and purpose of educational research grants, (b) evolving the relationship between educational researchers and educational administrators, (c) shifting research questions from "What works?" to "What is likely to work in this context?" to "What are the infrastructure supports needed for scaling?", and (d) reconfiguring the relationship between local, state, and federal education agencies and the communities they are a part of.

A focus on improvement in this way could support continuous learning and innovation that is grounded firmly in problems of educational practice. It would move away from a system that is stronger in support for evaluating program impact and weaker in supporting continuous improvement (Peurach, 2016). Building system capacity in this way could harness the potential for nimble systems at the federal, state, and local levels that can respond and innovate using evidence based on the local context and student needs with the aspirational goal of ensuring equitable Pre-K–12 STEM learning opportunities for all students.

SUMMARY

The complexity of educational environments results in both embedded challenges as well as opportunities for successfully scaling and sustaining Pre-K–12 STEM education innovations. An array of catalysts—nature of the innovation, resources, professional learning, leadership, system capacity, and coherence—enable the implementation of STEM innovations to scale in more equitable and sustainable ways across various contexts. Policies and resources can reshape conditions to not only support individual actors, but also promote deeper, systemic change. Leaders can create conditions enabling teachers and system and school leaders to interpret, learn from, and then respond to messages about STEM innovations in substantive ways. The coherence of

STEM innovations with other educational improvement efforts influences the degree of organizational and individual change. It is also crucial to consider the need for system change and provide opportunities to not only support the building of individual and organizational capacity to scale and sustain STEM education innovations, but also to seek to continuously improve.

REFERENCES

Bryk, A. S., Gomez, L. M., Grunow, A., & LeMahieu, P. G. (2015). *Learning to improve: How America's schools can get better at getting better.* Harvard Education Press.

Bryk, A. S., Sebring, P. B., Allensworth, E., Luppesco, S., & Easton, J. Q. (2010). *Organizing schools for improvement: Lessons from Chicago.* University of Chicago Press.

Cobb, P., Jackson, K., Henrick, E., Smith, T., & MIST team. (2018). *Systems for Instructional Improvement: Creating coherence from the classroom to the district office.* Harvard Education Press.

Coburn, C. E. (2001). Collective sensemaking about reading: How teachers mediate reading policy in their professional communities. *Educational evaluation and policy analysis*, 23(2), 145–170.

———. (2003). Rethinking scale: Moving beyond numbers to deep and lasting change. *Educational Researcher*, 32(6), 3–12.

———. (2006). Framing the problem of reading instruction: Using frame analysis to uncover the microprocesses of policy implementation. *American Educational Research Journal*, 43(3), 343–349.

Cohen, D. K., & Mehta, J. D. (2017). Why reform sometimes succeeds: Understanding the conditions that produce reforms that last. *American Educational Research Journal*, 54(4), 644–690.

Desimone, L. M., Porter, A. C., Garet, M. S., Yoon, K. S., & Birman, B. F. (2002). Effects of professional development on teachers' instruction: Results from a three-year longitudinal study. *Educational Evaluation and Policy Analysis*, 24(2), 81–112. https://doi.org/10.3102/01623737024002081

Elfers, A. M., & Stritikus, T. (2014). How school and district leaders support classroom teachers' work with English language learners. *Educational Administration Quarterly*, 50(2), 305–344.

Elmore, R. F. (1996). Getting to scale with good educational practice. *Harvard Educational Review*, 66(1), 1–26.

———. (2016). "Getting to scale . . ." it seemed like a good idea at the time. *Journal of Educational Change*, 17, 529–537. https://doi.org/10.1007/s10833-016-9290-8

Ertmer, P. A., Ottenbreit-Leftwich, A. T., Sadik, O., Sendurur, E., & Sendurur, P. (2012). Teacher beliefs and technology integration practices: A critical relationship. *Computers & Education*, 59(2), 423–435.

Fullan, M. (2016). The elusive nature of whole system improvement in education. *Journal of Educational Change*, 17(4), 539–544. https://doi.org/10.1007/s10833-016-9289-1

Frank, K. A., Zhao, Y., & Borman, K. (2004). Social capital and the diffusion of innovations within organizations: Application to the implementation of computer technology in schools. *Sociology of Education*, 77(2), 148–171.

Garet, M. S., Porter, A. C., Desimone, L., Birman, B. F., & Yoon, K. S. (2001). What makes professional development effective? Results from a national sample of teachers. *American Educational Research Journal*, 38(4), 915–945.

Grissom, J. A., Egalite, A. J., & Lindsay, C. A. (2021). How principals affect students and schools: A systematic synthesis of two decades of research. *The Wallace Foundation*, 2(1), 30–41. http://www.wallacefoundation.org/principalsynthesis

Grubb, W. N. (2008). Multiple resources, multiple outcomes: Testing the "improved" school finance with NELS88. *American Educational Research Journal, 45*(1), 104–144.

———. (2009). *The money myth: School resources, outcomes, and equity.* Russell Sage Foundation.

Grubb, W. N., & Allen, R. (2011). Rethinking school funding, resources, incentives, and outcomes. *Journal of Educational Change, 12,* 121–130.

Honig, M. I. (2012). District central office leadership as teaching: How central office administrators support principals' development as instructional leaders. *Educational Administration Quarterly, 48*(4), 733–774.

Honig, M. I., & Hatch, T. C. (2004). Crafting coherence: How schools strategically manage multiple, external demands. *Educational Researcher, 33*(8), 16–30.

Hopkins, M., Spillane, J. P., Jakopovic, P., & Heaton, R. M. (2013). Infrastructure redesign and instructional reform in mathematics: Formal structure and teacher leadership. *The Elementary School Journal, 114*(2), 200–224.

Jackson, K., Cobb, P., Rigby, J. G., & Smith, T. M. (2018). District instructional leadership. In P. Cobb, K. Jackson, E. Henrick, & T. M. Smith (Eds.), *Systems for instructional improvement: Creating coherence from the classroom to the district office* (pp. 193–208). Harvard Education Press.

Johnson, S. M. (2019). *Where teachers thrive: Organizing schools for success.* Harvard Education Press.

Kazemi, E., Calabrese, J., Lind, T., Lewis, B., Resnick, A. F., & Gibbons, L. (2024). *Learning together: Organizing schools for teacher and student learning.* Harvard Educational Press.

Kazemi, E., Resnick, A. F., & Gibbons, L. (2022). Principal leadership for school-wide transformation of elementary mathematics teaching: Why the principal's conception of teacher learning matters. *American Educational Research Journal, 59*(6), 1051–1089.

Kolbe, T., Steele, C., & White, B. (2020). Time to teach: Instructional time and science teachers' use of inquiry-oriented instructional practices. *Teachers College Record, 122*(12), 1–54. https://doi.org/10.1177/016146812012201211

Kraft, M. A., & Novicoff, S. (2022). *Instructional time in US public schools: Wide variation, causal effects, and lost hours* (EdWorkingPaper No. 22-653). Annenberg Institute for School Reform at Brown University.

Krainer, K., Zehetmeier, S., Hanfstingl, B., Rauch, F., & Tscheinig, T. (2019). Insights into scaling up a nationwide learning and teaching initiative on various levels. *Educational Studies in Mathematics, 102,* 395–415.

Lowrie, T., Leonard, S., & Fitzgerald, R. (2018). STEM practices: A translational framework for large-scale STEM education design. *Educational Design Research, 2*(1).

Maass, K., Cobb, P., Krainer, K., Potari, D. (2019). Different ways to implement innovative teaching approaches at scale. *Educational Studies in Mathematics, 102,* 303–318.

MacLeod, L. (2020). Shaping professional development of educators: The role of school leaders. In M. A. White, & F. McCallum (Eds.), *Critical perspectives on teaching, learning and leadership: Enhancing educational outcomes* (pp. 189–217). Springer. https://doi.org/10.1007/978-981-15-6667-7_10

Marshall, S. L., & Khalifa, M. A. (2018). Humanizing school communities: Culturally responsive leadership in the shaping of curriculum and instruction. *Journal of Educational Administration, 56*(5), 533–545.

McDonnell, L. M., & Elmore, R. F. (1987). Getting the job done: Alternative policy instruments. *Educational Evaluation and Policy Analysis, 9*(2), 133–152.

McLaughlin, M. W., & Mitra, D. (2001). Theory-based change and change-based theory: Going deeper, going broader. *Journal of Educational Change, 2,* 301–323.

Munter, C., & Wilhelm, A. G. (2021). Mathematics teachers' knowledge, networks, practice, and change in instructional visions. *Journal of Teacher Education, 72*(3), 342–354. https://doi.org/10.1177/0022487120949836

National Academies of Sciences, Engineering, and Medicine (NASEM). (2020). *Changing expectations for the K–12 teacher workforce: Policies, preservice education, professional development, and the workplace.* The National Academies Press.

———. (2022a). *The future of education research at IES: Advancing an equity-oriented science.* The National Academies Press.

———. (2022b). *Science and engineering in preschool through elementary grades: The brilliance of children and the strengths of educators.* The National Academies Press. https://doi.org/10.17226/26215

National Research Council. (2015). *Identifying and supporting productive STEM programs in out-of-school settings.* National Academies Press.

Niederhauser, D. S., Howard, S. K., Voogt, J., Agyei, D. D., Laferriere, T., Tondeur, J., & Cox, M. J. (2018). Sustainability and scalability in educational technology initiatives: Research-informed practice. *Technology, Knowledge and Learning, 23*, 507–523.

Olson, K., Lannan, K., Cumming, J., Macgillivary, H., & Richards, K. (2020). The concerns-based adoption model and strategic plan evaluation: Multiple methodologies to understand complex change. *Theory and Practice, 31*(3), 49–58. https://files.eric.ed.gov/fulltext/EJ1274351.pdf

Pareja Roblin, N., Schunn, C., & McKenney, S. (2018). What are critical features of science curriculum materials that impact student and teacher outcomes? *Science Education, 102*(2), 260–282.

Peurach, D. J. (2016). Innovating at the nexus of impact and improvement: Leading educational improvement networks. *Educational Researcher, 45*(7), 421–429.

Peurach, D. J., Russell, J., Cohen-Vogel, L., & Penuel, W. R. (Eds.). (2022). *The foundational handbook on improvement research in education.* Rowman & Littlefield.

Puntambekar, S., Gnesdilow, D., Dornfeld Tissenbaum, C. D., Narayanan, H. N., & Rebello, S., (2021). Supporting middle school students' science talk: A comparison of physical and virtual labs. *Journal of Research in Science Teaching, 58*(3), 392–419.

Sabelli, N. H., & Harris, C. J. (2015). The role of innovation in scaling up educational innovations. In *Scaling educational innovations* (pp. 13–30). Springer.

Sarama, J., & Clements, D. H. (2013). Lessons learned in the implementation of the TRIAD scale-up model: Teaching early mathematics with trajectories and technologies. In T. G. Halle, A. J. Metz, & I. Martinez Beck (Eds.), *Applying implementation science in early childhood programs and systems* (pp. 173–191). Brookes.

Schneider, J. (2014). *From the ivory tower to the schoolhouse: How scholarship becomes common knowledge in education.* Harvard University Press.

Sun, M., Wilhelm, A. G., Larson, C. J., & Frank, K. A. (2014). Exploring colleagues' professional influences on mathematics teachers' learning. *Teachers College Record, 116*(4), 1–30.

Tyler, B., Estrella, D., Britton, T., Nguyen, K., Iveland, A., Nilsen, K., Arnett, E., & Valcarcel, J. (2020). *What education leaders can learn about NGSS implementation: Highlights from the early implementers initiative* (Evaluation Report No. 14). WestEd.

Wilhelm, A. G., Chen, I.-C., Smith, T. M., & Frank, K. A. (2016). Selecting expertise in context: Middle school mathematics teachers' selection of new sources of instructional advice. *American Educational Research Journal, 53*(3), 456–491. https://doi.org/10.3102/0002831216637351

Woulfin, S. L. (2015). Catalysts of change: An examination of coaches' leadership practices in framing a reading reform. *Journal of School Leadership, 25*(3), 526–557.

Woulfin, S., & Gabriel, R. E. (2020). Interconnected infrastructure for improving reading instruction. *Reading Research Quarterly, 55*, S109–S117.

Woulfin, S. L., & Gabriel, R. (2022). Big waves on the rocky shore: A discussion of reading policy, infrastructure, and implementation in the era of Science of Reading. *The Reading Teacher, 76*(3), 326–332.

Woulfin, S. L., & Spitzer, N. (2023). The evolution of coaching as a policy instrument: How a district engages in organizational learning. *Educational Policy*, *38*(6), 1386–1417.

Woulfin, S. L., Donaldson, M. L., & Gonzales, R. (2016). District leaders' framing of educator evaluation policy. *Educational Administration Quarterly*, *52*(1), 110–143.

Woulfin, S., Stevenson, I., & Lord, K. (2023). *Making coaching matter: Leading continuous improvement in schools*. Teachers College Press.

Woulfin, S. R., Dawer, D., McKenzie, L., & Pernetti, M. (2024). [The ecosystem of actors influencing the implementation of STEM innovations]. Paper commissioned by the Committee on Pre-K–12 STEM Education Innovations. https://nap.nationalacademies.org/resource/27950/Ecosystems%20of%20Actors%20Influencing%20the%20Implementation%20of%20STEM%20Innovations_Woulfin%20Dawer%20McKenzie%20Pernetti.pdf

Yoon, S. A., Miller, K., Richman, T., Wendel, D., Schoenfeld, I., Anderson, E., & Shim, J. (2020a). Encouraging collaboration and building community in online asynchronous professional development: Designing for social capital. *International Journal of Computer-Supported Collaborative Learning*, *15*, 351–371.

Yoon, S. A., Miller, K., Richman, T., Wendel, D., Schoenfeld, I., Anderson, E., Shim, J., & Marei, A. (2020b). A social capital design for delivering online asynchronous professional development in a MOOC course for science teachers. *Information and Learning Sciences*, *121*(7/8), 677–693.

Young, V. M., House, A., Sherer, D., Singleton, C., & Wang, H. (2016). Scaling up STEM academies statewide: Implementation, network supports, and early outcomes. *Teachers College Record*, *118*(13), 1–26. https://doi.org/10.1177/016146811611801310

Zeichner, K. (2010). Rethinking the connections between campus courses and field experiences in college- and university-based teacher education. *Journal of Teacher Education*, *61*(1–2), 89–99.

9

Conclusions, Recommendations, and Research Agenda

The committee was tasked with reviewing the evidence on the interconnected factors that foster and/or hinder the successful implementation of promising Pre-K–12 science, technology, engineering, and mathematics (STEM) education innovations at local, regional, and national levels. As the committee reviewed the evidence around promising innovations, they explored the barriers to widespread and sustained implementation of such innovations and provided recommendations to address these barriers. Through the committee's analysis of the research and evidence of promising Pre-K–12 STEM education innovations, the committee examined the landscape of the public Pre-K–12 education system including the various actors at different levels of the system (federal, state, local, and regional), including their roles and responsibilities. To understand the current state of STEM education within public schools, the committee examined the history of federal and national STEM education improvements.

In an effort to understand the barriers to "widespread and sustained implementation," the committee interrogated the evidence on scale and the factors that foster and/or hinder the successful implementation of promising, evidence-based, Pre-K–12 STEM education innovations (to include programs, practices, models, and technologies). Through this interrogation of evidence, the committee recognized an inherent tension between the configurations of actors, decision makers, and financial resources involved in the development of an innovation and those involved in the implementation.

As the committee carried out their work, they recognized that although individual innovations are important and necessary contributions to the broad Pre-K–12 STEM education system, they may not be sufficient in leading to the kind of system change that the committee believes is needed for all students to have differentiated and equitable access and opportunities to engage in STEM learning. And, systemic change is needed. **If a potential aspirational end goal is to have a durable educational system that can continuously improve itself through cycles of reflection, innovation, implementation, and improvement,** the committee makes the following consensus conclusions and recommendations based upon the available evidence to achieve this aspirational goal. The chapter concludes with a discussion of remaining research gaps.

CONCLUSIONS

What follows are the committee's conclusions based on the review of the available evidence on the interrelated factors that enable or constrain the scalability of promising Pre-K–12 STEM education innovations, organized by themes. The committee first characterizes the complex Pre-K–12 education landscape—noting the roles and responsibilities of those actors in the implementation of STEM education innovations—as a starting point before describing the history of STEM education improvements. Then the committee goes on to articulate the conceptualization of scale as multidimensional, which includes spread, depth, sustainability, and ownership, and the implications for collecting evidence of the supporting conditions for promising Pre-K–12 STEM education innovations to scale. Lastly, the committee then describes conclusions related to the enabling and constraining factors for scaling and sustaining Pre-K–12 STEM education innovations.

Pre-K–12 Education Landscape and History of STEM Education Improvements

Numerous educational reform efforts at the federal and state levels have attempted to change the nature of STEM instruction and disrupt persistent inequitable patterns regarding students' short- and long-term STEM outcomes. As described in Chapter 2, structural features of the U.S. education system present barriers as well as opportunities for STEM education innovations to take root and scale. Each of the multiple, nested levels of the education system contains regulations, ideas, and resources related to STEM education innovations. And various actors, positioned across multiple levels of the education system and facing different institutional and organizational conditions, deploy their agency while enacting STEM innovations. These actors not only engage in different responsibilities but also hold different levels of power and authority for motivating the implementation of various innovations.

Conclusion 1: Actors across the formal Pre-K–12 educational system not only have different spheres of influence but also have power and decision making at different levels (e.g., local, state, federal). This can result in misalignments across levels due to divergent constraints, potentially impacting the implementation, scaling, and sustaining of promising Pre-K–12 STEM education innovations.

The formal Pre-K context is different from the formal K–12 education system in important ways, and there is not clear alignment or coherence of policies, standards, and teaching practices from Pre-K into the K–12 system. Chapter 2 contains a description of the formal Pre-K system and the linkages to STEM education. Each state designs its own Pre-K system through authorizing legislation and funding, and determines eligibility, quality standards, and monitoring. Because of this, the governance is highly variable and fragmented. There are a number of ways in which states have attempted to enhance integration of STEM in their Pre-K policies; however, attention to STEM in Pre-K is sporadic. A few states and districts have developed a scalable and sustainable approach to integrating STEM fields through curriculum, professional preparation, and professional learning and development[1] of Pre-K teachers and administrators.

Conclusion 2: There is a lack of coherence in STEM education across early childhood, in part due to the disconnect that exists between preschool programs and the K–12 education system. Prior to elementary school, young children are served through a variety of programs (e.g., federal programs like Head Start, state-funded Pre-K, and various community agencies), which vary in their alignment to K–12.

Conclusion 3: Promising research and development efforts in early childhood have emerged in the past decades. However, more research is needed to understand how early STEM education innovations can be scaled and sustained to promote STEM learning in preschool and strengthen children's later learning in K–12.

Chapters 2 and 3 describe the role of federal agencies in STEM education improvements. Historically, the U.S. federal government has played an indirect and influential role in education while states and local education agencies have direct control. Even today, the federal government exerts

---

[1] As noted earlier in the report, the terms "professional learning" and "professional development" are both in current usage, though various users may prefer one to the other and may intend to indicate different approaches or types of activities. Because various local, state, and national education agencies; funders; and other organizations may use one or the other, the committee's recommendations include both terms.

limited control over schooling, with few direct throughlines to communities and classrooms. Yet researchers and practitioners point to multiple ways that federal legislation, guidance, and leadership affect local systems and activities. For example, early initiatives made significant advancements in leveraging science and mathematics curricular resources to improve STEM education at scale, but their potential to drive transformative and sustained improvements is limited without continuous, long-term funding, and easy-to-manage distribution channels.

Conclusion 4: The federal government and states have implemented different efforts with the goal of improving STEM education (e.g., systems change, standards, accountability). Although these efforts, particularly those with robust and coordinated plans, have shown promise and lead to improvements, few have been sustained once funding was reduced.

Conclusion 5: The decentralized system not only lacks the means to propagate large-scale improvement across the country but also presents a challenge for the ways in which the federal government can incentivize large-scale, sustained, and well-resourced improvement efforts.

The passage of the No Child Left Behind (NCLB) Act in 2001 marked a number of critical changes in the federal education policy landscape and significantly increased the role of states in holding schools responsible for the academic progress of all students. Chapter 3 describes how different federal pushes have ushered in a new era of high-stakes assessment in mathematics (and English language arts). This intense focus on math assessments led to a narrowing of the curriculum, with teachers often feeling pressured to "teach to the test." Science and engineering learning became even more deprioritized, with instructional time and resources frequently diverted from these subjects to improving math and reading scores. This increased focus on student performance and achievement has fundamentally altered STEM education.

Conclusion 6: Across the Pre-K–12 spectrum, the distribution of emphasis placed on different STEM disciplines has restricted opportunities for some content areas and in some grades. This presents different innovation and implementation challenges for STEM education innovations within formal Pre-K–12 educational settings.

Notably, the education landscape includes actors beyond those most closely connected to formal spaces. Out-of-school time experiences take place in a vast range of environments and situations, including youth development programs, museums, libraries, zoos, botanical gardens, science centers, and community centers. Chapter 3 describes the role that these spaces can play in supporting STEM education improvement efforts. For example, programs within out-of-school time settings often have flexibility to design learning experiences that reflect the interests and identities of the learners and communities they serve. Moreover, partnerships between K–12 and out-of-school time settings can enhance connections to support the teaching and learning of STEM through the development of resources. Additionally, Chapter 3 acknowledges many of the other actors in the system (e.g., families, communities, business/industry, professional societies to name a few) who can have influence on what happens in schools, including the development and implementation of Pre-K–12 STEM education innovations. This larger circle of actors can play an important role in advocating for change; however, they may need to be proactive and persistent as they seek to be recognized and understood. Decision makers and implementers within the formal education system who seek out partnerships with an expanded group of actors can gain a variety of supports for effectively adapting and sustaining innovations in their local contexts.

Conclusion 7: Out-of-school spaces (e.g., museums, science centers, libraries) not only provide opportunities for learners to engage in Pre-K–12 STEM education innovations but also are important spaces for their development. These settings can support experimentation and, the development of resources (e.g., professional learning, curriculum) that can translate into formal Pre-K–12 educational settings, as well as serve as backbone organizations in scaling efforts.

Conclusion 8: Actors and participants closely connected to formal spaces, including those traditionally underrepresented in the development and implementation of Pre-K–12 STEM education innovations, can play important roles in shaping what is (or is not) happening in schools.

Scaling and Sustaining Promising Pre-K–12 STEM Education Innovations

In the design of innovations, conceptualization of scale is diverse, and there is variability in the criteria to assess whether, and in what ways, an innovation has "scaled." Chapter 4 recognizes that most discussions of scale focus solely on increasing numbers, or spread; however, scale is multidimensional and includes other dimensions such as considerations of the depth of implementation, sustainability, and shift in ownership. Assessments of scale often focus on surface-level indications of adoption (e.g., number of beneficiaries, presence of materials, time spent using the materials), with little attention to depth, sustainability, and ownership. Spread alone does not support educators or researchers in knowing whether an innovation is resulting in the desired improvement and for whom, whether the innovation is sustained as enactors change, and why or why not.

> *Conclusion 9: The notion of scale is multidimensional (i.e., spread, depth, sustainability, and ownership); however, assessments of scale to date most often focus on the spread of innovations. Additional research is needed to better understand these other dimensions of scale.*

Conceptualizing scale as multidimensional recognizes that some innovations are specifically tailored for a particular population, place, and/or problem of practice. Moreover, Chapter 4 illustrates that not all efforts to scale an innovation will explicitly attend to each of these dimensions, nor will they give equal weight or priority to the dimensions on which they focus.

> *Conclusion 10: Pre-K–12 STEM education innovations can be designed for different purposes. They can be designed to have deep impact with a more local focus, designed explicitly for large-scale impact with less attention to depth, or designed to be some combination of both. Targeted innovations can be just as impactful as those designed for broad reach.*

The four dimensions of scale discussed in Chapter 4 are intertwined in complex ways. And the more ambitious an innovation is, the more challenging it may be to sustain if it necessitates a substantial change to "business as usual." Research has shown that if the innovation involves superficial or minor changes to current practice, its adoption and assimilation by practitioners is more easily achieved. However, superficial change is inherently fragile. Innovations that entail substantial change to current practice represent a formidable challenge that demands time and significant investment in professional resources to accomplish. It requires a change of culture. But once achieved, it provides a foundation for sustainability.

> *Conclusion 11: In the identification and selection of Pre-K–12 STEM education innovations, a tension exists between innovations that are easy to spread despite limited evidence of impact and innovations that are harder to implement yet show robust evidence of impact.*

Federal funding agencies have historically prioritized sequential studies of scaling innovations (i.e., pilot studies, efficacy studies, effectiveness studies, scale-up studies), whereby the innovation is implemented in tightly prescribed ways, in increasingly heterogeneous sites and/or populations, and in service of specified outcomes. However, federal funding is limited to investigate the sustainability of innovations (see Chapters 4 and 5).

CONCLUSIONS, RECOMMENDATIONS, AND RESEARCH AGENDA 245

Conclusion 12: Current funding structures encourage scalability after innovations are designed, tested, and proven efficacious; however, funding to ensure and study how innovations can sustain is limited, and therefore less is known about the mitigating factors for scaling and sustainability of innovations.

Chapter 6 begins with a discussion of how computer technologies have had profound impacts on education, especially as access to computers and the internet have increased in K–12 education settings. Tools and technologies rarely fully communicate meaning or information about how they can be best used, especially to support learning and cultural practices. Many other factors, such as pedagogy underlying curricula, participatory structures, and teachers play an essential role in helping students understand how and why these tools have been designed in certain ways and how they can be used to promote reflection, solve problems, and accomplish goals. Therefore, it is important to interrogate promising, evidence-based innovations for the features that support (and constrain) their scalability and sustainability.

Conclusion 13: Multiple forms of technology (e.g., simulations, models, visualizations, immersive environments, artificial intelligence technologies, dashboards for classroom orchestration) have shown evidence for supporting Pre-K–12 STEM learning and teaching. Although technology is being used to promote learning in Pre-K–12 STEM education environments, the impact of particular forms of technology on the scalability and sustainability of innovations needs to be better examined and understood.

Drawing from an examination of the literature as well as a synthesis of program information, Chapter 7 highlights the factors that support the conditions for scaling. For programs to successfully scale, it is important that they include a proven core program (that is clearly stated) with ample room for adaptation to different contexts and learners. This flexibility can support educator autonomy, which can aid in motivation and buy-in. The program also needs to align with the priorities set by policy, organizations, and individual practitioners. For example, showing how the program is aligned with standards can help with uptake by showing how implementing the program can be incorporated into existing practices and help achieve goals for learners. Providing support for practitioners through professional learning opportunities is important for capacity building and program adoption. However, there also needs to be support from the organization via an investment in resources and continued support. In some cases, this might mean focusing on a bigger shift in the organization or policies to establish a system where the essential principles of an innovation can be adopted and sustained. In this way, an organization's capacity for adopting any new program could be strengthened. Lastly, partnerships can be valuable for scaling in a variety of ways. Having external organizations partner with districts, schools, and teachers can provide in-depth insights into specific contexts to guide development and improvements. Moreover, external partners can also be valuable sources of resources, funding, and support.

Conclusion 14: The extant literature suggestions that some characteristics that allow a promising innovation to spread and sustain over time include:

- *A strong, core program with ample room for adaptations for different contexts and learners*
- *Alignment of goals, policies, and practices*
- *Development of individual capacity and organizational support*
- *Development and support of partnerships and networks*

Enabling and Constraining Factors

In understanding how Pre-K–12 STEM education innovations arise, take root, and spread it is important to recognize that there is an important distinction to be made between the configurations of actors, decision makers, and financial resources that are typically involved in the development of evidence-based innovations as compared to the configurations that come into play as innovations are implemented, sustained, and spread across settings and populations. Many funded projects are not sustained in a significant way beyond their original instantiation because of this (see Chapter 5). Although these innovations may generate important research evidence of impacts on STEM learning or other desired outcomes in their original context, they lack a functional dissemination model that reaches directly into classrooms or other educational settings. As noted above, partnerships play a key role in the scaling and sustainability of promising Pre-K–12 STEM education innovations.

Conclusion 15: In the design of innovations, there can be a disconnect between the landscapes of innovation and implementation.

Conclusion 16: Mature innovations often involve collaborative, iterative cycles of design across multiple sites and an extended period of time. Different aspects and phases of this work generally require the participation of actors with different experience and expertise.

Innovations that have shown promise for scaling and sustaining are often developed with input from practitioners about the needs of educators and students and with explicit attention to the varying contexts in which the innovation could be implemented. Chapter 5 points to the research that shows that promising innovations with good evidence of efficacy often lack characteristics and features that would make them easier to be adopted and implemented more widely. It goes on to note that the original designers may lack incentives, knowledge, or expertise to build them out in more full-featured formats.

> *Conclusion 17: Promising innovations often have limited impact because their research and development are isolated from realistic contexts. The designs and methodologies prioritize artificially narrow or rigid interventions or conditions to obtain strong evidence, but then potential adopters or adapters lack information about how the innovation could be adapted for a particular context or goal(s).*

As introduced in Chapter 5 and then taken up in Chapters 7 and 8, the complexity of educational environments results in embedded challenges that can negatively affect successful scaling and sustainability efforts. If a program is designed to align with specific policies or to meet specific goals, there can be a large threat to scaling and sustainability when policies or priorities change and are no longer in line with the direction of the program. Scaling and sustainability are aided by the buy-in and capacity building of individuals and organizations. If individuals championing the program at an organization or those trained to implement it leave, it can hinder continuity and efforts scale the program. During scaling efforts, it can be difficult to also update materials, as doing so may require additional development and testing. This can lead to materials that are out-of-date with the latest advances in STEM fields. Once a program has scaled broadly it is challenging to monitor and evaluate. When a program is being implemented and adapted in many different contexts, it is difficult to draw conclusions across sites and learners. Additionally, the cost of evaluating something at this scale in a deep way can be prohibitive.

> *Conclusion 18: Challenges to scaling promising Pre-K–12 STEM education innovations include changes to policies and priorities, staff turnover, keeping materials updated, cost, and monitoring implementation and outcomes at scale.*

Policy structures and design features, resources, infrastructure, and leadership influence the STEM innovation implementation activities of various actors. Certain levers hold the potential to increase the agency of district and school leaders to more deeply implement STEM innovations, as described in Chapter 8. Policies and resources can reshape conditions to not only support individual actors, but also promote deeper, systemic change. Leaders can create conditions enabling teachers and system and school leaders to interpret, learn from, and then respond to messages about STEM innovations in substantive ways. The coherence of STEM innovations with other educational improvement efforts influences the degree of organizational and individual change. By aligning with—or building upon—other improvement strategies and reducing the "too-muchness" of educational reform, coherence can catalyze the implementation of STEM innovations. An array of catalysts—nature of the innovation, resources, professional learning, leadership, system capacity, and coherence—enable the implementation of STEM innovations to scale in more equitable and sustainable ways across various contexts.

Conclusion 19: Critical factors that need attention during implementation include: the nature of the innovation, resources (e.g., funding, materials, and time), professional learning for educators, leadership, system capacity, and coherence. For innovations to scale and be sustained, it is critical to attend to these key factors during implementation so that these factors are supportive of, rather than hindrances to, educators' enactment of innovations.

Chapter 8 also acknowledged the need for system change through the building of individual and organizational capacity. Providing high-quality professional learning supports for those charged with enacting the innovation is necessary but not sufficient for supporting sustainable implementation at some scale, especially if the innovation entails substantial change to the enactors' current beliefs, knowledge, and/or practice. The sustainability of an innovation is easily threatened by turnover in the enactors. Thus, whether the innovation entails a minor or substantial change to "business as usual," it is critical to build in structured opportunities to "onboard" new enactors. One strategy is to identify and grow a cadre of experienced educators who are provided with resources (e.g., time, compensation) to create ongoing opportunities for new members to learn about the innovation.

Conclusion 20: The preparation and development of preservice and inservice teachers and school leaders does not routinely include building internal capacities to continuously identify, evaluate, and implement new high-quality instructional resources and practices to adapt them for the needs of different students.

RECOMMENDATIONS

The committee was tasked with identifying barriers to widespread and sustained implementation of promising, evidence-based Pre-K–12 STEM education innovations and to make recommendations to the National

Science Foundation, the U.S. Department of Education, the National Science and Technology Council's Committee on Science, Technology, Engineering, and Mathematics Education, state and local educational agencies, and other relevant stakeholders on measures to address such barriers. A prevailing issue emphasized by the committee is the need for coherent, systemic reform efforts that can build toward a nimble system that can innovate and respond to challenges as they emerge. This includes developing the capacity of all participants in the design, implementation, scaling, and sustaining of Pre-K–12 STEM education innovations whether at the level of individuals or a system that connects across multiple levels so that there is increased sharing of knowledge across levels of the system. For example, if an individual teacher is entering into a research-practice partnership, they may need support from the school, access to resources and time, and professional learning opportunities that allow them to fully engage in the research process. A school is more likely to be able to provide these types of experiences to the teacher if the school itself is embedded within a system that has the necessary resources for the work to be carried out. And federal agencies can be a source of funding to establish and build structures so that these infrastructure supports can be maintained.

Based upon the committee's conclusions, the following recommendations are intended to be steps toward changing the current "business as usual" to a system that can effectively and efficiently plan, implement, evaluate, and adjust Pre-K–12 STEM education innovations.

Building Capacity and Monitoring Progress

The first four recommendations point to roles that federal agencies can play in building capacity within states to support implementation efforts. Chapter 8 highlights the need for individual and organizational capacity as supporting conditions for the scalability of promising Pre-K–12 STEM education innovations. To build capacity, there needs to be significant investment in the professional learning and development[2] of teachers, as they are the frontline in the implementation of STEM education innovations, as well as significant investment in building partnerships within the system to support organizational capacity. Building connected systems of teachers and administrators, curriculum specialists and developers, technology specialists, community learners and partners, and researchers and creating new roles and

---

[2] As noted earlier in the report, the terms "professional learning" and "professional development" are both in current usage, though various users may prefer one to the other and may intend to indicate different approaches or types of activities. Because various local, state, and national education agencies; funders; and other organizations may use one or the other, the committee's recommendations include both terms.

spaces for them to work and learn together is foundational for supporting organizational capacity. Moreover, as acknowledged in Chapter 3, previous systemic efforts showed greater promise when given the opportunity to build strong plans, many of which require time to take shape and then be implemented.

Recommendation 1: The U.S. Department of Education should allocate funding for teacher professional learning and development in all STEM disciplines, to include science, technology, engineering, mathematics, computer science, and other emerging STEM-focused subjects (e.g., data science). As part of the funding allocation, states will need to provide a plan for the use of funding for professional learning and development that is based on established best practice (e.g., curriculum-embedded, sustained over time), metrics to achieve the goals (e.g., measures of quality teacher professional learning and development), and data that show evidence for achieving those goals. The funding should be renewable up to ten years, and if states have not shown improvement by year four, they must revise their plan.

Recommendation 2: The National Science Foundation should develop a new generation of Pre-K–12 STEM education systemic initiatives, with the goal of building infrastructure, capacity, and expertise to harvest promising evidence-based innovations, prepare them for wider implementation in new settings, and fund backbone organizations to organize the resources and support systems needed to carry out the implementations in schools. Funding should have a long enough time horizon (e.g., renewable up to ten years) for new structures and relationships to be iteratively refined and to take root in ways that could be sustained.

Recommendation 3: In alignment with the authorizing language of the CHIPS and Science Act of 2022 (P.L. 117–167, Sec. 10395), the National Science Foundation's Directorate for Technology, Innovation, and Partnerships should partner with the Directorate for STEM Education (EDU) to fully leverage the expertise of the EDU Federal Advisory committee and ensure the inclusion of program officers with expertise in Pre-K–12 STEM education in the evaluation of proposals related to supporting multidisciplinary research centers for scaling promising Pre-K–12 STEM education innovations.

Recommendation 4: In an effort to facilitate coordination across federal agencies that implement, scale, and sustain Pre-K–12 STEM education innovations, the National Science and Technology Council's Committee on STEM Education (CoSTEM) should identify key metrics for scaling and sustaining innovations and identify an appropriate schedule for reporting them to the public, exploring where the data should be reported (e.g., science.gov, National Center for Education Statistics, National Center for Science and Engineering Statistics) to keep the data ever green. CoSTEM should use these data to inform future iterations of the strategic plan and coordinate consistent investments across the federal agencies.

Building a Research Infrastructure for Scalable and Sustainable Innovations

The committee also points to the need for additional research for better understanding the interrelated factors associated with sustaining Pre-K–12 STEM education innovations. The next three recommendations point to how to address those gaps in the research base, particularly for understanding issues of sustainability of innovations.

Recommendation 5: The U.S. Department of Education and the National Science Foundation should create a new funding category that allows for the study of sustainability of STEM education innovations, which could allow for a deeper understanding of the dimensions of scaling. This should include developing system-level measures of STEM education innovations that attend to the inter-related actors, structures, and interactions that shape how innovations take hold in multiple, diverse contexts for different learners with an eye toward equity.

Recommendation 6: The U.S. Department of Education and the National Science Foundation should encourage practice-initiated partnerships and planning grants that will connect teams of researchers, designers, and practitioners with expertise and experience in different aspects of innovation development and implementation, either within a project or across successive related projects. These projects should include considerations of implementation and adaptation for different learners across multiple, diverse contexts early in the development process.

Recommendation 7: The U.S. Department of Education and the National Science Foundation should continue to encourage research and development in early STEM education: specifically, efforts that tackle integrating professional learning and development opportunities with curricula that address the many domains of learning that educators are expected to promote in early childhood, planning grants to support practice-initiated partnerships, and focus on coherence and alignment across preschool and elementary.

State and Local Actors: Systemic Change and Continuous Improvement

The next five recommendations are directed toward state and local actors in the Pre-K–12 education system. The recommendations focus on including strategies for making processes for continuous improvement the norm and creating partnerships to connect and align all of the relevant roles and forms of expertise. In the building of networks and partnerships, it is necessary to take the time to figure out common goals/purposes and how to align them, and to frame the efforts to achieve the desired outcomes. Relatedly, within the formal education system, understanding who has decision-making power for a given initiative is important and may vary across locations (see Chapter 2).

Recommendation 8: School and district leaders should adopt and/or evaluate a networked continuous improvement framework, emphasizing iterative assessment and refinement of strategies to meet the evolving educational landscape. This involves a cycle of planning, implementing, evaluating, and adjusting, with engagement of pertinent individuals to ensure ongoing relevancy. Data-driven analysis and feedback mechanisms should allow for real-time monitoring and responsive adaptation. Embracing this approach fosters a culture of innovation, learning, dexterity, responsiveness, and resilience within the schools and across the district.

Recommendation 9: To understand the implementation and scaling of Pre-K–12 STEM education innovations, state and district partners should develop data systems that capture information about opportunities to learn including time for instruction, allocation of resources and funding, access to and enrollment in Pre-K–12 STEM education innovations, and qualifications of teachers and characteristics of teachers. These data should be disaggregated to examine trends by subgroups of students and by school characteristics.

Recommendation 10: To ensure continuous improvement in Pre-K–12 STEM education innovations, school and district leaders should engage with professional learning and development providers to offer curriculum-embedded, ongoing opportunities within and across years that includes specific emphasis on new teachers to ensure that their learning is commensurate with those who participated in opportunities in years prior.

Recommendation 11: Local school and district leaders should initiate and sustain partnership agreements across all levels of the STEM education learning ecosystem (e.g., teachers, teacher educators, education researchers, designers of Pre-K–12 STEM education innovations, families, etc.) in order to combine STEM education expertise and local knowledge to attend to specific problems of practice and advance sustained development and implementation of promising, evidence-based Pre-K–12 STEM education innovations.

Regional Actors and Impact

The final set of recommendations acknowledge some of the broader range of actors that can have regional impact as they support the implementation, scaling, and sustaining of Pre-K–12 STEM education innovations.

Recommendation 12: Leaders of local and regional Pre-K–12 system should work to strengthen learning opportunities in STEM education among key actors in the STEM education learning ecosystem (e.g., teachers, school/district leaders, school board leaders, teacher educators, professional development providers, universities and colleges, museums, nonprofits, families, etc.) with an emphasis on building relational connections among communities and sharing knowledge.

Recommendation 13: In their support of Pre-K–12 STEM education innovations, the federal government, philanthropic organizations, and business and industry should provide support to projects that include designers of curricula partnering with education leaders, teachers, families/communities, and researchers to co-design resources that are evidence-based, meaningful, accessible, and able to be feasibly implemented to support STEM teaching and learning. Attention should be given to features that can lead to meaningful STEM learning, while also considering components needed to ensure resources can be sustained and adapted for use by others.

RESEARCH AGENDA

In addition to providing what is known about the scaling of Pre-K–12 STEM education innovations, the committee was asked to identify gaps in the research that can aid in a better understanding of the interrelated factors that support and hinder the widespread implementation of Pre-K–12 STEM education innovations. Through their analysis of the literature, the committee identified four crucial areas: (a) attending to all dimensions of scale, (b) focusing on scale early in the development process, (c) documenting evidence of impact across varied learners and contexts, and (d) examining systems-level impacts. Across these crucial areas and potential questions, it is important to consider the methodologies employed, as both quantitative and qualitative methods are needed (sometimes simultaneously) to unpack the effects of the innovation at multiple levels. (For a deeper discussion of methodologies, see Chapter 6 of the 2022 National Academies of Sciences, Engineering, and Medicine report *The Future of Education Research at IES: Advancing an Equity-Oriented Science*).

Research Area 1: Attending to All Dimensions of Scale

The committee presents a multidimensional framework for scale that includes spread, depth, sustainability, and ownership. With changes in funding as described in earlier chapters, there has been increasing attention to understanding the scaling of innovations, with particular emphasis on the dimension of spread. Fewer studies have focused on the other dimensions of scale, including the relationship between the different dimensions. For example, how is depth related to scale? How is ownership related to sustainability? What are the connections between scalability and sustainability given that sustainability is included as a dimension of scale?

In addition to understanding each of the dimensions and their relationships, additional research needs to focus on ways of assessing scale and sustainability of Pre-K–12 STEM education innovations that attend to the depth of implementation and sustainability, and in relation to populations, geography (and other aspects of spread), and the impact on communities. In assessing these various dimensions, there needs to be attention to variability and how enactors and enablers respond to unwanted variation. This could allow for a deeper analysis of the conditions that allowed a particular innovation to be sustained. This might include teacher narratives combined with quantitative analyses of innovations they have developed/shared/continued to use that reflect the reality of innovations in the classroom (including limitations of the innovations that were present). Through this research, there would also need to be greater emphasis on the systematic tracking of the various factors and conditions—this could help with understanding how innovations can better learn and grow as the implementation context changes over time.

Research Area 2: Focusing on Scale Early in the Development Process

There has been a history of funding research that emphasizes a particular sequence: pilot studies, followed by efficacy studies, then effectiveness studies, and finally, scale-up studies. Not surprisingly, given this history and trajectory of funding, not all projects have considered the various dimensions of scale or the particular challenges in implementation identified in Chapters 5–7 early in the development phase. This includes having an eye on support for professional learning of educators or the creation of resources that can be adopted in schools. That is, what are the plans for an innovation to scale (and sustain) beyond the local context? Having this information collected early in the process would aid in understanding challenges in implementation, and these constraints could be built into the scale-up design process. Potential questions could include:

- What are the decision-making processes, contexts, resources, and conditions that support or hinder district and school leaders to make decisions about scaling and sustaining Pre-K–12 STEM education innovations?
- When should innovations scale and when should they not?
- What should one pay attention to when thinking about how programs start partnerships and how does this play out across the different types of funded studies?
- How are innovations adapted as they are scaled and sustained, included enabling and constraining factors?

Research Area 3: Documenting Evidence of Impact Across Varied Learners and Contexts

As elevated throughout portions of this report, STEM outcomes are not the same for all kinds of cultural communities and place-based contexts. A number of the innovations discussed in Chapter 6 had been intentional in attending to understanding the impact of the innovation across varied learners and contexts. However, this research is limited and necessitates considering how the research is conducted. For example, it may be that there is a need for developing and/or leveraging new statistical methods for analysis and using larger sample sizes. Moreover, not all methods will be quantitative (see National Academies of Sciences, Engineering, and Medicine, 2022).

There is a need to investigate how researchers and educators have identified a variety of ways to measure, assess, and evaluate differentiated STEM learning outcomes for various groups of learners (e.g., students from rural communities, bilingual students, neurodivergent students, and tribal nations). This necessitates practical, affordable methodologies and multiple forms of assessment for gathering evidence of the purposes of STEM in differing contexts, what counts as success, and "what works for whom and under what circumstances" in a medium timeframe. Looking across contexts, it is important to identify the major drivers (e.g., contributors at the regional, state, and local levels) and the differences in their motivations and ability to scale and sustain Pre-K–12 STEM education innovations (e.g., differences between rural, suburban, and urban contexts as related to the enabling and constraining factors identified throughout the report).

Research Area 4: Examining Systems-Level Impacts

Expanding research-based knowledge about productive strategies to support the scaling and sustaining of Pre-K–12 STEM education innovations requires investment in research that documents not just the learning that occurs within individual innovations, but also the innovation's system-level impacts and how the *system* is learning. For example, in what ways have policy shifts resulted in significant changes to the STEM learning ecology and at what level (district, state, regional, national)? What are some indicators that the system is learning? Beyond understanding how an individual innovation could have an impact on the system, there is also a need to understand robust community-level outcomes. Community-level goals, such as neighborhood resiliency, building community capacity to adapt to changing social and ecological systems, more access to healthy drinking water, increased biodiversity, and a sense of community belonging, often seem to be lacking in STEM learning outcomes. Community-level desires can be foundational measures of system-level educational impacts. These include questions such as, How is the program supporting community-level goals and outcomes? How is this program supporting broader social and ecological health and wellbeing?

Finally, in thinking about scale, the committee noticed a lack in outcomes that support STEM learning programs networking and learning with each other. Some Regional Education Labs are exemplars of how this might be done, and further work is needed into how we know that local system is in fact learning. What kinds of system-level measurements could help advance and enhance STEM learning that supports diverse visions of wellbeing for children and families, more just and vibrant community life, and healthier lands and waters where they live?

FINAL REFLECTION

The committee was asked to examine the vexing problem of why federal and other investments in research and development have led to a wealth of innovative ideas and resources with excellent potential to improve STEM teaching and learning, but these innovations are often unable to be scaled effectively and equitably in new settings and to be sustained over time. To produce this report, the committee examined both successes and shortcomings of attempts to spread and sustain promising innovations, drawing on historical analyses, contemporary evidence, and first-hand accounts of actors and participants throughout the landscape of Pre-K–12 STEM education.

The committee concluded that barriers that stand in the way of widespread dissemination and sustainability of promising innovations are generally not individual failures but rather systemic ones. Most developers would like to see their innovations take root and spread, and most school leaders would like to access high-quality research-based innovations if they are responsive to school needs and can be tailored to local circumstances, but there is complicated terrain that must be navigated in between. The United States' historically decentralized system, where research and development take place outside of the Pre-K–12 educational system while implementation happens locally within districts and schools, has resulted in a malfunctioning and fragmented system. However, decentralization and local control need not imply isolation, disconnection, or tunnel vision.

In this report, the committee presents a variety of examples and models demonstrating how systemic efforts to increase collaboration and partnerships and to build permanent mechanisms for actors with different capacities and responsibilities that coordinate coherently can result in robust, durable, and ongoing improvements in STEM education. Building systemic capacity will not happen quickly and will require considerable and sustained investments of funding and leadership at every level of the educational system. But there is an urgent need to engage in this work to fulfill the promise of public education to youth and their families and communities, and to reap the benefits of future workers and citizens who are empowered with knowledge, competencies, and motivation gained from a world-class STEM education.

REFERENCE

National Academies of Sciences, Engineering, and Medicine. (2022). *The future of education research at IES: Advancing an equity-oriented science*. The National Academies Press. https://doi.org/10.17226/26428

Appendix A

Biosketches

COMMITTEE BIOS

CHRISTINE M. MASSEY (*Chair*) is a senior researcher in the Psychology Department at the University of California, Los Angeles, where she specializes in linking research in cognitive science to learning in public schools, higher education, and informal education. She has led multiple collaborative projects combining research investigating students' learning and conceptual development in science, technology, engineering, and mathematics (STEM) with the development of new curricula, adaptive learning technologies, and educational programs for students and teachers. Prior projects included the development of science curricula and teacher professional development for Pre-K–grade 1 and robotics programs for girls. Massey's current projects involve basic and applied research using principles of perceptual and adaptive learning to create learning software with applications in STEM and medical education. She was formerly the director of research and education at the University of Pennsylvania's Institute for Research in Cognitive Science and was a member of the national Institute of Education Science's Research and Development Center for Cognition and Science Instruction. Massey is an Eisenhower fellow and was a fellow in the Spencer Foundation/National Academy of Education's postdoctoral fellowship program. She received her B.A. from Wellesley College and her Ph.D. in psychology from the University of Pennsylvania. Massey has participated in the National Academies of Sciences, Engineering, and Medicine's study committees on *Defining Deeper Learning and 21st Century Skills* and *Designing Citizen Science to Support Science Learning*.

HYMAN BASS is the Samuel Eilenberg Distinguished University Professor of Mathematics and Mathematics Education at the University of Michigan. He previously was at Columbia University and has held many visiting appointments extensively in India and in France. Bass' mathematical work is in algebra, with connections to algebraic geometry, number theory, topology, and geometric group theory. His educational interests include mathematical knowledge for teaching, task design, mathematical practices, and the "mathematical horizons" of school mathematics. Bass is currently experimenting with instructional designs to help cultivate "connection oriented mathematical thinking." This involves an in-depth study of mathematical structure, and concept formation. He is also developing an undergraduate course on mathematics and social justice. Bass is past president of the American Mathematical Society and of the International Commission on Mathematical Instruction, and he has received the U.S. National Medal of Science. He is a member of the National Academy of Sciences, the American Academy of Arts and Sciences, the Third World Academy of Sciences, and the National Academy of Education.

JASON BLACK is associate professor in Business Information Systems at Florida A&M University (FAMU). He is also the campus director of the Blackstone LaunchPad @ FAMU (an Entrepreneurship Network sponsored by the Blackstone Charitable Foundation designed to foster and support entrepreneurship efforts at FAMU and in the community at-large), the co-director of the Program of Excellence in STEM (a multi-million dollar funded academic and research-centered grant focusing on increasing participation and advancement of underrepresented students in science, engineering, technology, and mathematics), executive director of the HBCU Data Science Consortium, and director of the Interdisciplinary Center for Creativity and Innovation (FAMU's entrepreneurship hub). Black holds a B.S. degree in computer information systems from FAMU, an M.S. degree in computer science from Georgia Tech, and a Ph.D. in computer science from Florida State University.

TINA CHEUK is an assistant professor of elementary science education at the California Polytechnic State University–San Luis Obispo. Her research centers on the development of culturally and linguistically diverse learners in science learning settings. Cheuk has previously served as a committee member in the development of California's Science Curriculum Framework and State Literacy Plan, and the revision of California's Bilingual Authorization Program Standards. Most recently, she is a panel member of the 2028 National Assessment of Educational Progress Science Assessment Framework Update Steering and Development Committees. Cheuk is a co-primary investigator of a 5-year U.S. Department of Education

Teacher Quality Partnership grant, creating a teacher residency program that expands pathways into special education and bilingual education in partnership with school districts in San Luis Obispo and Santa Barbara County. She began her career in education as a fifth-grade science teacher in the South Bronx, followed by service as a secondary science teacher as a U.S. Peace Corps volunteer in Ghana, West Africa. Cheuk holds a B.S. in chemistry and biochemistry from the University of Chicago, and a M.A. and Ph.D. in education policy from Stanford University.

CHRISTINE M. CUNNINGHAM is the senior vice president of STEM Learning at the Museum of Science in Boston. She aims to make engineering, science, and computational thinking education more equitable and accessible, especially for populations that are underserved and underrepresented in science, technology, engineering, and mathematics (STEM). Cunningham's research focuses on articulating frameworks for precollege engineering education and exploring affordances of engineering for learners. She is the founding director of Youth Engineering Solutions and Engineering is Elementary, which develop equity-oriented, research-based, field-tested STEM curricula and professional learning resources for Pre-K–8 youth and their educators. Under her leadership, these resources have reached more than 20 million youth and 200,000 educators. Previously, Cunningham was a Professor of Practice in Education and Engineering at the Pennsylvania State University. She serves on a number of advisory boards that currently include the National Assessment Governing Board. Cunningham is a fellow of the American Society for Engineering Education and has received numerous awards including the American Society of Engineering Education K–12 and Pre-College Division Lifetime Achievement Award, the Institute of Electric and Electronics Engineers Pre-University Educator Award, and the International Society for Design and Development in Education Prize, and her work was recognized with the prestigious Harold W. McGraw Jr. Prize in Education. She holds joint B.A. and M.A. degrees in biology from Yale University and a Ph.D. in education from Cornell University. Cunningham has previously been a committee member of five National Academy Committees, most recently chairing the Inclusive, Diverse, Equitable Engineering for All Committee.

XIMENA DOMINGUEZ is the executive director of learning sciences and early learning research at Digital Promise. Across research and development efforts, she and her team aim to make early learning experiences more accessible and equitable for historically excluded young learners by centering families' funds of knowledge. More specifically, Dominguez's work involves co-designing and evaluating early science, technology, engineering, and mathematics (STEM) innovations in partnership with families from diverse cultural and linguistic backgrounds, educators in public early childhood programs, curriculum developers, and educational media designers. In addition to studying how young children's interests, community assets, and everyday experiences can be leveraged to meaningfully promote STEM learning across home and school, she and her partners explore when and how STEM domains can be feasibly and meaningfully integrated with each other and with other learning disciplines to promote learning broadly. Across these efforts, Dominguez explores the affordances of technology and media for supporting early STEM teaching and learning—documenting how digital tools can be designed to strengthen (not replace) the hands-on, socially rich, and collaborative learning that is key early in childhood. In addition to leading grants from federal agencies and philanthropic organizations, she currently leads Digital Promise's strategic effort on multilingual learners. She earned an M.S. in education from the University of Pennsylvania and a Ph.D. in applied developmental psychology from the University of Miami. Dominguez also serves as ad hoc reviewer for multiple early childhood journals and recently served as a member of the National Academies of Sciences, Engineering, and Medicine's consensus study, *Science and Engineering in Preschool Through Elementary Grades: The Brilliance of Children and the Strengths of Educators*.

KARA JACKSON is a professor of mathematics education at the University of Washington, Seattle. Her research focuses on (a) elaborating critical distinctions in secondary mathematics teachers' perspectives and practices that matter for advancing equity and (b) investigating and supporting schools and districts to design and implement coherent systems of support that enable teachers to develop ambitious and equitable teaching. Jackson taught secondary mathematics in Vanuatu as a Peace Corps volunteer and was a mathematics specialist, supporting both youth and their families, for the Say Yes to Education Foundation in Philadelphia. Jackson's scholarship and practice is grounded in long-term partnerships with teachers, coaches, and leaders in schools and districts. Jackson's research has been supported by a National Academy of Education/Spencer Postdoctoral Fellowship, the Spencer Foundation, the National Science Foundation, and the Carnegie Foundation for the Advancement of Teaching. She completed her bachelor's degree in mathematics at Bates College and her doctorate in education, culture, and society with an emphasis in mathematics education at the University of Pennsylvania.

AMERY MARTINEZ works in the Department of Career and College Success supporting and expanding Career and Technical Education career pathways for Denver Public Schools (DPS). He has held various positions within education and industry during his career, including working as a design and architecture professional, licensed bilingual educator, instructional technology coach, and district innovation coordinator. Additionally, Martinez served as the K–8 computer science specialist for the New Mexico Public Education Department where he worked on the creation of the state computer science endorsement and competencies. He managed the K–8 computer science grant program based on the New Mexico computer science strategic plan, which was designed to support school districts across the state with providing equitable access to computer science education. Martinez is the lead for the DPS CSforAll Accelerator program, a strategic initiative focused on accelerating high-need communities in their progress toward fundamental standards-aligned computer science education and increased access to interest-driven computer science learning opportunities. In addition to his professional expertise, his personal experience as a first-generation college graduate contributes to his equity driven mindset relatable to colleagues and students. He holds a master's degree in architecture and urban design from University of California, Los Angeles, and a bachelor's degree from the University of New Mexico

KRISTEN D. McKINNEY currently serves as an educator in the Sedalia 200 school district where she focuses on innovation through assessment at the high school level. Prior to this role, she worked at the Missouri Department of Elementary and Secondary Education (MO DESE) where she focused on implementation of *Framework*-adapted, three-dimensional learning standards and oversaw the development of the science assessments within the Missouri Assessment Program. McKinney also served as co-chair of the Assessing Student Learning Ad Hoc Committee for the Council of State Science Supervisors, the Missouri state lead for the Advancing Coherent and Equitable Systems of Science Education (ACESSE) work, and a member of the Short Performance Assessment Learning Community. Since taking the position in the Sedalia200 school district, she has transitioned to an associate role with the Council of State Science Supervisors. As the director of science for MO DESE, McKinney received recognition for the Conservation Intersection Award and the Presidential Citation Award. She holds a B.S. in biology with a minor in chemistry from Missouri Valley College, M.A. in teaching from the University of Central Missouri, M.Ed. in K–12 building leadership from Northwest Missouri State University, and an Ed.S. degree in educational technology and curriculum from the University of Central Missouri.

MEIXI is a Hokchiu assistant professor in Comparative Education and International Development at the University of Minnesota–Twin Cities and former middle school mathematics teacher. Over the past decade she has collaboratively designed schools and learning systems to restore school-land-community-family relationships and advance collective Indigenous futures in the United States, Thailand, and Mexico. Meixi interweaves comparative

Indigenous education with the learning sciences and community-engaged design research to support the creation of land- and water-based curriculum and school assessments with families' stories, technologies, and place-based knowledge systems. Broadly, she studies (a) children's ethical development within micro-moments of interaction in STEM education in relation to sociopolitical/ecological phenomena and (b) the possibilities of innovating schools to become sites of healing, wellbeing, and regeneration for Indigenous young people, families, and their lands. Meixi was named a National Academy of Education/Spencer Postdoctoral Fellow and Presidential Postdoc in American Indian Studies at the University of Minnesota. She earned her B.S. in education and social policy at Northwestern University and Ph.D. in learning sciences and human development from the University of Washington.

THOMAS T. PETERS serves as executive director of South Carolina's Coalition for Mathematics & Science, a science, technology, engineering, and medicine (STEM) Learning Ecosystem Community of Practice that has been in continuous service to the state for 30 years. His professional expertise includes curriculum design and implementation, teacher professional development, and systemic approaches to educational innovation in STEM. Peters is a recipient of the Outstanding Leader in Science Education Award from the National Science Education Leadership Association and the Richard C. Riley Award from the South Carolina Council of Teachers of Mathematics. He holds B.S. degrees in both teaching biology and ecology/ethology/evolution, as well as an M.S. and Ph.D. in science education, all awarded from the University of Illinois at Urbana-Champaign.

ANTHONY J. PETROSINO serves as the associate dean for research and outreach in Southern Methodist University's Simmons School and professor of the learning sciences in the Simmons Department of Teaching and Learning. He is also emeritus from The University of Texas at Austin where he was an Elizabeth G. Gibb Endowed Fellow. Petrosino has received research grants from the National Science Foundation, the Department of Education, and the McDonnel Foundation for Cognitive Studies. His research interests include students understanding of experimentation, teacher education in STEM, and the development of expertise in STEM disciplines. Petrosino is co-founder of the nationally recognized UTeach Natural Sciences Program. He has been a NASA Space Grant Fellow as well as a McDonnell Post-Doctoral Fellow funded through the Cognitive Studies in Educational Practice Program by McDonnell Douglas. Petrosino's articles have appeared in the *Journal of Science Education and Technology*, *The Journal of the Learning Sciences*, *Mathematical Thinking and Learning*, *Educational Computing Research*, *The Journal of Engineering Education*, and *The American Educational Research Journal*. He received his M.Ed. from Teachers College, Columbia University in educational administration and his Ph.D. at Vanderbilt University where he was a member of the Cognition and Technology Group at Vanderbilt.

ROBERT J. SEMPER currently serves as the chief learning officer for the Exploratorium, providing strategy and oversight to the science and education work of the institution and representing the Exploratorium to the broader world of science, science centers and science, technology, engineering, and medicine (STEM) education. Over the years he has had a career developing exhibits and exhibitions onsite and worldwide, creating teacher education programs, producing publications, films, online media and communication programs, expanding the informal science education field and leading major initiatives including the recent relocation of the institution to Pier 15/17. Before joining the Exploratorium, Semper taught physics at St. Olaf College and conducted solid state, elementary particle and nuclear physics research at Johns Hopkins University, Lawrence Berkeley National Laboratory, and University of California, San Francisco. He is the author of many journal articles and invited papers and conference talks, and he has been principal investigator on over 50 federally and privately funded projects that include developing new online and media resources, experiments using technology to enhance the museum visitor experience, and programs for teachers and museum educators. Semper was selected as a member of the Federal STEM Education Advisory Panel, which evaluated and offered guidance on the federal government's Strategic Plan for STEM education. He was also a Schumann fellow at the Harvard Graduate School of Education and director of the creative collaboration between Apple Computer and Lucasfilm Ltd. formed to develop interactive multimedia education projects. Semper's awards include American Physical Society Fellow, American Association for the Advancement of Science Fellow, and the National Science Teaching Association Faraday Science Communicator Award. He received his Ph.D. in solid-state physics from The Johns Hopkins University.

MIRAY TEKKUMRU-KISA is a senior policy researcher at RAND. Two interrelated foci of Tekkumru-Kisa's research are (a) understanding and supporting professional learning and (b) measuring and improving instructional quality for ambitious and equitable science, technology, engineering, and mathematics (STEM) teaching. Her research efforts center around the design and study of responsive STEM and professional learning environments and involve working in partnership with educators across layers of the education system (e.g., schools, districts, and states) and building the capacity for continuous improvement. Tekkumru-Kisa has led and contributed to federally funded projects involving careful design of educational interventions that address problems of practice and challenges of policy implementation and help to extend theories of teaching and learning. Prior to joining RAND, she worked as an associate professor of science education at Florida State University. She earned her B.S. and M.S. in science and mathematics education from Bogazici University in Turkey, and her Ph.D. in learning sciences and policy from University of Pittsburgh. Before moving to the United States for her Ph.D., Tekkumru-Kisa was involved in national and international education improvement projects in Turkey.

MARCELO WORSLEY is an associate professor of computer science and learning sciences at Northwestern University. His research integrates artificial intelligence and data mining with multimodal interfaces to study and support human learning. Worsley directs the technological innovations for inclusive learning and teaching lab, which works with community and industry partners around the world to empower people and organizations through the design and use of equity focused learning tools. These tools include both pedagogical and technological solutions for in-school and out-of-school learning. His research has been selected for best paper awards at multiple interdisciplinary research venues. Worsley's work has also been recognized through a National Science Foundation CAREER award on bridging sports and computer science. He has a B.S. in chemical engineering, a B.A. in Spanish and Portuguese, an M.S. in computer science, and a Ph.D. in learning sciences and technology design all from Stanford University. Worsley also completed post-doctoral training at the University of Southern California Institute for Creative Technologies.

STAFF BIOS

AMY STEPHENS (*Study Director*) is the associate board director for the Board on Science Education at the National Academies of Sciences, Engineering, and Medicine. She has served as study director for several consensus studies on a variety of topics to include English learners in science, technology, engineering, and mathematics (STEM) subjects, preschool through elementary science and engineering education, the teacher workforce, and how STEM opportunities can cultivate interest and the development of competencies for computing. She is currently directing the study on Developing Competencies for the Future of Data and Computing: The Role of K–12. Prior to joining the National Academies, Stephens was a postdoctoral fellow for the Johns Hopkins University's Center for Talented Youth and prior to that worked at the Kennedy Krieger Institute. She received her Ph.D. in psychological and brain sciences from Johns Hopkins University with an emphasis in cognitive neuroscience.

SAMUEL CRAWFORD is a research associate for the Board on Science Education at the National Academies of Sciences, Engineering, and Medicine. Before joining the Board on Science Education, he was a senior program assistant for the Food and Nutrition Board at the Academies. He is currently supporting the Consensus Study for Thriving in a Changing Climate and the Standing Committee for Advancing Science Communication. Before joining the National Academies, Crawford was a Peace Corps Volunteer in Panama and a high school chemistry teacher in Maryland. He received his master's degree in EU Trade and Climate Policy from the LUISS Guido Carli University and Centre International de Formation Européenne.

BRITTANI SHORTER is a senior program assistant for the Board on Science Education at the National Academies of Sciences, Engineering, and Medicine. As a member of the board staff, she has supported studies focusing on science education, science communication, and STEM education in rural areas.

HEIDI SCHWEINGRUBER (*Board Director*) is the director for the Board on Science Education at the National Academies of Sciences, Engineering, and Medicine. In this role, she oversees a portfolio of work that includes K–12 science education, informal science education, and higher education. Schweingruber joined the National Academies starting as a senior program officer for the Board of Science Education. In this role, she directed or co-directed numerous projects including the study that resulted in the report *A Framework for K–12 Science Education* (2011), which served as the blueprint for the Next Generation Science Standards. Most recently, she co-directed the study that produced the report *Call to Action for Science Education: Building Opportunity for the Future* (2021). Schweingruber is a nationally recognized leader in leveraging research findings to support improving science and science, technology, engineering, and medicine education policy and practice. She holds a Ph.D. in psychology and anthropology, and a certificate in culture and cognition from the University of Michigan.

AUDREY WEBB is a program officer with the Board on Science Education (BOSE). Since she joined the BOSE staff in April 2023, she has supported two congressionally mandated consensus studies and the Collaborative on Advancing Science Teaching and Learning in K–12 (CASTL-K12). Before joining the BOSE team, she served as the K–12 science supervisor for the Nebraska Department of Education. In this position, she supported district selection and implementation of instructional materials for science, provided professional learning opportunities across the state, and supported the development of the statewide phenomenon-based performance assessment system, including large-scale, interim, and classroom formative assessments and implementation toolkits. Previously, Webb designed and implemented project-based curricula for secondary biology, physiology, and physical science in the San Francisco Unified School District. She holds a master of arts in education from Stanford University and a bachelor of arts in both biology and sociology/anthropology from St. Olaf College.